FIRE AWAY!
FIELDING TOUGH
QUESTIONS WITH FINESSE

FIRE AWAY!
Fielding Tough Questions with Finesse

Myles Martel, Ph.D.

IRWIN
Professional Publishing
Burr Ridge, Illinois
New York, New York

This book is based, in part, on *Mastering the Art of Q & A*.

This publication is designed to provide accurate and authoritative information in regard to the subject matter covered. It is sold with the understanding that neither the author nor the publisher is engaged in rendering legal, accounting, or other professional service. If legal advice or other expert assistance is required, the services of a competent professional person should be sought.

From a Declaration of Principles jointly adopted by a Committee of the American Bar Association and a Committee of Publishers.

Sponsoring editor: Cynthia A. Zigmund
Production editor: Paula M. Buschman
Production manager: Jon Christopher
Designer: Larry J. Cope
Art coordinator: Heather Burbridge
Compositor: AppleTree Graphics, Inc.
Typeface: 11/13 Palatino
Printer: Book Press, Inc.

Library of Congress Cataloging-in-Publication Data

Martel, Myles.
    Fire away! : fielding tough questions with finesse / Myles Martel.
      p.   cm.
    Includes bibliographical references and index.
    ISBN 1-55623-976-9
    1. Business communication 2. Questions and answers I. Title.
HF5718.M375 1994
658.4'5—dc20   93–1265

Printed in the United States of America
1 2 3 4 5 6 7 8 9 0   BP   0 9 8 7 6 5 4 3

To three men who have influenced my thinking and my career far more than I could ever express: Frank Ursomarso, Carl Hermann Voss, and Ralph Towne.

Preface

The questioning impulse in us is our deepest instinct. It is deeper than even our hunger for food. Deeper than the drive for sleep. Deeper than the drive for sex. This instinct to ask questions keeps intruding—even during sleep and sex.[1]

—Michael Novak
Noted Theologian and Author

The title of this book is inspired by a collection of mental images I have of business leaders, politicians, and other professionals who have begun their question-and-answer sessions with a confident "Fire away, I am ready" attitude. In many instances they were indeed ready to field even the most challenging questions with consummate finesse. In others, they were far less prepared than expected, often embarking on a perilous course.

This book is about fielding questions—especially tough, trick, and hostile ones—with finesse. Most of the insights and examples are drawn from my 20-plus years as a communication advisor to the world's business and political leaders. *Fire Away!* will help you to prepare for a host of significant communication challenges, including major speeches and presentations, financial analyst meetings, public hearings, government testimony, depositions, and media interviews, including crisis situations.

Although *finesse* is defined as "delicate skill; subtle discrimination; or refinement,"[2] my principal intent in choosing this term is to imply a high degree of clarity, credibility, and persuasiveness through the appropriate choice and control of the spokesperson, setting, ideas, words, tone, and body language.

Fire Away! is based on eight fundamental premises:

1. The question-and-answer (Q & A) session during or following a presentation can be as important, if not more important, than the presentation itself. Here audience members, especially those you want most to influence, seek clarification, reassurance, proof, confidence in your leadership, or whatever factor or combination of factors ultimately impact your performance.

2. Regrettably, presenters generally undervalue the importance of Q & A skills. This is due in part to their inability to sufficiently appreciate the critical difference between their comfort level in fielding questions and their persuasive effectiveness. This phenomenon is especially common when the Q & A session is conducted by persons who feel less than comfortable when making presentations. As a consequence, they are relieved that their presentation is over, and approach the Q & A too passively; they are not as proactive or persuasive as they need to be.

3. Q & A sessions are often fraught with risks, including the risk of:

A. Not knowing the answer to an important question
B. Making a misstatement or gaffe
C. Stepping into a trap
D. Offending the audience via an idea, phrasing, tone, body language, or any combination of these factors
E. Missing the opportunity to reinforce one or more key messages
F. Overanswering or underanswering a question
G. Being generally unimpressive
H. Being outperformed by a competitor

Any of these risks can translate into lost business, weakened relationships, poor representation of a deserving cause, and even a lost opportunity to advance one's career.

4. Q & A sessions, as implied above, frequently require strong advocacy skills. These sessions are, by nature, forums for advancing or defending positions, premises, proof, plus one's overall suitability for a leadership or management role. Therefore, most Q & A exchanges involve the process of persuasion—the process of influencing attitudes and, often, behavior.

5. Fielding questions with finesse requires abandoning any allegiance to fate, declaring war on risk, and replacing both with a strong, take-control, "I'm in charge of my Q & A performance" mentality. This mentality is to be buttressed by the following seven factors. Collectively, these factors contribute to finesse:

A. A well-analyzed target audience
B. Clearly defined goals and key messages
C. Careful preparation for anticipated questions
D. Skillfulness in negotiating or arranging for formats and environments conducive to your goals
E. A fine-tuned sense of your tactical options
F. Keen sensitivity to tone and body language
G. The ability to articulate ideas clearly and reinforce them convincingly

6. As globalization continues at an historic pace with unprecedented merger and acquisition activity, plus the rapid development of transnational business structures and strategies, Q & A finesse requires clear insights regarding the norms of the culture in which you are fielding questions.

7. Regardless of circumstance, truthfulness should never be compromised—no exceptions! Therefore, your principal tactical challenge in responding to tough questions is to gauge how open you should be—how much truth you need to disclose without compromising either your credibility, or your personal sense of integrity.

8. Understanding the process and principles of Q & A, combined with disciplined preparation and practice, is the best formula for a virtuoso performance on the firing line.

May *Fire Away!*, coupled with your commitment to enhance your finesse, bring you both added persuasive impact and lasting self-satisfaction.

Myles Martel
Villanova, Pa.

Acknowledgments

The cover of this book carries only the author's name; yet so many people were instrumental in helping make *Fire Away!* a reality. My most heartfelt gratitude is extended to:

My wife, Susan, and son, David, who were constantly supportive of my commitment to write this book, even when it encroached on time we needed to spend together.

Kathleen Tenuto, who prepared the manuscript with an admirably positive attitude and uncommon perseverance.

Roger Axtell, Dick Collins, Ellen Roberts, Mike Bailey, Norm Blanchard, Ed Baruff, Max Downham, Cees van der Wel, Henry Pollak, Theo Carnier, Henry Wendt, Ron Lehrer, Kelly Martin, John Tognino, Greg Bundy, Marc Holtzman, Mike Marino, John Venardos, Peter Rost, Anthony Graham, Ben Han, Dr. Sang Han, and Monique Martens for their invaluable input regarding Chapter 12, "Displaying Finesse Globally."

Dan Deslaurier, who converted my ideas of humorous Q & A situations into the cartoons you'll find throughout this book. Our collaboration was pure fun.

Larry Beaser, Esq., and George Kruger, Esq., for their fine counsel in helping me to develop, respectively, the preparation plans for the sections on testifying and being deposed (Chapter 15).

Paul D'Angelo and Andrew Kurtz, who undertook with enviable patience the challenge of critiquing, researching, and reformatting this book.

Sue Katz, my agent, who handled the contractual details with unquestioned competence and good humor.

Peggy Ruggiero, my executive assistant, who not only handled the administrative details of my firm smoothly as I was writing this book, but pitched in to assist me in putting the finishing touches on the research for Chapter 12, "Displaying Finesse Globally."

Cindy Zigmund, my editor, for her unflagging encouragement, guidance, and professionalism. Good editors are hard to find. I found a great one!

Contents

Chapter One

A Bird's-Eye View of the Firing Line

As a lifelong lover of baseball, I begin by using a baseball analogy to put this chapter, particularly the complexity of the question and answer (Q & A) interaction, in proper context. Understanding the major elements and dynamics of this interaction will help you to define your range of control as you clarify what to expect from the firing line.

- The person who poses the question is the pitcher.
- The batter's eye on the ball and swing are analogous to the respondent's skill in listening to and "making proper contact" with the question.
- The batter, by studying the pitcher and fielders in advance, is analogous to a respondent analyzing his audience.
- The batter, by digging in at the plate and observing the direction and intensity of the wind, attempts to control the environment that will ultimately affect the outcome of his swing. Similarly, respondents, by attempting to control format, setting, and so on, are seeking to maximize the impact of their answers.
- Both batter and respondent have target audiences, including some crucial ones in common, for example, senior management, consumers (fans), the competition, and the media.
- Both batter and respondent can depend on benefiting from practice and constructive feedback from seasoned coaches.

- Finally, and most significantly, perfection is an unrealistic standard for baseball as well as Q & A. A batter hasn't hit over .400 in more than 50 years (Ted Williams, .406, 1941). Therefore, your finesse, like a batting average, must be as slump-proof and as strong as possible.

The process of fielding questions cannot only be likened to a game; in many instances it may even help you to think of it as a game, especially if this mindset fosters a be-prepared mentality that stimulates your competitive juices. Yes, baseball is a complicated game, and so is Q & A. Regardless of whether you're a rookie or destined for the Fire Away Hall of Fame, I will clarify your expectations by posing a series of questions, most of which will be addressed in the chapters that follow.

YOUR AUDIENCE AND THEIR AGENDA

Let's begin by examining your audience. Is it the questioner himself? Do others need to be influenced by your ideas and your manner? Who are they? What is their role in affecting your outcome? How much can you learn about them in advance—their demographics, knowledge level, attitudes? How can you shape your responses to maximize your influence? How active do you expect them to be in questioning you? To what extent can you anticipate their questions? To what extent can you anticipate their tone? What is their agenda?

- To learn more about your point of view.
- To seek reassurance.
- To test your mettle.
- To discern your leadership and management skills.
- To discern your communication skills.
- To communicate their own points of view.
- To pursue their hidden agenda.
- Something else.
- Any combination of the above.

THE ENVIRONMENT

Now let's turn to the environment, a factor to be discussed in greater detail in Chapter 6. Do you hit better at home or away? (Most of our clients say that they feel more in control at home.) Does standing or sitting affect your performance? (Most of our clients feel that when norms permit, standing for Q & A helps bring out their best.) How might seating arrangements, lighting, decor, refreshments, and so on, affect your impact? How might the format itself, including who speaks, on what, and when, influence your performance? What other norms might prevail? For example, will questions be asked during or following your presentation?

YOUR RELATIONSHIP WITH THE AUDIENCE

A crucial aspect of your audience and their agenda is your relationship with them. Pitchers who don't like batters often try to "dust" them—force them to hit the ground with a pitch too close for comfort. Questioners can approach the Q & A with an analogous temperament. Or, in some instances, they can be charitable, providing opportunities for the respondent to shine.

The following three scenarios bring into focus two interrelated factors affecting the dynamics of Q & A: (1) the mutuality of the agendas of the questioner and respondent, and (2) the level of trust between you and your questioner, versus its potentially powerful opposite, suspicion:

- During the Senate Confirmation Hearings for Clarence Thomas, the Republican questioners, while attempting to appear even-handed, were nonetheless obliged to help reinforce his case, while his detractors, mainly Democrats, pursued the opposite agenda.
- During a Ph.D. candidate's orals, the advisor asks the candidate questions to facilitate the opportunity to reinforce his thesis. In this setting the candidate prays (as I did) that none of the professors has a less than supportive agenda.

- During an annual meeting in which the CEO is under fire for one or more issues, planned or unplanned supportive questions from sympathetic shareholders often surface to counterbalance the agenda(s) of vocal detractors.

YOUR AGENDA

What do you want the net impact of your performance to be? What messages will facilitate this outcome? What personality or image traits will influence or detract from your purpose? To what extent is your agenda overt versus covert? For example, overtly you may want to generate buy-in for your proposal, but covertly you may be seeking a promotion based on the strength of your performance. To what extent are your overt and covert agendas compatible with your audience's (acknowledging that discerning your audience's covert agenda may be difficult, if not impossible)? How will you tailor your performance for expected compatibility or incompatibility?

THE COMPLEXITY OF THE QUESTION

Like pitches (especially the fastball), some questions are simple and straightforward. Other pitches (e.g., the curve, slider, and knuckleball), like questions, are more complex. The complexity of questions is rooted in several factors, including, most notably, an assessment of the questioner's intent; the clarity of the question's phrasing and logic; the number of premises, facets, and facts within the question; and the intellectual challenge plus its memory or recall requirements.

THE COMPLEXITY OF YOUR RESPONSE

How well does the batter see the ball? Anticipate the type of pitch? How well do you hear, listen to, and understand a question? To what extent does it provide an opportunity for you to influence your target audience? How strong is your data base in responding to the question? To what extent should you be responsive or not? What special tactics should you employ to field trick and tough questions? How should you begin your response? What ideas should you present? What language should you select? To what extent do you need to amplify your responses with examples or other forms of support? How long should your responses be? To what extent should you be prepared for follow-up questions?

YOUR BODY LANGUAGE

Body language, including the tone you project, is not a linear process based on the notion that first one transmits a nonverbal message, then one responds. Rather, the exchange of body language or nonverbal cues between pitcher and batter, or between questioner and respondent, is simultaneous—and decidedly significant.

The Q & A process is complicated by the broad range of body language cues both consciously and unconsciously transmitted and interpreted by questioner, audience members, and respondent. The process is further complicated by the receiver's correct or incorrect assessment of their meaning and by the appropriateness of any party's adjustment to them.

To compound matters, significant differences in meaning are assigned to various cues on a culture-by-culture basis. For example, in our culture, forming an "o" with the thumb and forefinger signals "O.K." However, in countries like Brazil and Germany it is an obscene gesture. In Japan it is not uncommon for the Japanese to concentrate on a presentation with their eyes closed. In our culture, this a generally a sign of fatigue and often disrespect.

It should therefore come as no surprise that one of the key challenges to enhancing your finesse, especially on a global basis, requires proper interpretation and transmission of body language. This includes not only vocal factors, including tone, but such factors as stance, eye contact, gestures, overall body movement, attire, grooming, distance from the questioner, and pointing behavior.

THE FEEDBACK CYCLE

How many times have you answered a question and were not sure you satisfied your target audience? It happens all the time. Why? It may be attributable to your own deficiency in interpreting cues transmitted by the questioner or other target audience members, or it may be due to the virtual absence of any useful feedback being transmitted. This latter phenomenon may be related to three principal factors: (1) the questioner's characteristic stoic visage; (2) his deliberate attempt to avoid providing feedback as a way to test your confidence, your convictions, or both; or (3) the questioner not wanting to transmit cues of what the ultimate outcome of your persuasive advances might be, especially if other parties need to be consulted. If stoicism shakes your confidence, you can appear more nervous, succumb to overelaboration, or, worse yet, ask diffidently, "Did I answer your question?" and receive an unsettling "No!" Hence, controlling your confidence level through the host of principles discussed in this book will significantly enhance your finesse.

You now have the bird's-eye view of the Q & A interaction. My intent in sharing it with you is not to make it daunting. Rather, I want to stimulate your awareness regarding how many variables can—and often must—be controlled for you to win big on the firing line.

A BIRD'S-EYE VIEW OF THIS BOOK

This book addresses the questions posed in the preceding discussion and many more. The key concept stressed throughout this book is control. Control begins with your firmly rooted attitude that you have significant potential control over the outcome of a Q & A exchange. This attitude, described earlier as a strong, take-control, "I'm in charge of my Q & A performance" mentality, will be greatly reinforced by the principles presented in this book and the range of control they collectively represent.

This book is organized to take you from foundation concepts to practical principles applicable in most any Q & A exchange, to special challenges. The foundation is laid in Chapters 2 through

4, addressing such topics as the meaning of finesse, the role of roles, and the significance of listening and memory.

Fire Away! becomes more advice-oriented in Chapters 5 through 8, with practical discussions regarding how to analyze your audience; define precise message and image goals; and control your credibility, the format, and your message, including your words, the way you begin your response (called a *headline*), and the length and structure of your response. In addition, you will receive advice for situations when you don't want to answer, don't know the answer, or need to stall to retrieve it.

Chapters 9 through 13 focus on how to exercise control in special situations, including how to field hostile trick, tough, and entrapping questions; address crisis situations; adjust to cultural norms as you field questions globally; and facilitate questions when a deadly silence follows your presentation.

Chapter 14 presents sound advice for conducting practice sessions. It is followed by a set of comprehensive, user-friendly Preparation Plans to assist you in getting ready for a wide variety of high-stakes Q & A exchanges.

Chapter Two

The Foundation of Finesse

N ow that I have given you a bird's eye view of the firing line and this book, I will put you in the on-deck circle, as you not only await, but anticipate, your turn at bat. Like baseball, where the big leagues mean facing pitchers with the best "stuff," the big leagues of Q & A mean facing the toughest questions in difficult and often high-stakes circumstances.

As you will see in later chapters, your finesse is a final result of in-depth target-audience analysis plus your ability to sense overt and hidden agendas of questions, and persuasively articulate your goal-based responses. This chapter will focus on the broader factors influencing the relationship between you and your questioners, and other audience members. Specifically, during a Q & A session, you are locked in a dance of expectations and perceptions. These expectations and perceptions will be discussed in five parts: (1) the risks and rewards of finesse; (2) the role of roles; (3) the role of effective listening; (4) the roles of fear and overconfidence; and (5) setting your Q & A agenda.

FINESSE: RISKS AND REWARDS

Committing yourself to "finesse" can, in a sense, put you on the horns of a dilemma, for questioners often expect something quite contradictory from you in Q & A. On the one hand, they expect you to be prepared, clear, and credible; yet, on the other, they expect you to *simultaneously* project an image of answering questions in an open, authentic, and less-staged manner. Achieving finesse, therefore, involves the often formidable challenge of finding the right balance in satisfying the audience's expectations.

Politicians, especially during election season, are highly prone to the risk of not finding the right balance. For example, during the 1992 Democratic primaries, Bill Clinton was perceived by many as "too slick." This perception was not entirely a partisan shot, for several public opinion polls reflected this as a voter concern. Thus, whether Clinton articulately addressed "character" charges, such as his alleged marital infidelity, or substantive campaign issues, such as the economy, many voters nonetheless perceived him as pandering and shifty. As a result, he unwittingly invited the unfortunate epithet "Slick Willie." Crafted by his detractors in Arkansas, this label gained impetus during his presidential race, but began to diminish as Election Day approached.

Late in 1991 it was reported in several major newspapers that then-President George Bush and his press secretary, Marlin Fitzwater, actually scripted the questions in advance of his satellite-assisted Q & A sessions from the Oval Office. In one case, a microphone was left on after Bush finished responding to questions posed in advance by members of the Association of Christian Schools International. Bush was heard through the open mike complaining that he was thrown off because the questions were presented out of their pre-planned sequence. This level of "scriptedness" raised questions about the president's credibility, and, thereby, reduced his role in this Q & A session to that of a mere actor.[1]

Teflon

"Teflon" was the clever metaphor given to Ronald Reagan's finesse on the firing line. His capacity to deflect a question or comment, however tough or penetrating, and keep the audience on his side will remain one of the long-remembered assets that contributed to his well-deserved epithet, "The Great Communicator." As George Will remarked, Reagan is the only person who can "walk into a room, have the ceiling fall on him, and walk out without a fleck of plaster in his hair."

Wouldn't it be nice if we could purchase a can of Reagan Teflon that could envelop us with an impenetrable film to help repel potentially difficult or embarrassing questions? Although the ingredients of Reagan Teflon listed below can be part of the formula for achieving finesse, also be aware that Teflon can wear thin (as it did to an extent during Reagan's second term), and thereby undermine the potential rewards of finesse.

Ingredients of Teflon (the Reagan version)

- Popularity with the people.
- An affable, avuncular manner.
- A quick wit and a good sense of humor (including the capacity not to take oneself too seriously).
- A winning smile.
- A soothing voice.
- A generally at-ease manner.
- The capacity to sense the inherent danger/risk in a question.
- The ability to dodge and obfuscate artfully.
- The ability to memorize and compose on-the-spot compelling lines that capture the essence of your position.
- The capacity to maintain composure under duress ("grace under fire").
- An aura of respectability (in Reagan's case, generated by age).
- An aura of respectability (in Reagan's case, generated by the office he held and the resulting deference it generated).
- An ability to cultivate common ground (for Reagan, via his impressively expressed commitment to traditional American values).

Any attempt to blend these ingredients into a workable formula suited to someone else would be impossible, if not ridiculous (unless in preparation for a Ronald Reagan imitation). In fact, using any single ingredient of Reagan's Teflon often requires enormous self-understanding, patience, and practice. If one does not smile easily, trying to smile like Reagan in any kind of an engagement can become an immediate disaster. The same applies to a sense of humor. If a person doesn't have a sense of humor, 100 private lessons with Ronald Reagan, Jay Leno, or David Letterman are not likely to produce one. However, on the more positive side, we can cultivate one or more of the traits exemplified by Reagan, just not all of them in the manner he displayed them.

You might ask, "To what extent does finesse correlate with intelligence?" No doubt, intelligence can play an important role, especially in grasping the question vis-à-vis your agenda and demonstrating intelligent command of your subject matter. But finesse requires, among other things, sensitivity to one's audience, a factor not measurable by IQ. This point is best illustrated by the appearance on CNN's Daybreak show of Marilyn vos Savant who, according to the *Guinness Book of World Records*, possesses the world's highest IQ (228). During the call-in segment, an older gentleman began to pose a rambling, poorly focused, but politely stated question regarding advanced physics. Instead of mildly interrupting him with a cordial, nondefensive, "Sir, I'm sorry, I really don't have sufficient expertise in the area you are discussing," vos Savant broke in, rebuked him for being "too scientific," and told him to "lighten up" and ask something "more fun." Despite her astronomically high IQ, her FQ (as in "finesse quotient") was appallingly low.[2]

THE ROLE OF ROLES

Since an important aspect of your finesse is how well you gauge organizational politics or protocol, you are expected to anticipate, internalize, and play out roles during the Q & A. You need to play roles such as "leader," "expert," "crisis coordinator," "motivator," "advocate," "conciliator," "counselor," and "ratifier."

These roles, performed with finesse through the careful selection and skillful execution of your image goals (Chapter 3), can transmit powerful messages about your image and credibility, and help you avoid the negative facets of finesse.

The importance of roles is frequently highlighted during our crisis communication counsel and training. Men tend to have difficulty displaying credible empathy and compassion. In fact, their words, tone, and body language often appear stilted and, as a result, insincere (see Chapter 11). To break this tendency, we sometimes say to them, "Right now, you're not the corporation; you're the caring clergy, the country doctor, or the close friend of a person needing to feel that you and your corporation are not profit-mongers, but truly have a heart." Visualizing the role helps supplant the spokesperson's fears about the crisis, while he experiences fulfillment from being able to display genuine empathy and compassion.

THE ROLE OF EFFECTIVE LISTENING IN CULTIVATING FINESSE

Effective listening plays a crucial role in Q & A and, ultimately, in achieving finesse, for it forms the basis of good recall of the question as a prerequisite to an effective response. Effective listening is a four-step process involving hearing, attending, interpreting, and evaluating.

Hearing

During the summer of 1992 Billy Graham, the then-73-year-old evangelist, appeared before the Philadelphia press corps preceding a crusade he was to conduct at the city's Veterans Stadium. "What are your *fees*?" a reporter asked. Graham, who had told reporters to speak up because "My left ear doesn't hear too well," responded "The *theme* of the crusade is, there's hope." The reporter then followed up, "No, I understand what the theme is. What are they paying you?" Graham then got the message, responded, "Not one cent," and proceeded to explain that he didn't receive "a cent" for his speaking engagements, preaching, or royalties from his book.[3]

Graham's problem wasn't related to listening; it was pure and simple a hearing problem. Hearing is a prerequisite to listening— a physiological process in which the sensory receptors of the ear are stimulated by sound waves.

Barring a physical hearing impairment, the enemy of hearing is *environmental noise*. Environmental noise is any external sound that prevents you from hearing the question, and includes ringing telephones, loud voices, shutting doors, sirens and beepers, plus, of course, other conversations (which you may be partially listening to).

Attending

For effective listening to occur, you must mentally attend to words and messages. Attention requires mental effort. Thus, the enemy of attention is *mental noise*. Your mind may drift to a business or personal problem, you may lose focus because television cameras or microphones are being pushed in your face, you may be stymied by the complexity of a question, or you may be trying to retrieve the response as the question is being posed, and, as a result, tune out temporarily.

Interpreting

Interpreting verbal, visual, and gestural cues of a questioner or audience member is a crucial aspect of effective listening. When interpreting, you strive to make sense of a question, the motive(s) of a questioner, and the cues she transmits to help you understand the question. Interpreting, therefore, reinforces the idea that Q & A is a two-way, dynamic process. The versatility of your mind allows you to receive messages, read cues to help you interpret them, and send messages *simultaneously!*

Evaluating

The final stage of effective listening is evaluation. Evaluation is, in essence, a monitoring process that allows you to assess your own and the questioner's performances during the Q & A session. Evaluation often occurs as you are answering; that is, *you listen as you speak*. The following questions reflect the broad scope and complexity of the evaluative process:

- Did I hear the question correctly?
- Do I understand it? If not, should I ask that it be repeated or rephrased?
- Can I answer it? If not, what do I say?
- Why is the questioner asking this question? Should I ask her?
- What are the risks (personal, political, legal) surrounding a response to this question?
- Am I walking into a trap here?
- What roles am I expected to play?
- How responsive should I be?
- How long or detailed should my response be?
- To what extent does this question provide me with an opportunity to advance my persuasive goals?
- To what extent should I dissect the phrasing and assumptions of the question as part of my response?
- What image traits do I want to emphasize? (competence, compassion, etc.)?
- What positive, nonverbal cues should I transmit? What negative ones should I avoid?
- What inferences can I make, based on verbal and nonverbal cues, regarding interest in me, understanding of the information or issue, or the slant of a story? How confident can I be in these inferences?
- What inferences can I make regarding the resourcefulness, personality, and character of the questioner?
- Should I take "key word" notes?
- Are the "right" questions being asked?

During the real-life pressures of Q & A, your mind processes any combination of these evaluative decision points swiftly and simultaneously. In fact, it could be said that just as rapidly as a computer reads through its programs, so does your mind "read" through these evaluative "programs."

How Effective Listening Breaks Down

In big-league Q & A, the best memory in the world will not help you if (1) you do not adequately hear, attend to, and understand a question; (2) you are not sensitive to the questioner's intent; or (3) if you cannot sufficiently—and efficiently—evaluate your performance. Thus, poor listening can have a domino effect: it can cause you to mishear or misinterpret the question, remember the wrong things, be unaware that you are answering with inaccurate or irrelevant information and so on.

A memorable example: do you remember Gerald Ford's gaffe in the 1976 debate with Jimmy Carter when he repeatedly stated that there was no Soviet domination over Eastern Europe? If you do, you probably remember asking yourself and others, "Why did he say that?" Although it is difficult to determine precisely what prompted this answer, poor listening was definitely a factor. I repeatedly analyzed a videotape of the debate, and have drawn three specific conclusions. Each highlights how poor listening resulted in a gaffe that many political observers claim helped prevent Ford's return to the White House: (1) Ford's level of emotional intensity in delivering his response to the question was so strong that he was too focused on speaking and not listening; (2) as a result, he interrupted Max Frankel, the questioner, as he posed his follow-up question; and (3) in so doing, Ford failed to listen with his eyes and ears to Frankel's transparent verbal and visual cues that he had misspoken.

Poor Listening Habits

Of the many types of listening pitfalls, four are especially common in the Q & A setting: (1) feigned listening; (2) sporadic listening; (3) argumentative listening; (4) distracted listening.

Feigned listening. Feigned listening is when we make believe we are paying attention by maintaining eye contact, nodding our heads, saying "I see," and providing other nonverbal and verbal cues to indicate listening. This pitfall can be especially pronounced when the respondent is so prepared to respond that she acts attentive to the questioner while saying to herself, "Hurry up and finish so I can answer."

Sporadic listening. Sporadic listening is often used with feigned listening. It involves a tuning-in-and-out process in which your understanding is based on piecing together what you did listen to, however poorly or well. To an extent, Gerald Ford's listening before he committed his infamous gaffe was sporadic. While being asked a question, you may be engaging in sporadic listening as you rethink the answer you just gave, or rush ahead to respond to the question you *think* is being asked.

Argumentative listening. This pitfall, sometimes called *verbal battle*, involves preparing a counterargument as you listen to a question or answer. As you do, you may be missing the full spirit of what was asked. People especially prone to this pitfall (probably the most common one we run into in our practice) tend to be defensive in general, have difficulty depersonalizing an exchange, or both. The fear of forgetting the counterpoint can seriously compound this problem. Hence, problems related to listening and memory converge.

Distracted listening. How many times have you been conversing with someone when a radio or TV message catches your ear and your interest? Basic politeness prevents you from saying that the distraction is more important than the conversation. Therefore, you inattentively listen to both the person you're conversing with and the source of the distraction.

Your Body Language and Listening

Listening with your eyes is just as important as listening with your ears. As you are being questioned, which cue(s) common to Q & A is (are) present?

• *Interrupting questioner.* Impatience, defensiveness, aggressiveness, lack of respect for questioner or audience.

- *Looking down or away.* Possible sign of timidity, insecurity, dislike, difficulty with the question, the need for "private" thinking time.
- *Smiling.* Confidence, embarrassment ("You got me"), pleasure (that the question was asked).
- *Scratching head.* Discomfort, the need for thinking time, and yes, a simple itch.
- *Turning body away from audience.* Discomfort, defensiveness, the need for "private" thinking time.
- *Walking toward audience.* Confidence, a desire to engage, or create a more personal or intimate feeling.
- *Rubbing hands, or making "church steeples" with fingers.* Anxiety, tension.
- *Folding arms across chest.* Defensive or unable to find an appropriate relaxed position.
- *Tilting head and chin upward.* Confidence, arrogance.
- *Nodding head.* "I understand," "I agree," "Hurry up and finish."
- *Shaking head.* "I don't follow you"; "I disagree."
- *Holding chin before responding.* Reflection, sometimes indicating difficulty with the question.
- *Blinking.* Blinking frequency has recently become the focus of interesting and widely publicized research conducted by Joseph J. Tecce, professor of neuropsychology at Boston College.[4] His study revealed that a subject's eyeblink frequency tends to increase under stressful conditions (called *negative hedonic states*) and decrease under conditions of contentment and pleasure (*positive hedonic states*). Applying his hypothesis to the second Bush–Dukakis debate in the 1988 campaign, he found that Dukakis produced 75 blinks per minute (BPMs) while Bush averaged 67. Fifteen is considered normal for general conversation, whereas 35 is the norm for news-related television appearances.

The context can usually prove helpful in interpreting most body cues. But remember, if a cue is particularly pronounced and you are having difficulty interpreting it, you may want to ask a question about it, for example, "Why are you shaking your head?" If you don't, you may be limiting your potential as a quality listener.

Effective Listening and Remembering

Without a doubt, good memory skills are necessary in big-league Q & A. A good hitter in baseball is required to learn and remember the pitcher's repertoire of pitches and when they are used. In a Q & A session, you need to learn and remember:

1. The styles and expectations of your questioners, plus those of other targeted audience members.
2. The overall import of the question: its language, tone, logic, and facets.
3. Relevant net effects, substance, and image goals, and tactics (Chapter 3).
4. The content required for answering the question: ideas, evidence, events, feelings, etc.

Memory will be discussed in greater detail in Chapter 4, when I clarify its relationship to your finesse. Here, the important point is that your memory depends on solid preparation (Chapter 3) and the mental agility that effective listening affords you when the question is "fired."

Active Listening

To facilitate good recall and understanding of the questioner's intent, you can engage in "active listening." This technique involves restating your interpretation of their question. The questioner then provides feedback regarding whether or not you understood the question sufficiently, and clarifies the point(s) you did not understand. In a Q & A exchange between a feature reporter and an executive communication consultant, active listening might work like this:

Reporter:
What does an executive communication consultant do?

Consultant (*as active listener*):

Do you mean specifically what assignments we work on or how we address them?

Reporter:

What assignments you work on.

Consultant:

We prepare people for speeches, presentations, and media appearances, including crisis situations.

Reporter (*as active listener*):

You mean you write speeches and coach people to deliver them?

Consultant:

We mainly provide ideas for the speeches, often working closely with the speechwriter. Then we advise our clients how to deliver them. A good portion of our practice is also devoted to preparing them to face the media.

Reporter (*as active listener*):

So you don't necessarily write the speeches?

Consultant:

Correct. Often our role, in addition to coaching, is strategic.

Reporter (*as active listener*):

Strategic. What does that mean?

Consultant:

Analyzing the audience, defining precise outcomes for the engagement (called *net effects goals*), shaping the ideas, and phrasing and organizing the message to achieve the goals.

Reporter (*ending the active listening process*):

Now I understand.

As helpful as active listening might be in clarifying and preventing misunderstanding, plus its enormous value in instructional settings, too full a commitment to it can result in your relinquishing sufficient control of the exchange, thereby permitting the questioner to press you too much.

Your listening appraisal. A good way to determine how good a listener you are is to rate yourself. Use the following questions as but a sample. Place the number that corresponds to the most accurate response beside each question, then total them at the end to see how much improvement you need.

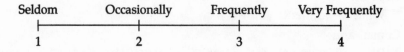

Seldom   Occasionally   Frequently   Very Frequently

1   2   3   4

1. ____ Make and maintain a commitment to listen attentively and nondefensively and to understand what is being said.

2. ____ Commit yourself to being perceived as a good listener.

3. ____ Maintain eye contact with the audience.

4. ____ Avoid playing with keys, pens, notes, or other objects during a conversation.

5. ____ Maintain contact with the audience instead of "walking" or turning away until the conversation has ended.

6. ____ Avoid excessive nodding or other improper body language aimed at expediting the completion of a statement or question.

7. ____ Create an environment free from unnecessary distractions and conducive to open communication.

8. ____ Avoid cutting the questioner off in midsentence.

9. ____ Transmit appropriate verbal or nonverbal cues to demonstrate understanding or misunderstanding.

10. ____ Take notes to aid listening patience and message retention.

Add the total number of points you assign to each item and rate your ability according to the following table:

40	Perfect
36–39	Excellent
33–35	Good/Very good
30–32	Fair
29 and below	Take notice!

Based on your self-assessment, establish specific listening objectives for yourself. Then, at a later point, take the survey again to track your development as a quality listener.[5]

THE ROLE OF FEAR

Although people are often more comfortable during Q & A than, for instance, during their presentation, fear in Q & A can be very real, especially if the situation is unusual and the stakes are high (e.g., an appearance on "Nightline" with Ted Koppel, a meeting with financial analysts, or a presentation for a major contract). Fear in Q & A, as in most any situation, can be your friend or foe. As a friend, it can motivate you to take the necessary steps toward achieving finesse. As a foe, especially an overpowering one, it can cause you to (1) procrastinate in preparing for Q & A, (2) underprepare, (3) not prepare, or (4) perform poorly.

How can you get the best of fear before it gets the best of you? Over the years, the following advice has been especially helpful to the people we advise:

• *Fear is controllable; declare a full-scale mental war on it.* If you think that fear is an external force that has invaded you like a virus, you're wrong. Fear is an emotional state that can't be conquered by pills or a needle. Your will power is the *only* antidote.

• *Pinpoint the source(s) of your fear.* Is it the fear of:

1. Forgetting?
2. Making a misstatement?
3. Losing your cool?
4. Being upstaged by another participant?
5. Being challenged?
6. Being generally unimpressive?
7. Something else?

If you have any—or even all—of these fears, take heart. Not only are they common, but they are controllable. By pinpointing your fears, you can pay closer attention to addressing them as you review briefing materials and engage in practice sessions. For example, the fear of forgetting, discussed in Chapter 4, can be combatted in several ways.

• *Set realistic expectations for yourself.* You are not expected to be an oral encyclopedia. Through in-depth audience analysis and counsel from trusted colleagues, you should be able to gauge accurately what and how much your target audience expects from you.

• *Value your base of knowledge.* Whether you are an expert on the subject or simply well-versed, you wouldn't be fielding questions unless you were regarded by the audience as having something of potential worth to share with them. Keeping this thought in mind throughout the Q & A will reinforce your positive mental attitude.

• *Appreciate your range of control.* Following the advice presented in this book will greatly broaden your range of control. And the more you feel in control, the less fearful—the more confident—you should be.

• *Don't participate in the Q & A until your sense of opportunity is stronger than your sense of risk.* Often a tall order, but a necessary one. If you are more focused on risks than opportunity (the achievement of your net effects goals, Chapter 3), you will probably be setting yourself up for failure. Stay singlemindedly focused on your goals, reminding yourself that your positive attitude is your lifeline to scoring on the firing line.

• *Don't let a few weak answers undermine your confidence and your competitive spirit.* I've seen it happen all too often. An executive allows one or two weak answers to get the best of her. Instead of fighting on to recapture any lost ground, she loses heart. If you identify with this tendency, you simply can't allow your loss of confidence to be harder on you than the toughest questioner. By summoning your competitive spirit, you might have a fighting chance of not only diluting the impact of your weak responses, but of turning out a performance generally regarded as impressive.

• *Practice, practice, practice.* Except for your willpower in achieving a positive mental attitude, thorough, systematic practice is the most important path to self-confidence and finesse. (This subject is discussed at length in Chapter 14.)

THE ROLE OF OVERCONFIDENCE

Overconfidence can be just as dangerous as fear. The overconfident executive is all too prone to place a low priority or say "no" altogether to preparation. Several factors may account for this: (1) fear disguised as overconfidence; (2) a general lack of appreciation for Q & A as a skill; (3) the tendency to feel comfortable in Q & A, and to therefore confuse being comfortable with being effective; (4) the executive's inability to distinguish between the Q & A skills required in situations in which she performed well and the more formidable one she now faces; (5) a lack of appreciation for the stakes of the situation; (6) an ego, reinforced by related or unrelated experience, that feeds the notion that she can influence most anybody.

It is difficult to give specific advice regarding overconfidence without knowing the person. However, dealing with factors 4 and 5 above may require that you help the executive understand the unusual challenges related to the upcoming Q & A exchange, including the stakes.

SETTING YOUR Q & A AGENDA AND NEGOTIATING THE "RIGHT" ANSWER

As stated earlier, how you evaluate your answers is a vital part of Q & A. However, the evaluations that seem to matter the most in Q & A are the questioner's expectations of what constitutes the "right" answer to her question. I say "seem to matter the most" for a reason: although a questioner always has the advantage of *forming* the question and setting her agenda, you are involved in *negotiating* the "right" answer.

Negotiating is an implicit mental approach where you use the Q & A session to set your agenda while seeking to meet—or exceed—your target audience's needs. I am referring, therefore, to a classical "win-win" scenario where both you and your audience "win." Your success during this negotiation depends on two factors. First, a thorough audience analysis will make you sensitive to the needs, interests, attitudes, knowledge level, questioning style, and expectations of your questioners—especially your target audience members. Second, well-defined net effects, substance, and image goals (Chapter 3) will create the working framework for your "win." These goals, put into message form, direct everything you do verbally and nonverbally during Q & A. A few negotiating scenarios:

The Media Interview

During a media interview, a reporter expects you to be a newsworthy source—to be cooperative, clear, truthful, and provide helpful information conducive to a good story (her "win"). In return, you expect to be treated fairly and to be neither misquoted nor quoted out of context (your "win").

Financial Analysts Meetings

When you appear before financial analysts, they expect you to disclose as fully as possible anything they regard as pertinent to assessing your company's strengths and weaknesses as an investment. They can press you hard—unrelentingly—regarding such issues as the rationales behind your organizational structure, commitment to research and development, financial performance and projections, and confidence in one or more existing or proposed product lines.

While engaging in an implicit negotiation with them, you must make your strongest case without tipping your hand to the competition, or divulging any sensitive information that might adversely impact employees, customers, shareholders, or other target audience members. As you do, the analysts must feel that your responses are reasonably candid, comprehensive, and collectively credible (their "win"). In return for meeting—or exceeding—their expectations, your "win" for your finesse during the negotiation is a favorable report circulated throughout the investment community.

A dramatic example of a poorly negotiated exchange between financial analysts and senior management of Chambers Development Company was reported in *The Wall Street Journal*. The company had recently approved an unorthodox accounting move that dropped shareholder earnings from 83 cents a share to 3 cents. The following excerpt from the coverage illustrates that the media are just as prone to report the respondent's behavior as the substance:

> Several analysts who attended a presentation by Mr. Knight (the Chief Financial Officer) and the elder Mr. Rangos (the Chairman and founder of the Company) two weeks ago in New York said the men were unusually brusque, and even ill-informed, when confronted with tough questions. Analysts said they booed Mr. Rangos when he attempted to blame them for the stock price's drop, and found Mr. Knight particularly abrasive when he was asked if Chambers would hire a new accounting firm.[6]

The remainder of this book is about how you can increase your negotiating potential in Q & A by capitalizing on your ability to take control of your behavior and substance and summon the inner strength to challenge your questioners to *fire away!*

Chapter Three

Behind the Scenes: Audience Analysis and Goal Setting

T he President of the United States has advance teams who visit a city or town days or weeks before his appearance. Their role: to determine the public's reaction to his upcoming visit; to do everything feasible to reduce the element of surprise; and to make sure that the setting, format, and timing of his message place him in the most advantageous light. Even if you do not have an advance team, you or someone designated by you (preferably a communications specialist) should do everything possible to understand your audience—whether your presentation is in-house or external.

This chapter provides you with practical advice regarding two critical steps toward achieving finesse: (1) how to conduct your audience analysis; and (2) how to use it as the foundation for defining your goals—for capitalizing on your control by setting your agenda for the Q & A exchange.

Few of us will forget the highly contested U.S. Supreme Court confirmation hearings in 1987 over the ill-fated nomination of Judge Robert Bork. During his 32 hours of testimony, Bork was asked by a friendly senator the most predictable question of all: "Why do you want to be on the Court?" Instead of presenting a patriotic essay about the honor and privilege of preserving freedom and the Constitution, Bork said that serving on the court would be "an intellectual feast." This answer was one of several that reinforced Bork's image as a cold-blooded ideologue. In fact, even a key supporter implied that he had not tailored his answers to his audience and the setting: "This was a political event, it was not a trial or a law school debate."[1]

No message can reach its potential impact unless it is tailored to the needs, wants, desires, values, or goals of an audience. The speaker who is too self-centered or too content-centered is normally doomed to mediocrity—or failure. Enter audience analysis.

Audience analysis is used to learn as much as possible in advance about your audience before you speak and field questions. This process applies to any type of engagement within or outside the organization. Audience analysis has three principal components: demographic analysis, knowledge level analysis, and attitudinal analysis.

The following scenario places the practical nature of audience analysis in perspective: You are a leading manufacturer of contractor pumps and have been invited to address a plumbing and heating contractors' convention session regarding "Aqua-Thrust," an innovative pump your firm has just manufactured. Before you prepare your remarks, you decide to secure answers to the following questions, classified according to the three components of audience analysis.

Demographic analysis

How many people are expected to attend?
How many will be plumbing versus heating contractors?
How many will be dealers?
How many will be your customers?
Will there be others?
How many are already using the "Hydro-Thrust" pump (the precursor to the Aqua-Thrust)?

Knowledge level analysis

How familiar are they with the basic design of a contractor pump?
To what extent do they have the technical background to understand the Aqua-Thrust design?
How familiar are they with the featured advantages of the Aqua-Thrust design over conventional pumps?

Attitudinal analysis

How satisfied or dissatisfied are they with the pumps they currently sell or use? Why?

How do they feel about the Aqua-Thrust pump? Why?

How do they regard your company? Your industry? You? Why?

MAKING YOUR AUDIENCE ANALYSIS WORK FOR YOU

Let's assume the following conclusions from the Aqua-Thrust audience analysis described above: you decide that your primary target audience consists of dealerships that sell to major contractors, and includes the major contractors themselves. You learn that their experience with and understanding of the Aqua-Thrust pump is minimal. Your audience analysis further reveals that although they respect your company, they know little about you. Finally, you learn that their attachment to the leading competitive product is moderate to extremely strong, mainly because of reliability and price.

These facts should promote the following two major tactical approaches to both the presentation and the Q & A:

1. Since the audience is not familiar with you, you will need to find ways to *cultivate your credibility* (Chapter 5).

2. Because your target audience's knowledge level of Aqua-Thrust is minimal, you will need to *educate as you persuade*.

To accomplish these tactics, choose language, concepts, and examples suited to your target audience's interest, experience, and level of understanding. Explain the advantages of Aqua-Thrust with fair-minded comparative references to the leading competitive product. Your persuasive challenge is to make your audience substitute a new criterion to evaluate the benefits of the Aqua-Thrust (e.g., faster water evacuation) in relation to its reliability and cost.

If Aqua-Thrust's reliability is strong and the price issue is nonexistent or modest, then the water evacuation capacity feature, if appreciably greater than the competitive product's, may offset concerns regarding price. If that's the case, you should highlight Aqua-Thrust's reliability, competitive price, and water evacuation feature early in the presentation, while underscoring the economic benefits of faster evacuation.

The basic lesson this example provides is that your audience analysis is crucial to both your presentation and Q & A as you select ideas, language, and examples, as well as shape and implement a pattern of organization.

OBTAINING INFORMATION ABOUT YOUR AUDIENCE

Four principal methods are available to you in conducting a quality audience analysis: telephone interviews, private meetings, informal contacts, and formal surveys.

Telephone Interviews

If you have an outside speaking engagement or plan to be making a presentation before a prospective or current client, picking up the telephone to ask one or more reliable sources a series of prepared questions can be one of your best investments in preparation time. In some instances, for example, a speaking engagement, you can prepare your secretary, assistant, or public information staff member to ask the questions. And don't worry about the impression such inquiries will make; in fact, the "right" questions asked in the "right" manner will probably convey your earnestness and sensitivity in preparing for the engagement.

Private Meetings

Although a private meeting can be helpful in conducting an audience analysis for major outside speaking engagements, it can be especially helpful for internal presentations. For example, if you are planning to make a major presentation and expect resistance from key audience members, meeting with them in advance can help you discern where they stand and why. Moreover, it can provide an opening for sowing the seeds for your persuasive advances.

Informal Contacts

Valuable audience analysis information can be obtained deliberately or occur spontaneously in the most informal settings—over coffee, at lunch, in the hallway, or on the way to work. The company grapevine can provide you with the latest information regarding who is or is not attending your presentation and what the current "pulse" is regarding it. However, before you accept any of this information as gospel, do your best to verify it. If you can't, and the information is crucial to your message, decide in advance how you should adjust your message just in case the grapevine proves itself reliable.

Formal Surveys

Formal surveys may seem a bit unorthodox, but I have used them successfully for several of my own speaking engagements. I draft the survey, and the host organization distributes it and returns it to me for tabulation and interpretation. I then base my remarks on it, often referring specifically to the data during both my speech and the Q & A session. The main advantages of this approach are specificity and accuracy. Rather than merely relying on the input of a few members of the host organization, you can secure data from most, if not all, of the audience.

AUDIENCE ANALYSIS AND TARGETING FOR INTERNAL PRESENTATIONS

Audience analysis tends to be underutilized in internal situations. Although executives frequently rely on general input regarding their audience or committee (such as whether they are for or against a particular proposal), all too often they fail to take their analysis to the next step—to determine the specific reasons *why*.

"Why" information is crucial to knowing how to preempt arguments within the presentation itself and to build on them during the Q & A. If we don't understand the "why's," we weaken the links between the benefits of our proposal and the audience's needs and, therefore, we shun the essence of persuasion.

During your internal committee meetings, who are the key people you need to "sign on" to get your proposal moving? The CEO? CFO? Chief counsel? Head of human resources? How do their positions and frames of reference influence the types of questions they ask? More specifically, *where* do they stand regarding your proposal? *Why?* How intensely?

Intensity can best be described according to the following scale:

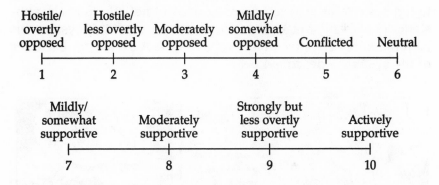

As you interpret data gathered from your audience analysis, you can normally rely on this widely accepted principle of persuasion: the greater the hostility, the less the susceptibility to persuasion, especially conversion. Therefore, one's persuasive energies should generally be concentrated primarily on people with opinions in the 4 to 7 range on the scale, unless the principal persuasive goal is reinforcement.

You may be asking, "What if my target audience members fall below the 4 range?" In such instances, you should not rely too heavily on the presentation and the Q & A session for the support you seek. Rather, you may need to develop a campaign built on internal lobbying and multiple presentations to persuade your audience to "buy into" your proposal.

Remember that your audience analysis is crucial to both your presentation and Q & A as you select ideas, language, and examples, as well as shape a pattern of organization. *To paraphrase the American Express ad, "Audience analysis is a must; don't leave home without it."*

GOAL SETTING

If audience analysis is about tailoring your message to the needs, wants, expectations, values, and goals of the audience, then goal setting is your way of defining precisely the persuasive impact you want to have on your audience, and, therefore, the starting point to controlling your messages. I have developed a three-tiered system for goal setting comprised of net effects goals, substance goals, and image goals. Properly executed, this system can be remarkably effective in any type of Q & A exchange. Each tier of the system is described below.

Net Effects Goals

Net effects goals refer to the end results you wish to achieve in response to your Q & A session—to the precisely defined impact you want to have on your audience. Normally, these end results or net effects are the same as those established for your speech or presentation. Net effects goals should be described in terms of attitude change and/or behavior change. Therefore, in defining these goals, ask the following fundamental questions: (1) what specific attitudes within my target audience must I modify to achieve maximum persuasive impact, and (2) should some form of behavior change also be linked to the attitude change I am seeking?

The following questions should help you define your net effects goals even more precisely:

Are you seeking:

1. Psychological support ("buy-in") from one or more target audiences?
2. An enhanced relationship with one or more target audiences?
3. An enhanced image?
4. Material support (financial, human resources, legislative, etc.)?
5. The diminution or elimination of competitive forces?
6. A combination of net effects goals?
7. Something else?

Once you both pinpoint the one or more questions above that capture your general intent and clarify their relative importance, then phrase your goal(s) as specifically as possible. For example, let's say that you are requesting an allocation for more staffing. Under these circumstances, questions 1 and 4 above would undoubtedly be prime net effects goals. However, so far they are only stated generally. More specifically stated, they would be: "To convince the three target members of the board who initially seemed most disinclined to my idea that the added staffing (five persons) is necessary. For this reason, they should approve a personnel appropriation of $315,000 plus benefits."

Net effects goals can be less overt—and even covert. For example, in preparing scores of executives to appear before the national conventions of their trade or professional organizations, I have discovered that the substance of their messages was frequently a secondary concern. Their primary concern: to make a sufficiently striking impression to enhance not only their visibility and expertise, but, their potential for a more attractive career opportunity with another firm as well.

Net effects goals should also be defined in terms of the behavior you should seek to *prevent* from occurring within your target audience. This is most important when dealing with sensitive and controversial matters, especially during a crisis (see Chapter 11). The following questions put the preventive net effects goal-setting step in perspective:

Are you seeking to prevent:

- Protest?
- Erosion of support (psychological, financial, etc.)?
- Deterioration of morale?
- Possible or anticipated misperceptions of fact?
- Release of sensitive or proprietary information?
- Speculation/rumor?
- The perception of negligence?
- Public concern or fear?
- The highlighting of a distracting/potentially embarrassing negative?
- Undue optimism or pessimism?
- Any combination of the above?
- Something else?

By identifying the appropriate preventive goal(s), anticipating responses to questions related to them, and actively keeping them in mind throughout the Q & A session, you can help avert a potentially difficult situation as you pursue your more positive or proactive goals.

Substance Goals

A substance goal refers to the specific attitudinal impact you seek within your target audience in response to each separate argument needed to help you achieve your net effects goal.

For example, if your net effects goal is to convince senior management to close down one of your manufacturing sites, some of the substantive goals might be to convince your audience that the site:

- Produces a product for which demand is declining.
- Has outdated equipment.
- Possesses a weak work force.
- Has an inhospitable tax structure.

The substance goals are interim *checkpoints* on your way to your ultimate destination, the net effects goals. Once you define your substance goals, you are therefore better positioned to discover the arguments that become the routes to those checkpoints. This process represents the essence of building a tight, persuasive case.

To illustrate briefly, using the example above:

Net effects goal (specific): To convince targeted members of senior management that the plant, located in North Gardiner, Maine, should be closed down indefinitely.

Substance Goal #1: To convince them that it is not needed.

Argument #1: Our current sites minus the North Gardiner plant can handle capacity well into the future.

Substance Goal #2: To convince them that the tax structure is no longer hospitable.

Argument #2: The recent municipal reassessment makes it economically unfeasible to operate in North Gardiner any longer.

Any net effects goal or combination of net effects goals requires an indefinite number of substance goals and arguments. Once these are determined, your role during the Q & A session is to reinforce those considered most potentially persuasive to your target audience. For example, in the illustration above, if your target audience is clearly persuaded that there is no further need for the North Gardiner plant, then the taxation argument is moot.

However, you can't always determine in advance precisely what your target audience's attitudes are and why they hold them. In this case, you may be obliged to adopt the "flypaper theory," advancing somewhat blindly a series of arguments based on your substance goals. You hope that, like flies on flypaper, some will stick on your target audience members and thereby result in your net effects goals being satisfied.

As straightforward as the preceding discussion may be, setting net effects and substance goals can be complicated, especially if multiple audiences need to be courted at once. For example, as I was advising the head of a national interest group that represents a somewhat controversial line of consumer products, it became clear to me that he had at least three different messages for at least *six* different audiences.

1. The consumer, legislators, regulators, and the secular press: "The product line is safe."
2. The financial analysts: "The product line should enhance sales and profitability."
3. The trade association members: "The product line, if subjected to extensive government regulation due to issues of safety, could undermine the financial stability of member institutions."

As you prepare your key arguments or messages based on your net effects and substance goals, keep the following questions in mind:

1. What target audiences will be immediately present and which might likely learn of my appearance?
2. Which target audiences are more important for this exchange?
3. Do my goals need to be reshaped based on my responses to 1 and 2 above? If so, how?
4. How much background understanding will my target audience need as I seek to reinforce a key message during the Q & A?
5. Are my major key arguments sufficiently distinct to prevent the perception of overlap?
6. Are they selected and phrased in a manner conducive to maximum persuasive impact?

7. Are the key arguments sufficiently limited in number to prevent confusion and possible dilution of my intended impact?

8. Is each major argument well substantiated? (See Chapter 7.)

Careful preparation based on these questions provides a stronger foundation for responding to questions properly, for remember— *the Q & A session is usually a forum for actively advancing your key messages.*

Image Goals

You may remember George Bush's need to counter his "wimp" image during the 1988 presidential race. Specifically, he was perceived by large segments of the media and the public as a weak, nice guy who lacked the courage of his convictions. To offset this image, his advisors encouraged him to sound more forceful, forthright, and even contentious. This latter advice resulted in his highly publicized combative exchange with the debate moderator Jim Gannon, of the *Des Moines Register*, during the pre-Iowa caucus debate. Bush projected a similar tone in an interview with CBS's Dan Rather a few weeks later.

You probably also remember Supreme Court nominee Clarence Thomas's appearance before the Senate Judiciary Committee in October 1991, to face charges that several years earlier he had sexually harassed a young female lawyer assigned to him. In riveting testimony following a highly credible, composed, and, to many, compelling appearance by his accuser, Anita Hill, Thomas displayed four prominent traits (defiance, anger, indignation, and hurt) as he refuted the charges as baseless, calling the hearings a "high-tech lynching." The collective force of these traits contributed mightily to his reversing a tide of negative public opinion and his confirmation by a narrow margin (52–48) three days later.

Setting image goals is hardly confined to the political arena. "Chemistry" is an integral aspect of any interaction, including Q & A exchanges. Image goals help you control the chemistry. To best understand image goal setting, you need to ask yourself the following four questions:

1. What traits do I need to project personally?
2. What traits should my company, division, industry, or profession project?
3. What traits should I consciously avoid projecting?
4. What traits should my company, division, industry, or profession avoid projecting?

The following image trait inventory, broken into two categories, Positive and Preventive Goals, can be especially helpful in responding to these questions.

Very frequently	Frequently	Occasionally	Seldom
1	2	3	4

Positive

1. Action orientation
2. Analytical ability
3. Approachability
4. Assertiveness
5. Believability/credibility
6. Candor
7. Charisma
8. Community orientation
9. Compassion/caring
10. Competence
11. Competitiveness
12. Composure/calmness
13. Confidence
14. Conviction
15. Cooperativeness
16. Courage
17. Decisiveness
18. Dependability
19. Detail orientation
20. Directness
21. Discipline
22. Energy
23. Enthusiasm
24. Fairness
25. Flexibility
26. Friendliness
27. Graciousness
28. Hard-working nature
29. Humorous nature
30. Imagination
31. Integrity
32. Kindness
33. Knowledgeability
34. Liking for people

35. Loyalty
36. Maturity
37. Neatness
38. Objectivity
39. Openness
40. Organized
41. Other-directed
42. Patience
43. Positive attitude
44. Reassuring
45. Relaxation
46. Respect for others
47. Righteous indignation

48. Security
49. Self-reliance
50. Sensitivity
51. Sincerity
52. Standards/values expectations
53. Strength
54. Tactfulness
55. Tenacity
56. Toughness
57. Trusting nature
58. Warmth

Preventive

1. Anger
2. Arrogance/aloofness
3. Condescending/ patronizing
4. Defensiveness
5. Detachment
6. Disdainfulness
7. Glib

8. Hostility
9. Impatience
10. Pedantic
11. Preachiness
12. Selfish/self-centered
13. Stress/tension/anxiety
14. Strident/shrill

Now that you have reviewed the image trait inventory, consider these insights and advice:

- *Image at times can take precedence over substance,* particularly when the audience is not well-informed or is confused about the subject, or when credibility is a more important decision-making criterion than content.

- *Do not adopt an image trait incompatible with your personality.* This is dishonest; moreover, you may be setting yourself up to be perceived as phony.

- *Bear in mind the most essential image traits* (generally no more than three) you need to project throughout the Q & A session.

- *Be prepared to modify the importance you assign to any given image trait* based on audience and circumstance.

Now let's see how all three aspects of goal setting—net effects goals, substance goals, and image goals—can help prepare you to build finesse and capitalize on your control on the firing line.

You are the CEO of a major pharmaceutical company that produces a widely used antidepressant. In recent months your company has been facing highly publicized criticism in the national media over the drug's safety record. Now, the Food and Drug Administration (FDA) has convened an advisory panel of experts to investigate the drug's safety. You have called together your top corporate advisors and outside consultants to prepare for the upcoming session. Your audience analysis has prepared you for:

- The concerns of the specific FDA panelists.
- The type of questioning you will face.
- The medical community's (including the affected patients') concerns.
- The public's concern.
- The potential media coverage.

Your next job is to define your net effects goal(s): to convince the FDA panel to conclude, without qualification, that the drug is safe. To achieve your net effects goal, you must combine your substance and image goals. Your substance goal is to prove the drug's safety through arguments based on methodologically sound and compelling safety studies and persuasive expert testimony. Your primary image goals are to demonstrate objectivity, candor, analytical skills, high standards, sensitivity to opposing viewpoints, and to avoid defensiveness.

Now you are prepared to use your audience analysis and goals to leverage control over your credibility (Chapter 5), environment (Chapter 6), and messages (Chapter 7). However, before discussing these aspects of control, let's take a look inside your mind at the process that stores all the information you've prepared—your memory.

Chapter Four

Memory Matters

MARTEL/DESLAURIERS

F ew people know very much about how memory works. This subject has intrigued—and baffled—philosophers, psychologists, and other researchers for centuries. The two basic functions of memory—storing and retrieving information—are so much a part of everyday life that, like walking or breathing, we usually take them for granted. Memory only becomes noticeable or problematic when we are learning to do something new, or find ourselves temporarily—or permanently—stumped.

Yet, certain activities require great amounts of learning through developed and rehearsed memory. Q & A is such an activity. My first word of advice: *never* take your memory for granted in preparing for a Q & A exchange. Consider, for example, the television show "Jeopardy." Contestants consistently impress us with their ability to recall information from categories like Meteorology, Greek Mythology, Gems, Biblical Names, or Alphabet Soup. The winner gets to return to the show; the losers receive consolation prizes, plus the thrill of having appeared on national TV.

Business-oriented Q & A, however, is not "Jeopardy." However, it is often fraught with memory-challenging risks that can jeopardize the fate of the respondent's goals, and even her career path in responding to questions from such categories as Justify that Budget! Explain that Proposed Downsizing! and Demonstrate Shareholder Value!

When preparing for a Q & A session, executives and politicians exhibit three major types of problematic behavior related to memory: (1) *overconfidence*, where smoothness and a good recall track record become confused with the specific memory requirements for the upcoming engagement; (2) *raw fear*, causing many of our best and brightest to shun adequate preparation altogether or to procrastinate to the point where their investment is too little, too late; and (3) *obsessive preparation*, that is, the need to know everything to succeed on the firing line.

Whether these behaviors apply to you or not, this chapter explains ways for you to capitalize on what I call *fire away memory*. *Fire away memory* links your memory skills (storing and retrieving information) to what you learned from in-depth audience analysis and precise goal setting (Chapter 3). Thus, the quality of your memory is not the key factor for an effective fire away memory per se; rather, the key factor is how well you use your memory to integrate your audience analysis and net effects, substance, and image goals into a coherent, control-oriented Q & A agenda that is readily accessible on the firing line.

A PRIMER ON FIRE AWAY MEMORY

You may recall from Chapter 2 that effective listening was linked to memory. There, I highlighted your need to remember:

1. The styles and expectations of your questioners, plus those of other targeted audience members.
2. Relevant net effects, substance, and image goals, plus the tactics based on them.

These factors—stored in memory—form the heart of fire away memory. The most prodigious memory in the world will not help you capitalize on your advocacy potential in major-league Q & A if you have not conducted audience analysis and formed net effects, substance, and image goals—*and* adequately stored these into memory.

Two other factors critical to effective fire away memory involve remembering:

3. The overall import of the question: its language, tone, logic, facts, and facets.
4. The content required for answering the question: ideas, evidence, events, feelings, etc.

Obviously, *retrieving* information on the firing line is certainly as important as *storing* it beforehand. And here we address two crucial principles regarding how memory works.

Fire Away Memory: Principle 1

Contrary to popular belief, your memory is not simply a storage chest in your brain into which you deposit material and withdraw it when needed. Rather, memory consists of fragments stored in a web of associations. To retrieve data from your memory, you need to activate one of the strands, a neurological process called *priming*. This leads to a crucial point: *memories are often reconstructed at the time of withdrawal*, depending significantly on how they are primed or stimulated by the question, the questioner's personality and rank or status, plus the context in which the question is asked. Therefore, the same basic question posed in different words, or reflecting a different tone, or both, could prime your memory differently and result in two responses varying in degree.

Fire Away Memory: Principle 2

Our memory is both *complex* and *imperfect*. Your brain is composed of miles of long, tentacle-like cells called *neurons*. It stores information as electrical impulses and converts stimuli into electrical "currents," or neural pathways, that become your memory. Countless neural pathways are spread throughout your brain—everything from tying your shoes to knowing the capital of Pennsylvania is encoded in a neural pathway.

Although your memory as a whole is huge, it can store only a small amount of new information at one time. To store great amounts of new information long term, it must pass from short-term memory into long-term memory.

SHORT-TERM MEMORY

Short-term memory applies to the number of items a person can perceive at once. It is, therefore, closely related to attention span. Short-term memory has a rapid forgetting rate—30 seconds or less. Your forgetting rate is illustrated by the number of times you need to reread a simple step required for assembling something you recently purchased, by your forgetting a telephone number right after you looked it up, or, in Q & A, by your forgetting the facet of a clearly stated multifaceted question. Short-term memory has a limited capacity, approximately seven items for most people, regardless of age or culture.

You may be asking yourself, "What good is short-term memory?" It has four principal advantages:

1. It helps rid our mind of clutter by serving as a filter for forgetting what we don't need to remember.
2. It helps us to define our "world frames"—our current picture of the world. According to Dr. Kenneth Higbee, Professor of Psychology at Brigham Young University:

    Our process of visual perception actually skitters here and there about a scene, taking about five retinal images, or "snapshots" per second. Yet we do not discard an old image every fifth of a second and construct a new scene of our surroundings. Rather, we integrate information from all the "snapshots" into one sustained image, or model, of the scene around us.[1]

3. It holds the goals we are pursuing at the moment.
4. It records topics recently mentioned in conversation.

LONG-TERM MEMORY

Long-term memory is usually divided into three types:

1. *Procedural,* involving how to do something.
2. *Semantic,* involving remembering factual information with no connection to when or where we learned it.
3. *Episodic,* involving personal events.

Long-term memory differs from short-term in three ways especially pertinent to Q & A:

1. It is less distractable—less disrupted by other activities.
2. Its capacity is virtually unlimited.
3. It is more vulnerable to retrieval problems, for retrieval from short-term memory is more automatic and instantaneous.

Higbee clarifies the relationship between short-term and long-term memory by likening short-term memory to an in-basket on an office desk, and long-term memory to the file cabinets:

> The in-basket has a limited capacity; it can hold only so much information before it must be emptied to make room for more. Some of what is removed is thrown away, and some is put into file cabinets; however, nothing is put into file cabinets without first sorting through the in-basket.[2]

RETRIEVING

How many times have you experienced the frustration of trying to recall a word, name, or thought that was on "the tip of your tongue?" You search anxiously only to be stymied by the inability to retrieve what you already know. This is only one of the many problems associated with retrieving or recalling information. Clearly, retrieving information, especially from long-term memory, plays an important role in the memory process. As we have seen, you *reconstruct* the content of your long-term memory when you retrieve it. (This is because information had to get transformed through deep processing to become stored in long-term memory.)

Recognition and *recall* are the two basic types of retrieval. *Recognition* can take the form of *simple recognition* or *complex recognition*. In simple recognition, the task is merely to say you recognize something or not. Complex recognition involves a kind of grouping process whereby you recognize a chunk of information simultaneously. An example of this would be the way you recognize someone. You do not look at a person's eyes, ears, nose, and mouth *separately*, but as a single unit.

Recall is more varied. The four major types of recall are:

1. *Free recall:* remembering the items in any order.
2. *Serial recall:* remembering the items in the same order they were presented.
3. *Ordered recall:* remembering the items in any order while reporting the position that they were presented.
4. *Probed recall:* remembering the items by being given some kind of cue.

Other types of recall are more contextual, dealing, for example, with recall of words, visual images, episodes, procedures, or facts.

Probed recall is probably the most prevalent type for Q & A. You take cues from questioners, and use them to advance your agenda. Serial recall is often appropriate for responding to the multifaceted question plus any other type of question containing more than one premise (Chapter 10).

STRENGTHENING YOUR FIRE AWAY MEMORY: A 16-POINT PROGRAM

The preceding primer on fire away memory sets the foundation for more specific advice regarding how you can enhance yours:

1. Set realistic expectations for your fire away memory by analyzing carefully what your target audience members expect from you, and in what degree of detail.

2. Recognize that net effects, substance, and image goals (Chapter 3) are, in effect, a memory device—a map or blueprint that provides a coherent and therefore memorable structure for your Q & A exchange.

3. Audit your listening skills, including your ability to concentrate on the question and the relevant cues of the situation. What steps do you plan to take to strengthen your listening skills?

4. Audit your powers of absorption and retrieval. For example, can you better recall what you read, see, or hear? Do certain circumstances influence your response to this question (e.g., time of day, location, state of relaxation, etc.)? How well do you remember events, numbers, people, or specific elements of a conversation? Test yourself in various pertinent situations.

5. Make sure your briefing materials are conducive to memorability. Do the anticipated questions appear in the materials? Are suggested "headlines" (Chapter 7) presented? Do the materials contain a reasonable quantity of information? Are they laid out well on the page— without appearing too crammed? Are key points highlighted? Are charts used to reinforce your visual memory?

6. Space your study of the briefing materials over time. Cram sessions are normally too risky for high-stakes engagements.

7. Consider using key ideas and facts for a high-stakes engagement in one or more meetings preceding it. Doing so helps embed them into your long-term memory, and facilitates retrieving them more easily.

8. To prevent yourself from overtaxing your memory, select colleagues who possess greater command of the details to be "on call."

9. Pause and reflect before answering the more challenging questions. Calm reflection often produces a response that better accesses your long-term memory.

10. If using a lectern, consider placing a seating chart on it to help you remember names. (Ronald Reagan did this during his debates and news conferences.)

11. Consider taking brief notes while being questioned to capture the key words of a question, the elements of the response you're afraid you'll forget, or both.

12. Consider repeating key terms of the question (but not the "damning premise," Chapter 10) to reinforce first your short-term memory of it and, ultimately, your faithfulness in responding to it.

13. Consider using notes without becoming too dependent on them. (In such high-stakes settings as financial analysts meetings and annual meetings, senior executives sometimes rely on Tele-PrompTers™ and computer monitors built into their lecterns to cue them regarding the appropriate response.)

14. Don't underestimate the value of graphics used during your presentations, or held on reserve for the Q & A, to prompt your long-term memory, including your speed of retrieval.

15. Make sure your practice sessions fit both your management and learning styles (Chapter 14).

16. In the final analysis, if your retrieval apparatus fails you, become comfortable using such lines as: "I don't recall, but I can make that information available to you shortly," and "I don't have the exact number, let me check into that and let you know." In so doing, ask yourself if you should seek an opening to reinforce your net effects goals. For example: "Although I can't tell you what our exact sales figures were in 1987—and I will let you know what they were as soon as possible—I can tell you that they have increased at an average of approximately 8 percent a year since then." (See Chapter 8 for a fuller discussion of this approach.)

By committing yourself to at least a majority of the steps presented above, you can be sure that your memory will be far better prepared to help you achieve finesse on the firing line.

Chapter Five

Control Begins with Credibility

No single factor in the dynamic relationship between the source of a message and its audience is more significant than credibility. No matter how clear, logical, insightful, sensitive, or eloquent a message may be, if it is not credible, its potential impact will be compromised. Whenever you are making a speech or presentation, or fielding questions, you are activating one or more of the following five channels of credibility:

1. Your own personal credibility.
2. The credibility of your ideas.
3. The credibility of your corporation.
4. The credibility of your division, department, or company within the corporation.
5. The credibility of your business, profession, or industry.

If you were an executive of a large pharmaceutical company asked to defend the safety and effectiveness of one of your highly controversial cardiovascular products on a national television talk show, you should do everything possible to cultivate at least three channels of credibility:

1. *Your own personal credibility:* Are you a physician? Are you a cardiologist? Do you have family care experience? How familiar are you with the research behind your product? How prepared are you to defend the fact that the pharmaceutical firm issues you a weekly paycheck?

2. *The credibility of your ideas (the safety and efficacy of the product):* How much confidence can we derive from the research? How legitimate are the complaints? How widespread are they? What is the Food and Drug Administration's reaction to the complaints?

3. *The credibility of your corporation:* What is your corporation's record in dealing with controversial products? Do the public or the media regard your past conduct as responsible? If the product is regarded as one of the pillars of your corporate success, how would you respond to accusations that your motives are more profit-oriented than consumer-oriented?

The two remaining credibility channels, the credibility of your division within the corporation (pharmaceuticals) and the credibility of your industry as a whole, might also be activated by a question such as: "Are big drug firms prematurely marketing unsafe and ineffective products?" The effective persuader understands which channels of credibility need to be cultivated and to what extent. And the effective persuader knows how to leverage his credibility to make a less than palatable point or proposal more acceptable.

MAJOR COMPONENTS OF CREDIBILITY

Eight traits constitute the principal components of credibility: character, candor, competence, confidence, composure, empathy/compassion, cooperation, and compatibility.

Character

Character is the keystone of credibility. If we feel that the speaker's character is flawed, particularly our perception of his truthfulness, then our ears are likely to deafen to even the most inspired thinking. Witness the catastrophic loss of trust experienced by Gary Hart, Jim Bakker, and Jimmy Swaggert, three of America's dominant political and religious personalities whose transgressions of character either destroyed or severely weakened their followings.

More recently, questions of character aroused great fervor among journalists, politicians, and the public during the 1992 presidential campaign. The "character issue" enveloped Bill Clinton in such a way that he had to spend great amounts of energy defending it. In a related vein, George Bush was unable to defuse the criticism that he knew more about the Iran-Contra arms-for-hostages deal than he had claimed. And Ross Perot's summer withdrawal and October re-entry into the campaign caused what many regarded as insurmountable obstacles to his continued credibility as a candidate.

Character, particularly trustworthiness, can be more obvious by its absence than by its presence. Normally, we accept a person's word unless we have reason to feel otherwise. If we do feel otherwise, we sense that the person's motives conflict with ours. This helps explain why we may feel skeptical when buying a used car, real estate, etc.

Although character can be conveyed through references to one's religious activity and teachings, we should be careful not to parlay it too explicitly. Doing so could promote the impression of self-righteousness ("wearing it on your sleeve") or the inference that we are compensating for a hidden character flaw. Prior reputation, not self-proclamation, is therefore the best means to convey character. If this reputation is not known by the audience before an engagement, then the introducer can cover it in a manner that prevents the speaker from being perceived as too self-serving or egotistical.

Candor

When I think about how time promotes historical perspective I turn to Harry S. Truman, a man whose presidency overflowed with controversy. Yet today Truman ranks among the more admired presidents. He epitomized the plain-spoken man from Missouri. His style in conversation and in public speaking was direct, crisp, unadorned, and, in fact, often candid to the point of being brutal. For example:

Reporter:

Mr. President, I see that among the candidates for the Nobel Peace Prize are President Perón of Argentina and my colleague Mr. Drew Pearson. Were either of them nominated by the government of the United States?

Truman:

I can say categorically that they were not. Probably nominated themselves.

Candor may indeed bruise feelings, but its potential to promote credibility is enormous, for the candid person expresses himself in a manner seemingly oblivious to hidden meaning and hidden agendas. Candor is an especially desirable quality for spokespersons and for almost anyone who faces tough questioning. The candid communicator is prone to give the impression of truthfulness; he does not appear to be masking the truth in a sea of well-honed phrases that reek of the company line.

An excellent example of candor surfaced in an interview between a no-holds-barred *Newsweek* reporter and media-shy Jack Welsh, General Electric's CEO since 1981:

Reporter:

When you began slashing jobs at GE in the early '80s, you got the name "Neutron Jack." Was that nickname useful somehow?

Welch:

It had no redeeming features. None. I hated it; I still hate it. Because frankly it didn't [reflect] what we were doing. We were trying to get ahead of the wave. For the last five years, there have been headlines every day: 40,000 [laid off] here, 30,000 out of here. The only thing different was that they were 10 years ago. And . . . that we were perceived to be a very healthy company. Chrysler was going through a [similar] revolution, but it was well accepted, because the press had portrayed Chrysler as a train wreck.[1]

Analysis:

Notice that as soon as Welch candidly revealed his emotions over the "Neutron Jack" epithet, he switched to his agenda, justifying GE layoffs in the early 1980s. This response was clearly a "win" for both the reporter and Welch.

A caveat: prefacing your response with a "to be candid," or "to be honest" will usually communicate the opposite of candor. It may cause your audience to infer that some, if not most, of your communication lacks candor, and therefore credibility.

Competence

As we assess a person's credibility, the factor that normally influences us the most is our perception of his competence. Competence implies that experience or study has given this person a vantage point for making statements worthy of our trust.

Appraising competence can be complicated. Take, for example, a contested presidential primary in which a wide field of contenders woo the voters' support. Some of the candidates may be members of Congress, some former cabinet members, one or more a current or former vice president or governor. As we review their varied candidacies, we establish conscious or subconscious subjective criteria to make a decision based largely on competence (e.g., leadership experience and results, grasp of the issues, proposed programs, and vision).

During a Q & A session, competence can be communicated in three principal ways: (1) by the perceived insightfulness of a response; (2) by the instant grasp of facts or points on which to build a response; and (3) by references to experiences, accomplishments, or results that the audience values or admires.

Many persons I advise have difficulty referring to their accomplishments. Some hesitate mainly due to personal style; others are concerned that such references may sound too immodest or self-serving. However, if one's natural style is reasonably down-to-earth or nonegotistical, the likelihood of sounding conceited or self-serving is usually remote.

Generally, the greatest resource for intentionally conveying competence is by referring to travel, meetings with important people, books or articles read or written, research, personal association with significant events, media appearances, speaking engagements, and seminars attended. In fact, skillfully handling such references can help elevate your perceived level of competence to one of expertise.

Confidence

My clients tell me that they generally feel more confident during the Q & A exchange than during a speech or presentation. There are four reasons for this: (1) a question implies audience interest or relevance, something the speaker often feels uneasy about during his formal remarks; (2) the Q & A tends to be more personal or one-on-one than the presentation, prompting a more comfortable, conversational style—one that contrasts with the need to sustain verbalization imposed by more formal remarks; (3) questions, however challenging or benign, tend to get our competitive juices flowing, normally resulting in a more comfortable and expressive style; and (4) the Q & A forum has an important ego-gratification component—it allows you to display your expertise.

Although the Q & A session may often be conducive to confidence and greater comfort, it has obvious risks: making a misstatement, having your theory or basic premise dissected or decimated, and not knowing the answer to a question your target audience feels you should know. (See Chapter 8 for advice regarding how to combat fear and overconfidence.)

The confident image and the three "Vs". A respondant's confident image inspires his audience's confidence. In fact, if we don't sense a confident image, the person's credibility may actually be at risk. The confident image has three interdependent dimensions. I call them the three "Vs": *verbal, vocal,* and *visual.*

The verbal dimension. What factors contribute to a confident verbal image in responding to questions?

- *Sounding decisive* at the beginning of the response as opposed to wimpy, wishy-washy, or meandering.
- *Producing the appropriate word or expression* with little difficulty.
- *Not pausing too long before responding.* (However, a brief, thoughtful pause is often advisable.)
- *Avoiding inelegant fillers* or vocalized pauses such as "um," "er," "you know," and "like."
- *Displaying conviction*—a sense of personal identification and commitment—in expressing ideas.

- *Avoiding unnecessary qualifiers,* such as "I think," "I feel," "I believe"—expressions also referred to as *authority robbers.*
- *Infusing the phrasing with energy.* This energy is produced by using sentences of short and medium length versus ponderously long sentences (a friend of mine calls them *anacondas*), and by using words that connote power or activity. For example, note the big difference that changing only one word makes in the semantic strength of the following sentences:

    "Our sales growth last year was strong."

    "Our sales growth last year was explosive."

The relationship between confidence and short sentences is well illustrated by Philadelphia Eagles owner Normal Braman in response to a reporter's question regarding rumors that he wanted to sell the team. Note also how the brief question at the end caps both his confidence and the credibility of his response:

No one has offered to buy the Philadelphia Eagles. Further, no one has spoken to me about selling the team. And beyond that, I am not interested in selling the team. The Eagles are not for sale. Can I be more clear than that?[2]

The vocal dimension. The vocal dimension has five major components: articulation, rate, emphasis, projection (volume), and pitch.

- *Articulation* refers to our capacity to enunciate clearly versus its opposite extreme, mumbling. Mumbling not only undermines our ability to understand, but also weakens our sense of the speaker's authority and conviction.
- *Rate or speed of speech* has fascinating implications for perceived confidence. We normally speak between 140 to 160 words per minute. If we speak slowly, we might be perceived as careful or circumspect, but if we speak too slowly, we may appear unconfident, dim-witted, or both. If we speak quickly, we could be perceived as confident or verbally facile. However, if we speak too quickly, we could appear nervous.
- *Emphasis,* including the amount of energy you inject into a word or phrase, helps to communicate your level of conviction or commitment, an important dimension of your confidence and

overall credibility. This conviction, properly expressed, can give contagious energy to your ideas, thus enhancing their believability. For example, John F. Kennedy, in his first debate with Richard Nixon in 1960, delivered an eight-minute opening address at an average of 220 words per minute, almost 40 percent faster than our normal speaking rate. Was he talking too fast? Absolutely not. His emphasis patterns, accentuated by repetition and pausing, contributed to an arresting cadence, and helped produce a supremely confident vocal image.

• *Volume* or *projection* helps promote the speaker's confidence and conviction. As soon as the Q & A session begins, you should *project* your invitation for questions in a confident voice: "And now I'll be pleased to answer your questions." This approach outdistances the diffident and qualified, "I'll try to answer your questions if you have any."

• *Pitch* involves how vocal sounds fall along a musical scale. When we say that a speaker is monotonous, we are referring to a flat pitch level, regardless of whether the sounds produced are spine-chillingly high or as low as the bass in a jazz combo. Confident vocal expression requires the ability to vary pitch to communicate our range of emotions more fully and stimulate our audience's attention and interest. Moreover, broadening your range of pitch can result in a greatly enhanced sense of self-expression.

The visual dimension. Our eyes play a large role in evaluating a person's confidence, especially since so many visual cues are related to presence. Nonverbal communication is so important to the oral message that some theorists estimate that as much as 93 percent of the emotional content of the verbal message is transmitted via nonverbal communication.[3]

• *Attire and grooming* Neat grooming and attire imply self-respect. Poor grooming or untidy or wrinkled attire can imply an even stronger negative message.[4]

• *Posture and position* Slouching over the lectern as a human dust-cover might make you more relaxed and feel more engaged, but an erect posture behind the lectern or, when possible, in front of it can transmit a powerful message of openness and confidence.

• *Eye contact* Fair or unfair, many people regard lack of eye contact as a sure sign of lack of confidence. Worse yet, many people regard it as a sign of deceit. Eye contact is important for three principal reasons: (1) it projects confidence, thereby promoting credibility; (2) it makes communication more personal; and (3) it permits you to read the questioner's or the target audience's feedback, thereby allowing you to adjust your answer if they haven't heard you, are disinterested, act bored, don't understand, or disagree with you. Eye contact can be especially effective if you confidently direct a portion of your response to a target audience member particularly interested in the issue at hand. By going eyeball-to-eyeball with this person, you are more likely to secure his support.

• *The smile* Many executives I advise have difficulty smiling while making speeches and presentations and fielding questions. I attribute this to three basic causes: (1) a tendency to be more focused on the risks the engagement represents than on the opportunity—including the opportunity for enjoyment—it offers; (2) a fear that smiling could transmit a negative message; for example, that he is not taking the message or the audience seriously enough; and (3) a lack of understanding that an appropriate smile can convey not only confidence, but can also project a sense of friendliness, leading to trust and approachability. Usually the executive begins to smile after I encourage him to relax his facial muscles, to visualize a more positive relationship with his audience, and to value the credibility implications of a genuine smile. Success is even greater if my observations are reinforced by a videotape replay of his stoic, dour—or sour—visage that contrasts with a smile that appears more authentic than the executive expected.

• *Gestures* Most people I advise have little difficulty gesturing during a Q & A session (although they may have difficulty gesturing during the presentation itself). Gestures send important messages; they can convey confidence and conviction, and significantly complement your emphasis patterns. Placing one hand in your pocket while gesturing with the other is normally appropriate, although it may be too casual for formal settings and in certain cultures (Chapter 12). When appearing on TV, avoid far-reaching gestures; instead, keep your hands close to your body and away from your face.

• *Distractions* Some time ago I advised a trim, mature, impressive-looking executive how to field questions. His listening behavior was excellent; his posture was appropriate; and his answers were informed, responsive, and to the point. Only one thing was wrong—during his responses he played with his keys and pocket change, behavior picked up and amplified by his microphone. Not only was this a distraction, it was also a confidence robber. Other distractions capable of undermining our perception of a presenter's confidence are playing with notes or a paper clip, taking too many sips of water, crossing one's chest (defensively), walking away from the audience (reflectively or defensively), scratching one's head, playing with one's mustache, being easily distracted—the list goes on. However, if these behaviors are brought to the presenter's attention, they usually can be controlled.

Composure

Few of us will forget the contradictory image projected by Alexander Haig, Jr., secretary of state, on March 30, 1981 (the day Reagan was shot), when he said forcefully, while shaking and perspiring heavily, "I am in control [of the White House] here. . . ." And few Philadelphians who followed the energy crisis in the early 1970s will forget the oil executive who, when accused by the media of being a party to manipulating the crisis, blew his cool on live TV with, "That's the dumbest f---ing question I ever heard."

If a Hall of Shame were erected for all the bright, talented people who dramatically lost their composure in a demanding Q & A exchange, we would need to build a skyscraper. And while it is easy to criticize or ridicule someone for losing composure, we must understand the factors that can lead to its loss.

Loss of composure is generally brought on by a highly tense state in which a question or comment is the "straw that broke the camel's back," by an assault—real or perceived—to one's ego, or by both. This condition is often exacerbated by a sudden sense of lost control manifested as frustration—frustration that you don't know what to say, or how to say it.

Composure detractors. Consider the following specific factors that can lead to loss of composure during a media interview, annual meeting, public hearing, debate, or other encounter:

- The accumulative tone of the questioning challenges your credibility—and assaults your ego.
- You are confused as to the amount of force you want to display in response. For example, should you question or attack the questioner?
- The questioning is getting repetitious, implying a lack of belief in what you are saying.
- The aggressiveness of the questioning and/or the restrictiveness of the format is preventing you from having enough time to think and to present your key messages.
- The questioner has disclosed a surprising piece of disturbing information you wish you had learned earlier.
- As you're responding to the questions, you're rethinking a previous response, deciding whether or not you wish to retract or build on it.
- You don't know an answer to a question that you and the audience realize you should know. As a result, you feel embarrassed, or worse, humiliated.
- The hot television lights, the TV cameras, and other distractions are making you even more uncomfortable.
- Beads of perspiration are starting to appear on your face, and you worry about their impact on your credibility and overall image.

Although Chapter 9, Finesse in Hostile Territory, will provide more in-depth advice regarding composure vis-à-vis hostility, two pieces of advice seem especially appropriate here:

If you're angry, count to five.
If you're really angry, count to ten.
                    —Thomas Jefferson

Do your best to keep your ego out of the picture. Depersonalize the situation while responding to the issues at hand. Yes, this is a tall task, but you really don't have a choice—other than the Hall of Shame.

Empathy/Compassion

As the CEO of the Coast of Maine Clam Chowder Company (CMCCC) you learn that one of your larger shipments of chowder is contaminated, resulting in approximately 70 people suffering from food poisoning, five of whom are listed in critical condition. With little hesitation you recall the entire shipment, although media pressure is mounting for you to recall every can of chowder you've produced. Your sense of disappointment and frustration defies description: a full recall could seriously weaken the financial stability of CMCCC—even put it out of business. Yes, you feel sorry for the victims, but your emotions are focused more on the many years you've devoted to building the business, on your employees, and particularly on the business risks you are facing. Your spokesperson has convinced you that you should call a news conference to update the media on CMCCC's intentions. How should you proceed?

Step 1 is obviously to put aside any illusions that your main position should be to focus on the economic risks of the full recall. Step 2 is to define a consumer-oriented approach to the entire crisis, beginning with an opening statement that should emphasize these points: you are very sorry about the misfortune facing the victims and their families, you have a reputation for being a responsible company that has long manufactured a quality product, and your customers have been crucial to your good reputation and success. Your actions have the customers' interests—particularly their health and safety—uppermost in mind. By projecting empathy and compassion, you have now set the tone for a news conference that should help cultivate your corporate credibility.

Credibility, empathy, and compassion: how are they related? Empathy and compassion, properly expressed, help reinforce your trustworthiness, and thus your credibility. If you demonstrate genuine empathy toward me, I am more likely to find you trustworthy and, therefore, more credible.

How often do you find empathy or compassion missing when you expect it the most?

Car Owner:

This is the third time in the last six weeks I've brought my car to you to fix the same problem. I'm a salesperson and I need the car for my livelihood. How can I be sure it will be fixed right this time?

Insensitive Service Manager:

What can I say?

Sensitive Service Manager:

I'm sorry you're having these problems and I understand your frustration, Ms. Tenuto. I will personally see that this problem is addressed by our most experienced mechanic, and do everything I can to make sure that it will be fixed right this time.

In many Q & A situations, the questioner may be more interested in your expression of empathy than in your answer. The question, therefore, may be merely a vehicle to solicit your reassurance, empathy, or support.

Commuter to Transit Official:

I'm late for work three out of five days a week. Why can't the trains run on time?

Transit Official:

I'm sorry that you've been late for work. Getting people to work on time is extremely important to us and we're doing everything we can to improve our on-time performance. (Optional) For instance, we've purchased 35 new cars and constructed a modern maintenance facility to reduce equipment failure and make it more likely that your train will be on time.

Analysis:

The transit official handled this well. This commuter was less interested in learning why the trains don't run on time. In fact, he may know that equipment failure is the main reason. What he really wanted was an opportunity to vent frustration and to judge or solicit the transit official's empathy.

Cooperation

Cooperation is an important component of credibility, especially in media relations. Reporters expect company spokespersons to be respectful of their deadlines and responsive to their requests for interviews, background information, and research. By being cooperative, the spokesperson is conveying two implicit messages: first, that he and his company have nothing to hide; second, that he values a positive working relationship with the media.

Being cooperative also has a credibility-preserving function related to control. Consider this scenario: a reporter requests information that you are reluctant to provide because it will probably embarrass your company. However, you realize that the reporter could secure the same information from a source outside the company. Should you cooperate? Probably, especially since not cooperating might injure your relationship with the reporter, possibly causing the company to be even more embarrassed by the manner in which the information will be used.

Compatibility

Compatibility, projected mainly by sociability or likability, is an important component of credibility. Compatibility is especially important if you are deciding whether or not to include a person on your team or are choosing someone, for example, a customer service representative, who needs to establish good chemistry with others. Good chemistry can influence one's comfort level in asking questions, and can thereby enhance approachability, a key factor in facilitating Q & A.

What main factors, then, promote our liking of another person? Psychologist Eliot Aronson, in his study, *The Social Animal*, concludes that we achieve compatibility with people whose attitudes and interests are similar to ours; who offer genuine praise and perform "no-strings-attached" favors; who have special talents or competencies and such qualities as loyalty, kindness, and reasonableness; and, of course, who like us in return.[5]

In encounters where the speaker is not well known by his audience, compatibility is mainly conveyed via five factors: a general sense of friendliness; common-ground references to shared perceptions, values, and experiences; good humor; a sense of direct contact with the audience; and a general sense of comfort and self-assurance without the impression that he is taking himself too seriously.

WIT, HUMOR, AND CREDIBILITY

During the widely telecast briefing following the Allied victory over Saddam Hussein's Iraqi forces, General Norman Schwarzkopf, when asked about Hussein's talents as a strategist, put his wit on full display for the tens of millions who savored the victory with him:

> As for Saddam Hussein being a great military strategist, he is neither a strategist nor is he schooled on the operational art, nor is he a tactician, nor is he a general, nor is he a soldier—other than that, he's a great military man. I want you to know that.[6]

No doubt about it, Schwarzkopf's response was credibility-enhancing. But what is the relationship between humor or wit and credibility? Effective humor or wit cannot only lighten up an otherwise heavy exchange, it can buttress the audience's sense of the respondent's intelligence, competence, candor, confidence, and liking for them. Moreover, it can reciprocally enhance the respondent's likability, as it undoubtedly did for Schwarzkopf.

Few major personalities have been as effective in displaying their wit during Q & A as President John F. Kennedy during his televised news conferences. Without question, wit was integral to his charisma and his memorability:

Reporter:
> Mr. President, back on the subject of presidential advisers, Congressman Baring of Nevada, a Democrat, said you would do much better if you got rid of some of yours—and he named Bowles, Ball, Bell, Bunche, and Sylvester.

Kennedy:
> Yes, he has a fondness for alliteration and for Bs. And I would not add Congressman Baring to that list as I have a high regard for him and for the gentlemen that he named. But congressmen are always

advising presidents to get rid of presidential advisers. That is one of
the most constant threads that runs through American history and
presidents ordinarily do not pay attention, nor do they in this case.[7]

Brevity and Wit

Waiter to Groucho Marx:

"How did you find the steak, sir?"

Groucho:

"Oh, quite by accident. I moved that piece of tomato and there it
was."[8]

Reporter to Former Acting Secretary of State Lawrence Eagleburger:

"Why did you name each of your sons Lawrence?"

Eagleburger:

"First of all it was ego. And secondly, I wanted to screw up the Social
Security system."[9]

Yes, the two examples above and several sprinkled throughout
this book demonstrate that brevity is indeed the soul of wit. This
reality provides you, the respondent, with an enormous potential
advantage, for often humor in Q & A is most effective when it is
brief and spontaneous. As you assess your ability to capitalize on
this advantage, don't lose heart if you're not a good joke teller.
Being able to tell a joke and displaying clever wit are two different
skills. In fact, many of the wittiest people I know couldn't tell a
joke even with a cue card.

Anticipating Openings for Wit

Although the strength of effective wit is attributable to the perception, if not the reality, of spontaneity, certain openings for wit
can be anticipated. Properly planned and executed, wit can appear spontaneous, as illustrated by the following examples. However, the potential effectiveness of each example depends largely
on the target audience's respect and liking for the respondent.

1. *When you don't know the answer to an obviously tough question.*

To audience: "Would any of you like to answer that one for me?" or "I'm leaving now."

To questioner: "With that question I can no longer put you in my will."

2. *When the question is patently unfair.*

Said with a smile: "I deeply appreciate the evenhandedness of your question," or "Would you like to make that more passionate?"

3. *When the question is loaded with facets.*

Putdown with a smile: "While you're at it, would you like to ask another?"

At night: "When will they be turning off the lights and locking the doors?"

To staff member: "*Name*, please book me on a later flight, I now have some work to do."

Despite its obvious assets, humor or wit carries a fair share of risks, especially the risks of not working and offending. Therefore, the following advice can be helpful:

- If you are not a witty or humorous person by nature, *attempting to be during an important Q & A exchange is not the place to begin.*
- *Many people often fail at humor when they attempt it as a means of curtailing their own anxiety.* Despite such an inclination, it is far better to attempt wit or humor when you're relatively at ease than when you're anxious. Under these circumstances, what you may suddenly think—or pray—is funny, often isn't. Further, your delivery, including your timing, may also be undermined by your anxiety.
- Few people have mastered the art of the putdown (see preceding Kennedy example). *If this isn't your forte, seek other forms of humor*, or play the whole exchange straight.
- *Don't flirt with bad taste.* It can hurt your credibility far more than exquisite humor can help it.

In the final analysis, when in doubt, avoid attempts at humor. Remember, humor is often more of a luxury in a Q & A exchange than a necessity. The necessity is to pursue your net effects, substance, and image goals. Therefore, don't let an unnecessary mis-adventure with humor undermine your essential purpose. Abiding by this advice takes discipline, but that's crucial to achieving Q & A finesse.

CULTIVATING YOUR CREDIBILITY

In the spirit of control, it is wise to ask yourself if you are doing your utmost to project credibility during your Q & A session or media interview. The following specific questions should prove helpful:

- Without being too self-serving or egotistical, are you prepared to fold into your responses credentials that qualify you to speak on the topic?
- Do you use examples enough in your responses—especially examples that can impress the audience with your breadth of experience and success?
- Do you take sufficient advantage of common-ground opportunities to highlight in a genuine way similarities in attitudes, feelings, and experiences between you and your audience?
- Do you project the impression that you have done your homework for the audience you are addressing—an impression that gives them the feeling that you have made a special investment on their behalf?
- Do you take pains to make sure the audience appreciates the personal value of your point of view and senses your genuine interest in them?
- Do you project the proper image of respect and liking for the audience? Do you smile easily? Can you display humor or wit to promote a sense of "oneness" with them?
- Do your responses have a sufficient ring of authority and conviction?

If you can answer most of these questions in the affirmative, your potential for finesse will be greatly enhanced. After all, the firing line is a much more hospitable place when your finesse is buttressed by firm control of your credibility.

Chapter Six

You Can Control the Firing Line

The Q & A environment can greatly influence your net effects goals. Therefore, your finesse depends greatly on your ability to control the firing line. This encompasses appropriate ways of beginning and ending a Q & A session, and controlling the Q & A setting, format, and timing.

INVITING QUESTIONS AND SETTING THE PROPER TONE

You have just completed giving what you and your audience obviously regard as an impressive speech. One reason for its success, apart from its relevance and insightfulness, was the energy you invested in delivering it—so much so that you feel tired, perhaps even exhausted. In fact, if you had your druthers, you might leave. But you can't, for a sea of hands is ready to appear as soon as you invite questions.

The manner in which you invite questions can greatly influence how the audience will perceive you in the more up-close, interpersonal Q & A environment. Specifically, the tone, quality, and quantity of their questions depends on how you invite them. Your image goals play a key role in defining your tone or manner. Do you want to be approachable or aloof? Do you want to be casual or more formal? Do you want to establish a strong common bond with the audience, or do you want to play the more-distant expert role to the hilt? Consider these lines and the tone they suggest:

- "Are there any stupid questions?" (Actually used by the superintendent of a military school); "John, your program chairperson, told me that I should spend a few minutes answering your questions."
  Analysis: Horrendously patronizing.
- "Do you have any questions for my answers?" (Used humorously by then-Secretary of State Henry Kissinger to open a press conference); "And now I'll be pleased to evade your questions." (Used humorously by a friend who heads a leading Hispanic interest group); "I know it's hard to ask the first question, so let me begin by taking the second one." (Used humorously and effectively by many speakers over the years.)
  Analysis: Humor can be an effective way to invite questions; however, there are risks. Using humor as a substitute for achieving credibility can backfire (see Chapter 5).
- "Are there any questions?"
  Analysis: It is better to avoid implying that there might not be—to be more positive (see the last version below).
- "And now I'll try to answer your questions."
  Analysis: The word *try* may signal lack of confidence, although in some situations it may be appropriately humble.
- "And now I'll be pleased (delighted, happy) to answer your questions"; "And now I'll welcome your questions."
  Analysis: These are more positive and generally more appropriate, although the speaker's facial expression and inflection must support the positive tone of her words.

If a positive, active Q & A session is important to you, you can actually set the tone for it within the speech itself by stating early (preferably immediately after announcing what topics or issues you plan to cover), "Following my remarks, I'll look forward to your questions." Note here that the speaker subtly shows respect for her audience by referring to their questions, not to her answers.

Announcing the Q & A within the speech itself reflects another dimension of control: it can signal the audience that the speaker prefers no interruptions until the end. However, this preference may not be honored in certain situations—before intensely hostile audiences, and in meetings in which the norm is "question or challenge at will."

Two other tactics can help prevent you from being interrupted by questions. First, if your presentation is short (e.g., under 10 minutes), you may wish to announce its approximate length as you begin, hoping your audience possesses the requisite patience to allow you to finish. Second, you may choose to break a longer presentation into segments with a short Q & A exchange at the end of each segment. For example, you might break a 45-minute presentation into three 15-minute segments. The effectiveness of this approach depends largely on your ability to know when and how to end each of the exchanges. Therefore, plan in advance the lines that will help you return to your presentation.

CONTROLLING THE SETTING

A client of mine, the president of a highly respected laboratory, was invited to appear on national television as an expert on medical testing. As we prepared for the interview, we explored how we could "control" the visual image—the setting in which the interview would take place. One possibility was inside the laboratory. However, the laboratory, while impressively large and clean, had few pieces of equipment to strongly reinforce one of his key messages: technical sophistication. Another possibility

was to stand at the entrance to the building, under the name of
the laboratory. Yet, this would not be too impressive either, especially in inclement weather. The third possibility, the executive's office, was finally selected because it was, at least, a comfortable setting for him. This visual image was to be buttressed
by supplying the network with aerial views of the laboratory plus
videotapes from the sister laboratory on the West Coast, where
more sophisticated equipment was housed. We therefore took
control of the setting.

How much latitude for controlling the setting do you have in
planning for important meetings and media appearances? To clarify this, you might ask if the room is large enough. Are the lighting and electrical conditions appropriate? Are the facility and
room conveniently accessible? Do you have ample opportunity to
use visual aids? Are furnishings congruent with the personal
image you intend to project? Is the room decorated in a manner
that supports your key message or theme? Is the seating ample
and comfortable? Do seating arrangements allow you to be seen
easily?

An excellent example of the value placed on controlling the
environment is the 1992 annual meeting conducted by the finan-
cially beleaguered, London-based advertising giant Saatchi &
Saatchi. Its revenues for the year were flat, and its debt was in
the hundreds of millions of pounds. Matthew Doull of London's
Daily Telegraph describes the setting:

> Unlike last year's event, held just before Saatchi's life-saving refi-
> nancing was unveiled, this year's affair was as smoothly stage-
> managed as a party political rally.
>
> Shareholders entered the darkened conference room at London's
> Marriott Hotel to the same strains of Purcell that piped Mr. Major to
> his podia during the election campaign. The directors gathered on the
> stage, their silhouettes gently backlit. Even the temperature had been
> carefully calculated slightly on the cool side, reinforcing the cinematic
> atmosphere.
>
> The music died and chairman Maurice Saatchi found his spotlight
> before beginning the meeting.[1]

Following the meeting, Doull asked a shareholder how he felt
about his investment. The shareholder replied, "I feel a little bit
better than when I came in."

CONTROLLING THE FORMAT

The format you select for a Q & A session can not only influence how a message is received, but can actually convey its own messages. The following case studies put this point in perspective.

Case Study One: Capitalizing on a Team Presentation

A few years ago I prepared the executives of a large manufacturing firm to make a full-day presentation to their board of directors. The program had three purposes: (1) to broaden the board's understanding of the business; (2) to give them confidence that the firm's strategy was on target; and (3) to showcase their management team.

During the planning stages, the president stated that he didn't want the board to feel that the program was a one-way "propaganda campaign" or "snow job." He therefore decided to reserve lengthy Q & A periods following each major presentation, expecting the announced length of the Q & A sessions to communicate the management team's openness and confidence in their command of the issues.

This format increased the probability of at least three risks: (1) a member of the management team might make a misstatement; (2) unhealthy disagreement could surface between management and the board; and (3) a team member might not know the answer to an important question. Despite these risks, the team drew confidence from the president's assurance that they could perform well within the more open format. Following extensive preparation, they did.

Case Study Two: Controlling the Process of Persuasion

Another example representing a keen understanding of the importance of controlling the format involves the management of a large membership organization I represent. They decided to propose to their membership a plan to restructure the organization dramatically. The plan had been carefully thought out. However, the concrete need for it was difficult to sell, as it was based on future assumptions and hard-to-quantify arguments.

Part of the organization's strategy to secure membership approval was to "pre-sell" the plan in a series of meetings with key members. To do so, the plan's advocates took two major tactical steps: first, to diminish the possible perception of too hard a sell, their pre-sell meetings were focused not only on the plan, but also on other issues of concern to members; second, several of the meetings were restricted to groups of 6 to 8. This prevented an opponent from making a persuasive statement that might have otherwise influenced a larger group of members.

Other Issues of Format Control

The following questions illustrate other issues of format control:

- Do you want to answer questions until people stop raising their hands, or do you want to end the session (possibly with the help of a program chairperson) on an appropriate upbeat note?
- If you are on a panel, what speaking position do you prefer? Or does appearing on the panel (versus being a featured speaker) diminish your status?
- Are certain topics off limits to your audience for legal, personal, security, or proprietary/competitive reasons, or because of a lack of sufficient expertise? If so, be prepared to maintain control by saying so—and be prepared to hold the line.
- Should you appear on a panel or show with an adversary? In this case, will the appearance do more to neutralize your adversary's impact or elevate her legitimacy?

Format Control and Media Interviews

Controlling the format, as the following example highlights, also applies to media interviews. A few years ago I received a call from the spokesperson of a public official I serve. The official had been accused by the media in headline stories of "junketeering"—

using taxpayers' dollars for unnecessary foreign travel. The situation had become so intolerant that the official decided to put a halt to media interviews; that is, until a well-recognized reporter requested one more.

This reporter promised the official one more opportunity to tell his side of the story. We agreed to the interview, but stipulated that it be confined to the official's travel, and not be focused on other controversial issues with which he had been linked. We also requested that the reporter, in explaining the official's terms of acceptance, not say that he "refused" to discuss the other issues; rather, the reporter should indicate that the interview was granted on the proviso that it focus only on the travel issue. By negotiating the format, we increased the official's latitude of control in clarifying his position.

One of the better examples of format control I've seen occurred in 1980 on the television show, Donahue. Phil Donahue's guest for the entire one-hour show: Irving Shapiro, chairman and CEO of Du Pont. Throughout the program, Donahue tried everything conceivable to paint Du Pont as too profit-oriented. Shapiro, a portrait of impressive intelligence, composure, control, and strength, held his ground firmly despite Donahue's badgering (which, by the way, frequently appeared to me to be desperate).

Toward the end of the show, Donahue challenged Shapiro regarding why Du Pont had stopped selling Zerex antifreeze, claiming the reason was related to consumer complaints. The following transcript illustrates how Shapiro negotiated right on the spot the opportunity to state his position, and won:

Donahue:

And your point is that my reference to the problems that developed with some coolant systems that used this antifreeze is what? Unfair, isolated, or not important?

Shapiro:

I think it is overstated. I know what you're referring to and, if you want me to get into that, I'll give it to you in spades, but I don't want to get nailed with the accusation without time to deal with it.

Donahue:

O.K., except I don't want to be thought of as unfair for raising something that is on the record. I mean, complaints are on the record?

Shapiro:

If you raise it, then give me time to respond.

Donahue:

I see, so I guess to be fair I should give you the option as to whether or not to respond. My hope is that you won't take the time, but you have a point—if I raise it, I should give you the opportunity to speak to it. So what's your choice?

Shapiro:

I'll speak to it.

Donahue:

Isn't that what you want to do?

Shapiro:

Sure, I'll speak to it.

Donahue:

That's not going to be boring? (Audience laughter) No, you're right; you got me. You have the floor.[2]

Shapiro then presented his case clearly, calmly, and succinctly—and without interruption.

CONTROLLING THE MESSAGE

Timing Is Everything

The tireless axiom "timing is everything" may be at most only a slight exaggeration in its relevance to you as a communicator. That's because timing can significantly affect three important factors: (1) *the size and make-up of your audience*; (2) *their level of active participation*; and (3) *the overall impact of your message*.

Audience size and make-up. Imagine yourself as the CEO of a major food company planning to announce via a news conference a new, revolutionary, low-fat, low-cholesterol food product. Recognizing that timing is key to generating maximum coverage, you select a day when you don't expect a major competing story that will prevent reporters from attending your news conference (e.g., the scheduled announcement of a verdict in a major case, Election Day, etc.). As well, you select a day when viewership and/or readership is normally strong, and an hour when you can take full advantage of the day's—or the next day's—news cycle.

Political debates pose a good example of the importance of timing. The candidate who needs the additional exposure a debate affords would prefer that it occur on the most popular channel during prime time on the evening her target audience would most likely tune in. Her opponent, if obligated to debate, generally wants the complete opposite.

Level of audience participation. The influence of timing on the second factor, the audience's level of participation, can be especially significant if you seek a good amount of give and take between speaker and audience. For this reason, you develop a format conducive to two-way communication. This format should be sensitive to the audience's personal schedules and their fatigue factor. For example, I have seldom seen good Q & A sessions follow a weekday luncheon address that ends after 12:45. At this time of day people are usually more interested in returning to work. Moreover, the meal may have created a physiological reaction (called *post-prandial fatigue*) that saps their energy and eagerness to participate in the Q & A.

In some instances your timing tactics may be focused on limiting two-way communication. For example, if you're the CEO of a publicly held company facing horrendous financial problems, you may want your annual meeting to be as short as possible without drawing attention to your intent. Therefore, if you have a choice of beginning at 10:00 or 10:30, you will probably opt for 10:30 since noon or close to it may be perceived by much of your audience as a sensible time to end (although you should not bank on such assumptions). In addition, you may decide to lengthen the various meeting addresses to limit exposure to potentially embarrassing audience questions.

The impact of your message. The third factor related to timing, the overall impact of your message, is brought into focus by this scenario: you are planning a three-day national sales meeting with an address at some point from your chairperson, a decidedly inspirational speaker. Where do you place her in the program? At or near the beginning to set the tone? Somewhere in the middle to help offset any drag in the program? At the end to send the sales troops home on a powerful note? Not an easy decision. However, by raising questions such as these, you are reflecting your appreciation for the need to exercise control over timing.

CONTROLLING THE SOURCE

Corporations invest a great deal of energy deciding on a spokesperson for their advertising campaigns. General questions include: should the spokesperson be a well-known sports or entertainment personality, a corporate executive (e.g., Lee Iacocca, Victor Kiam, Frank Perdue), an unknown actor, or some combination of the above? Other important decisions include how long the spokesperson should appear, with whom and when, what the spokesperson should say and how it will be said, and, most important, what overall image should be projected. These decisions are complicated, based on the expected appeal of the spokesperson and how it should translate into persuasive impact and, ultimately, corporate profits.

These assessments are becoming more scientific than subjective. Increasingly, corporations are relying on focus groups for input in identifying the best spokesperson, not only for commercials but also for media appearances. Groups of eight to ten people meet to view videotapes and discuss the relative strengths and weaknesses of each spokesperson. In fact, one technique involves each focus group member using an electronic device that registers and averages emotional reactions on a graph.

Although you may not have the luxury to test via a focus group a spokesperson for an upcoming presentation and Q & A session or a series of media appearances, you will need to select the best spokesperson(s) available: men and women whose credibility meet the criteria discussed in Chapter 5 and whose communication skills and understanding of the issues are unmistakably strong.

Controlling the Source in a Crisis Situation

Controlling the source has special pertinence in crisis situations (see Chapter 11). Consider this comparatively simple scenario: a public school bus carrying 43 students from public, private, and parochial schools slips on the ice and rolls over an embankment at 7:45 one wintry morning. Ten students are rushed to a hospital for treatment of lacerations and broken bones.

In this situation alone the following persons might be pressed into service by the media as spokespersons: the bus driver, representatives from the school system providing the bus, school teachers and administrators, the students themselves, parents and other family members, police, fire and other rescue personnel, attending physicians, and eyewitnesses. Yes, a huge chorus of discordant voices could end up speaking before cameras, lights, and microphones regarding what happened and why. This simple situation explains why corporations normally assign a minimal number of spokespersons to any situation, crisis or otherwise. By controlling the source they can better control accuracy, consistency, and, ultimately, credibility.

THE TEAM PRESENTATION

A fair measure of my consulting practice is devoted to preparing people for team presentations, whether they are addressing an internal meeting, a current or prospective client, convention or seminar, or making a media appearance, such as a talk show or news conference.

Successful team presentations require four major dimensions: (1) a consistent theme and set of key messages; (2) a sense of unity among the presenters and the presentations; (3) the absence of unnecessary repetition; and (4) smooth handling of the Q & A. The following example clarifies this.

As the CEO of the Haddonfield Hat Company, you, your COO, and your CFO have decided to appear before an influential group of financial analysts. Your principal net effects goal is to convince them to write a favorable report of your firm as an investment. Specifically, your substance goals are to persuade them that "hats are back" and you have the fiscal strength, marketing savvy, and manufacturing support to sustain this trend.

To be successful at Q & A, you and your team need to be facile in handling three tactics: *the handoff, the piggyback play,* and *"blowing the whistle" on your own teammate.*

The Handoff

This tactic involves delegating a response. As you do, you have two options: (1) to provide a basic answer before asking your colleague to provide the details—an option that highlights your knowledgeability and thereby your competence; and (2) to introduce your colleague in a manner that clarifies why she is in a better position to provide the answer or elaboration. As you hand the ball off, avoid appearing defensive, especially when you do not know the answer.

The "sticky ball" is an interesting variation of the handoff. Suppose you are asked why a major line of hats failed—a predictably tough question. Although you can answer the question fully, you hand it off to the COO to distance yourself from the failure. The sticky ball is fraught with risks. The analysts could perceive you to be "sticking" the sticky ball to your COO. Moreover, unless the COO agreed in advance to field this question, she may be so miffed with you that she decides to bolt Haddonfield Hat and form Camden Chapeaus.

The Piggyback Play

Your COO has done a nice job responding to an important question regarding your advertising campaign; however, she left out one big point that prompts you to "piggyback" onto her answer. As you do, make sure you are using the right line:

- "Jo failed to make one important point."
  Analysis: This response showcases your team by declaring their failures, thereby inviting the disrespect of both the analysts and your colleagues.

- "Let me add to what Jo has said by . . ."
  Analysis: Fine.
- "Jo's answer reminded me of an additional point."
  Analysis: Perfect (if fully honest).

The execution of the handoff and the piggyback play can be smoother if the participants decide in advance who will be mainly responsible for which topics. However, during the actual exchange, be careful not to tune out a question apparently intended for another team member. Despite the division of labor, you may be required to answer it or to comment on it following an initial answer. Again, effective listening is key!

"Blowing the Whistle" on Your Own Teammate

Your COO has just declared during an early summer meeting with analysts that a new and promising line of hats will appear in the fall. However, she means spring. What do you do? Regardless of her position, if you can't signal her subtly that she misspoke, *gently* correct her, especially if the misstatement relates to an important issue. You may simply interrupt and say, "Jo, you mean spring," or wait until she finishes and say, "Jo, you meant to say spring," or "Jo meant to say spring." Humor may even be appropriate to relieve the tension produced by the misstatement: "Jo is more enthusiastic about this line of hats than I realized; she's moved us up by two seasons." Be careful, though, that the humor is not too heavily laced with a put-down tone.

KNOWING HOW AND WHEN TO END

A terrific speaking engagement, news conference, or media interview can quickly turn into a disaster if it runs on for too long. Not only might the audience's patience be taxed, but the risks of generating unnecessary controversy, making a misstatement, and not ending your performance on a positive note can quickly escalate.

Finesse, once again, is linked to control. Specifically, how much control is available to you directly, or through others? Consider these three approaches: (1) *pre-established endings*; (2) *the brief epilogue*, or *recap*; and (3) *expressing gratitude*.

Pre-established Endings

You may ask the program chairperson to inform the audience that you will be available for a Q & A session of approximately X minutes following your speech. You may also request that she explain why you can't stay longer, for example, you have a plane to catch, another meeting, etc.

In establishing the length of the Q & A, you may want to offer somewhat less time than what is actually available (without appearing too stingy). This gives you the option to expand the Q & A session. If this occurs, your additional time with the audience can be regarded as a bonus, one that can boost your credibility, particularly through cooperation and compatibility.

Make sure the program chairperson understands that she, not you, is to end the session. You do not want to be perceived as "leaving the host's table prematurely." However, to ensure that the program doesn't go on any longer than necessary, consider establishing a nonverbal signal system with the program chair. For instance, you may give her a quick look either when it's time to end the program, or to inform the audience that you will answer only one, two, three, or the less-definite "few" more questions.

Before you leave the stage to mingle or catch that plane, do your best to end on a positive note. If the last question was negative and your answer was not especially positive or strong, field one more question if the audience seems supportive of both you and the additional question. Alternatively, you may want to arrange for the last question to be a plant. If so, make sure that it is not a patent plant (e.g., the CEO's spouse); this won't go over well with most audiences.

The Brief Epilogue

An important option for ending your program is the brief epilogue, a recap of the major ideas discussed during the Q & A exchange that link back to your net effects, substance, and image goals. To illustrate this option, imagine that you are about to complete your appearance before a public zoning hearing where, in the face of active, tough questioning, you have advocated a 150,000 square foot expansion of your factory.

> This evening you have asked a lot of questions that reflect your understandable interest in protecting your rights and the attractiveness of your neighborhood. You have asked about a smokestack, and I have assured you that there won't be one. You have asked about our building design, and I have shown you our plans to blend it into the environment. You have asked about additional traffic, and I have assured you that it will be minimal. There isn't a question or concern I haven't addressed. We have demonstrated over the years that we want to be a good neighbor, and we'll do everything reasonable to continue to be. I ask for your support.

This approach is usually effective. It demonstrates the respondent's respect for the audience, confidence in her ability to address each issue satisfactorily, and commitment to be a good neighbor. Further, it explicitly asks for support, linking back to the essential net effects goal. One caveat: be careful not to reintroduce or highlight an issue to which you have a less than persuasive response.

Expressing Gratitude

Your final option in ending the Q & A exchange involves expressing the appropriate amenities: "Thank you" (appropriate for most situations); "I found your questions most enlightening"; "I wish you a most productive and enjoyable conference"; "Plan to visit us if you're in our area"; etc. When delivering lines such as these, you add to your finesse when you feel and sound authentic while displaying full eye contact. Therefore, as you end the Q & A exchange, remain focused on your net effects goals, particularly your image goals.

Chapter Seven

Your Firepower

Your audience analysis is now complete and your net effects, substance, and image goals are embedded in your fire away memory. You have capitalized on controlling your environment, and have planned how to display your credibility. You're in the batter's box and it's time to show your stuff. Your firepower—controlling the clarity, conciseness, and length of responses; using effective headlines; and forging your goals into coherent and persuasive arguments by exercising your tactical options—is crucial to your finesse.

CONTROLLING YOUR WORDS

Four principal factors influence how you control the phrasing of your message: (1) being clear; (2) being concise; (3) controlling connotations; and (4) gaining and sustaining the audience's attention.

Being Clear

Question to a Ph.D. in communication:

What is clarity?

Answer:

Essentially, clarity is a phenomenon characterized by idiosyncratic selective perceptual behaviors that result in a conscious or subconscious state of recognition that a message or its constituent elements is relatively devoid of factors that tend to facilitate cognitive confusion in the receiver.

Image message:
Pedantic, pretentious—you name it!
Clarity quotient: (*without careful rereading*)
Low.

How ironic it is that this hypothetical Ph.D. in communication can't be clear in defining clarity. But that's the point. Clarity is a challenge facing all of us, regardless of intelligence, education, position—or knowledge about communication.

Let me ask the question again: "What is clarity?" In simple terms, clarity means that a message is understood with minimal confusion. What factors from the preceding example promote confusion and thereby undermine clarity?

- Answers or sentences that are too long or complex (preceding example: 42 words).
- Answers or sentences that contain too many concepts (preceding example: at least five).
- Answers containing jargon (preceding example: "selective perceptual behaviors," "cognitive confusion").
- Answers containing highfalutin language when simpler, more direct terms would be more effective (preceding example: "idiosyncratic" = unusual/uncommon, "constituent elements" = components/parts, "devoid of" = free from, "facilitate" = promote, "cognitive" = mental).
- Answers that are too abstract or not sufficiently concrete (preceding example in its entirety).

The absence of structure or direction to a response also undermines clarity, as the following example shows.

Question:
As an executive communication consultant preparing people for challenging situations, what would you consider to be their major needs?
Answer 1:
There are so many different challenging situations: annual meetings, ambush interviews, talk shows with your adversary sitting next to you, public hearings, and the like, I'm not sure what their major needs are, but off the top of my head, I would say that they need to learn how to handle these situations a lot better.

Analysis:

Just fair. First, you don't get an immediate sense that the question is going to be answered (*introducing a sense of confusion and a possible loss of attention*). Second, the answer is a nonanswer, merely a mirror of the question.

Answer 2:

Three major needs come to mind: (1) the need to understand the enormous range of control they can exercise in such situations; (2) the need to define precisely what goals they intend to accomplish vis-à-vis their target audience; and (3) the need to develop an enhanced sense of confidence and competence through practice, experience, and systematic feedback.

Analysis:

The response had direction from the very beginning because of the definitive *headline*, "Three major needs come to mind." (*Headlines* are covered in detail later in this chapter.)

Is the question clear? Answers hold no exclusive claim to lack of clarity. Questions can just as easily prompt "What did you mean by that?" reactions. In fact, the same factors that produce unclear answers also produce unclear questions: undue length, too many concepts or facets, jargon, confused syntax, highfalutin language, and abstractness.

But the real question is: "What are the root causes of the vague question?" Four major reasons come to mind: (1) a questioner may think he can crystallize his question by talking it out; (2) the questioner, torn between displaying his own knowledge and probing the depths of your mind, produces a schizoid statement/question; (3) the questioner may be deliberately vague in order to observe your ability to focus your response (e.g., a reporter may be open-ended and vague to promote a more meandering response filled with opportunities for follow-up questions); and (4) the questioner's general communicative style may be vague; thus, the question merely reflects that style.

Being Concise

In most Q & A situations, *conciseness is a virtue*, especially if it is not mistaken for curtness, defensiveness, or lack of knowledge or depth.

Question to CEO:

Do you expect this year's sales to improve over last year's?

Answer:

Absolutely!

Analysis:

This concise answer:

- Communicates confidence and authority.
- Demonstrates a respect for the audience's time (versus the "How long is he going to keep us here?" reaction).
- Makes a response easy to follow, placing little strain on the audience's attention span.
- Provides an opportunity for follow-up or additional questions.
- Increases your chances of being quoted by the media—especially the electronic media.

Enough said? Not quite; be sure to read the section "The Long versus the Short Answer" later in this chapter.

Controlling Connotations:

"Weigh what you say" is one of the more popular expressions in our seminars. It not only conveys the importance of carefully assessing what you say, but, just as important, how you say it. The word is the smallest weighable commodity in a response, yet the potential impact of the right or the wrong one can break any scale.

Question to CEO at financial analysts meeting:
How would you evaluate your sales growth over the last quarter?

First optional response:	"Strong"
Second optional response:	"Excellent"
Third optional response:	"Impressive"
Fourth optional response:	"Outstanding"
Fifth optional response:	"Explosive"

Each response may be intellectually honest, yet each connotes a different degree of satisfaction, pleasure, and pride. The one you eventually select depends significantly on your net effects, substance, and image goals vis-à-vis your audience analysis. For example, from an image perspective, if you want to project enthusiasm, "outstanding" or "explosive" would normally win hands down over the other alternatives. However, either or both may be too hyperbolic for a group of analysts whose professional style calls for a more conservative manner of expression.

"**Jargon patrol**". Most every field has its own jargon. In the pharmaceutical industry terms like "double-blind, placebo-controlled studies," "anecdotal reports," and "efficacy" are part of a research scientist's daily parlance. The financial services industry uses scores of terms that make little or no sense to the outside world, for example "puts," "calls," "swaps," and "hedging." Our field, communication, is no exception, with terms such as "boomerang effect," "inoculation," and "primacy-recency effect" (all, by the way, used—but defined—in this book).

Jargon, despite its frequently negative connotation, helps people within any given discipline describe phenomena more precisely and efficiently. However, jargon, as the opening example to this chapter illustrates, can also impede communication, especially if the audience does not understand the terms used, or has difficulty interpreting them based on context. Hence, the need for a "jargon patrol"—for on-going vigilance, by you and other reliable sources of feedback, for avoiding this tendency.

Inappropriate use of jargon occurs in two principal situations: (1) by people fully aware that their target audience may not grasp it; and (2) by people so accustomed to the jargon that they are oblivious to its limitations outside the discipline in which it is generally used. Use of jargon is the first situation in a tougher challenge for a "jargon patrol," for it is frequently driven by the presenter's insecurity, arrogance, or both. Insecurity impels the person to fulfill his ego needs by sounding erudite. Arrogance (often rooted in insecurity) takes the form of "if they don't understand my message, it's their loss."

As you get ready for the firing line, I recommend that you: (1) prepare a glossary of synonyms for jargon likely to be used in broader settings; and (2) assign one or more persons to a "jargon patrol" during the practice sessions. Taking these steps will not only enhance communication, it will also prevent the audience resentment often spawned by jargon-filled responses.

"Don't be a parrot."   In so many Q & A situations, unless you are vigilant, you can find yourself parroting the questioner's language. The danger of parroting if you repeat a damning proposition or negative premise is the possibility that you might reinforce a negative connotation in the audience's mind—*even if you are refuting the questioner's argument*. Further, if you parrot a reporter's damning premise, it could land up in print, or on the radio or TV. The following two examples demonstrate the value of a reflective or offensive response to a damning premise versus a reflexive or defensive one:

Question:
  I hear your product is dangerous. Is this true?
Reflexive (defensive) answer:
  It is not dangerous.
Reflective (offensive) answer:
  Our product is safe.

Question:

Doesn't your drug cause serious side effects?

Reflexive (defensive) answer:

No, I don't think it causes serious side effects.

Reflective (offensive) answer:

The safety profile of our drug is unqualifiedly strong.

These two examples yield the following advice:

1. *Listen carefully* to the question.
2. Rather than defensively repeat negative language or damning premises, *go on the offensive with language more suited to your net effects, substance, and image goals*—language more likely to register a positive connotation.

Gaining and Maintaining the Audience's Attention

Gaining and maintaining the audience's attention is a primary factor in controlling your message and demonstrating finesse. While clarity and conciseness can decidedly contribute to gaining and maintaining attention, they by no means ensure it. What else can be done to gain and maintain the audience's attention? Some practical advice:

- *Adjust your responses to your audience's frame of reference, speak their language, and refer to their experiences.* This will add to your common ground and thereby enhance your credibility (see Chapter 5).

  Question by a group of hockey players during a media interview seminar:

  Where should we look when we're appearing on a talk show? At the host? The live audience? Into the camera?

  Answer:

  Always keep your eyes on the person who is communicating. This is similar to the way you follow the puck. Looking at the live audience during the talk show, unless they're participating, is the same as looking at your fans when you're skating down the ice.

- *Paint "word pictures."* Help your audience visualize what you are talking about by appealing to their five senses.

  Question:

  What are the beaches like in St. Lucia?

  Answer:

  Gorgeous, intimate, and immaculate. The iridescent orange sunsets are especially enticing, giving a rich golden hue to the sand and a deep turquoise glow to the warm, inviting water.

  A fine business-related example of "word pictures" occurred during an interview between CNN's Deborah Marchini and Ralph Whitworth, president, United Shareholders of America. The issue: the growing accountability of boards of directors for the performance of the corporations they represent.

  Marchini:

  Now, the examples of General Motors, Oster Sunbeam, American Express, indicate that corporate boards may finally be waking up just a little bit. Why?

  Whitworth:

  Well, the reason is because of the pressure that you just discussed. The boards can't hold their noses any longer, is really what it is. And we're seeing the end of the pet rock directors. It's basically the embarrassment factor that is putting the pressure on these boards to finally live up to their responsibilities to shareholders.[1]

  Analysis:

  Whitworth responds directly and pointedly, affirming Marchini's premise. Note particularly the striking imagery of "holding their noses" and "pet rock directors." Then note how Whitworth ended the response by reinforcing his major substance goal for his target audience, shareholders who insist on a greater role regarding who sits on a board.

- *Be personal.* While responding to questions, consider using expressions that engage your audience. For example: "You may remember when . . . ," "How would you feel if . . . ?" and "I'm sure you know what it's like to . . ." or "I, too, am a parent and understand. . . ."

- *Be anecdotal.* By telling an anecdote well, you can paint "word pictures" and create curiosity, a major psychological stimulus to attention.

Question to me:

When was your first contact with Ronald Reagan?

Answer:

It came as a complete surprise to me. One summer evening in 1978, while watching TV in our bedroom, the phone rang. Upon answering it, I heard the voice say, "This is Ronald Reagan calling from California. I read your letter and decided to call rather than write." I had written him months earlier to ask a question regarding my book on political debates. Wanting to record the conversation, I asked if he wouldn't mind if I gathered my tape recorder and telephone jack (imagine my doing that today with a candidate for president of the United States). He politely said "Yes," and patiently waited for two or three minutes until I returned. I then expanded the call into a full interview.

Analysis:

This answer creates and maintains attention for two principal reasons. First, it provides an intimate glance at a person who automatically commands interest; second, it is reasonably graphic.

YOUR MAJOR RESPONSE OPTIONS

Whenever anyone asks you a question—any question—you have five possible response options. I will define each briefly and then elaborate:

1. *Respond only* to the question asked (i.e., to answer the question posed faithfully and pointedly, thereby providing no elaboration).
2. *Respond and insert* (i.e., to respond and then add information not directly called for by the question).
3. *Insert and respond* (i.e., to add information not called for by the question, and then respond to the question).
4. *Insert only* (i.e., to avoid the question consciously or subconsciously, responding instead with content not necessarily related to the question, and certainly not faithfully responsive to it).

5. *Ignore* (i.e., to behave in a manner either seemingly oblivious to the fact that a question was even asked, or patently unwilling to respond to it).

Your decision in selecting the appropriate option is important. As the following discussion clarifies, it depends on your net effects, image, and substance goals as they relate to your target audience, knowledge level, willingness to disclose, and time. As a general principle you should normally be faithfully responsive to the question, seeking openings to pursue your persuasive goals, especially when a faithful response (*respond only*) does not provide such an opportunity.

Respond Only

This option involves a faithful answer to the question, with no elaboration. For example, if the question simply calls for a "yes"-or "no"-type response, that is all you'll provide. If you're asked for the time, you simply say it's 5:55 (without adding that dinner will be in 20 minutes). If you're asked where you work, you mention the firm, its location, or both, but you don't reveal anything regarding your job.

"Respond only to the question asked" is typical advice given by lawyers as they prepare witnesses, plaintiffs, and defendants for depositions, trials, and quasi-judicial hearings. If followed, this advice reduces the risk that the person may overanswer the question—a situation that can open the proverbial "can of worms" and invite potentially damaging questions.

In a nonlegal context the *respond only* approach may be especially credible, for it can accentuate your faithfulness to the question and implicitly display your respect for the questioner and his question. However, if the response, including its tone, is too abbreviated or curt, a host of negative inferences can be drawn by your audience.

Financial analyst to pharmaceutical executive:
Aren't side effects responsible for the poor sales of your new anti-hypertensive drug—particularly its tendency to produce nausea?

Executive choosing *response only* **mode:**

No.

    Analysis:

    Too curt; generates a negative image while begging for a follow-up
    question.

Respond and Insert

This approach involves faithfully responding first to the question
and then adding an elaboration or, possibly, a totally unrelated
point. In most medium-to-high-stakes Q & A exchanges, you
should be constantly vigilant for openings to "bridge" from your
basic response to a proactive persuasive theme supportive of your
net effects, substance, and image goals.

Executive choosing *respond-and-insert* **mode to question above:**

    No. In fact, the side effects are limited to a very small percentage of
    the user population. However, since we need to do more to get that
    message across, we are planning to launch an aggressive campaign
    to highlight the drug's safety and efficacy.

    Analysis:

    Responsive, positive, active, direct, informative, and credibly con-
    fessional.

The following *respond and insert* example is from George Bush's
press conference of October 4, 1991:

Reporter:

    Mr. Bush, do you totally dismiss the testimony that the Senate heard
    this week that your nominee [to head the CIA], Bob Gates, cooked
    the analysis to CIA for political purposes?

President:

    If that's the charge, I totally dismiss it. I think it's an outrageous as-
    sertion against a very honest man, a thorough-going professional.
    And that's the worst charge that can be leveled against an intelligence
    officer. And I know Bob Gates, and I know he would never cook the
    estimates.[2]

    Analysis:

    Following a pointed and confident flat denial headline Bush added
    an insert based on his net effects goals (Gates's approval). How-

ever, Bush should neither have returned to the damning premise, nor repeated it (i.e., Bush *parroted* the "cook the estimates" premise). This simply accentuates the negative and ends the response on a defensive note.

Probably the finest example I've seen of *respond and insert* (and one which we show during our media and crisis communication seminars) occurred in the early 70s during the appearance of Dow Chemical's chairman Carl A. Gerstacker, on The Today Show. During the mid- and late-60s, Dow Chemical had been a focal point of Vietnam War protesters and others opposed to the company's role in making napalm. In the following exchange with The Today Show host Hugh Downs, Gerstacker maintained a friendly, credible, nondefensive demeanor as he responded to Downs' question on napalm, and inserted a highly positive message regarding Dow's activities. As a result, he defused the napalm issue within less than two minutes:

Downs:

On the subject of corporate conscience, and so forth, where it's bolstered by expediency—of course, it's all going the same direction and that's fine—but you at Dow Chemical quit manufacturing napalm in 1969, I believe. Was that the result of the public pressures and the fact that television had shown what napalm does?

Gerstacker:

No, Hugh. We have not been making it since May of 69 simply because we did lose the contract on a bid. We would be willing to make it again if the government asked us to make it because simply as long as our country is drafting young men and sending them out—while we don't like war; we don't like any wars—we think the young men should be supported so we would make it again. But Hugh . . .

Downs:

And no other reason though?

Gerstacker:

We don't make napalm. I'd rather talk about something we do make. Dow's in the life science business; for example, we have a measles vaccine that's been out since 1965. About 50 million U.S. children have been vaccinated. I think the key thing here again is that there are 5,000 children in the United States today who are not mentally retarded—all that anguish and all those years—because of this measles vaccine.

Downs:

You mean who otherwise would have been?

Gerstacker:

Who otherwise would have been mentally retarded. And, in Africa, the numbers are much greater and in the whole world, of course, it's many times the 5,000 in the United States. That's the kind of project I would like to talk about. And then we have our Italian drug company that has a new antibiotic called "Rifadin" which will probably eliminate tuberculosis in the world, as well as being the hottest new item for leukemia. You know the virus cause of leukemia is one of the hottest developments and a byproduct of Rifadin at variation is now considered by scientists as the hottest thing for the solving of leukemia. Those are the kind of products I'd like to talk about.

Downs:

I hadn't thought much about the overlap between what we call the pharmaceutical field and the chemical field. Pharmaceuticals are chemicals after all.

Gerstacker:

They certainly are.[3]

Insert and Respond

This approach is normally chosen when a question or comment just made requires a reaction *before* you faithfully respond. It is especially common in debates and other adversarial situations in which the parties must defend themselves. This scenario from a political debate illustrates the *insert and respond* approach:

Political candidate A:

My opponent has done nothing to support AIDS-related research subsidies other than dispense his nice-sounding rhetoric. Thousands of people with AIDS are dying as he buries his head in the sand.

Panelist:

What is your position regarding whether or not the city should have a greater say in the operation of our transit system?

Political candidate B:

Before I answer your question, let me set the record straight regarding my actions on behalf of the people afflicted with AIDS. . . .

Analysis:
Candidate B was wise to choose the *insert and respond* tactic if the AIDS issue is relevant to his target audience, particularly if Candidate A's attack appeared persuasive or, in political debate terms, "seemed to draw blood." This choice, however, is not without risk. Specifically, the moderator might strictly enforce the format with a reprimanding and potentially embarassing "stick only to the question asked." Or the moderator might be prompted by the *insert* to switch back to the AIDS issue, one that Candidate B might rather not discuss beyond his *insert*.

Insert Only

This option, an unfortunate mainstay of political communication, involves virtually disregarding the question and taking two possible routes: (1) actively discussing the question's subject area while avoiding a direct response to the question; or (2) abandoning the topic entirely to discuss another issue.

Insert only is frequently the preferred option when: (1) the question is inhospitable in content or tone; (2) the question is confusing; or (3) you lack or are unwilling to provide an answer. However, of the four response options (as opposed to the fifth option mentioned earlier, *ignoring* the question), it poses the greatest risk of inviting an embarrassing, "You didn't answer my question."

Occasionally you might choose to signal the questioner that an *insert* is on its way, using a version of the following: "The question you should be asking is . . . ," or, "The real issue is. . . ." The impact of this approach can vary widely: it can reflect finesse, or be patently nonresponsive or patronizing. Your success depends heavily on your tone, credibility, the questioner's tolerance, credibility, and audience expectations.

The *insert only* option is frequently used to answer the typical question, "On a one-to-one scale how would you rate _____?" If you don't want to be boxed in by giving an exact number, you may simply verbalize your value judgment (e.g., "terrific," "terrible") and do so with or without stating that you choose not to use the scale.

Question to a utility executive:

Has competition in the utility industry increased appreciably over the past few years?

Answer:

Competition is fierce. No longer can a utility regard its service territory as inviolate—as insulated from incursions by neighboring utilities.

Analysis:

The question per se is not answered. However, the executive proactively bridges to the theme of competition. This may be a more advisable approach than, for instance, responding first by saying that he didn't know whether or not competition had increased appreciably. After all, such a response might devalue the competence or knowledge component of his credibility, and thereby undermine the authority of his remarks regarding competition.

A good example of the finessed insert occurred during a live face-to-face television interview between Larry King and Julie Andrews.[4] When King asked Andrews, "How old are your children?" she, following a slight pause and flashing her characteristic charming smile, responded without elaboration, "They're all out of the nest."

Why wasn't she more responsive? Was this typical of her response style? Not based on my analysis of the interview. Had she forgotten their exact ages? Perhaps. Did she want to avoid providing a response that accentuated her age? Perhaps. Whatever her reason, King didn't follow up—nor did he apparently need to.

Ignore

Although *insert only* is a form of ignoring, *ignore*, as a response option, involves a conscious decision not to respond to the question at all. The situations discussed below put this option in clearer perspective.

As you are conducting a news conference, reporters may compete aggressively for your attention. As questions are fired, decorum—your control—tends to deteriorate. Despite your apparent loss of control, you can exercise a different form of control by acknowledging only those shouted questions suited to your persuasive goals, while attempting to duck the others.

This approach, however, is not without risk. A perfect example surfaced during the Arab-Israeli Peace Conference in November 1991 when Syria's spokesperson may have exercised too much control. Thomas Friedman, the *New York Times'* Middle East expert, expressed his reaction:

> Watching Mr. Sharaa's spokesman carefully pick out non-Israeli reporters to ask questions at a news conference was chilling. Any notion that Syria had come to Madrid because of "new thinking," or for any other purpose than to make peace with Washington, was dispelled by his performance.[5]

When asked a multifaceted question (Banana Peel 8, in Chapter 10), you may wish to respond to certain facets and consciously discard others. Hence, the act of discarding involves the art of ignoring.

A final *ignore* option is the "No comment," or its putdown cousin, "I refuse to dignify that question with a response." Either tack is fraught with risks, for the declared intention not to respond can beg a bushel of questions, including the classical, "What is he trying to hide?" Before exercising a potentially obvious and risky *ignore* tactic, ask yourself whether or not you can erect a credible boundary or fence to mitigate the risk (see Chapter 8).

"HEADLINES"

When we begin to listen to a response, we often stay tuned in or tune out based on the way it begins. If it begins on an interesting note, we are more likely to remain attentive. If the beginning sounds disturbingly nonresponsive or boring, we are likely to tune out or half listen. You cannot afford to have your target audience tune you out at the beginning of your responses (at least most of them). To do so is a virtual abandonment of the control you need for succeeding on the firing line. How do you capitalize on your potential for preventing tune-out, and for seizing control? By making a commitment to using "headlines," sentences at the beginning of your responses that either present the gist of your responses or help shape them. The following headline classification scheme and advice, based on research I've conducted regarding Q & A in a wide variety of business and political situations, work. By making a strong commitment to "headlines," your potential for achieving finesse can increase phenomenally.

- *The flat answer:* "Yes." "No." "Perhaps." "Right now."
  Advice: The flat answer often demonstrates faithful responsiveness, directness, confidence, and strength. However, it can appear curt when elaboration is expected. It can also appear defensive if the response is a flat "No," connoting denial, when elaboration is expected. For example, if a suspect is asked, "Were you in the store when the crime (committed in the store) occurred?" and he responds, "No," the "No," by itself lacks credibility, and thereby begs the follow-up question, "Then where were you?"

- *The response (via agreement or disagreement) to a premise contained within the question:* "You're right, our sales activity in this region is declining."
  Advice: Reinforcing the questioner's premise, even referring to the questioner by name, is generally effective. It communicates responsiveness, and helps build common ground between questioner and respondent. Overdone, it can appear to be pandering. Disagreeing, however, generally requires finesse (Chapter 8), although more forceful disagreement, expressed as righteous indignation, may be appropriate.

- *The framing statement:* U.S. Special Envoy to Somalia Robert B. Oakley, when asked to explain the difficulties of disarming gunmen in that country, responded, "There are three things important to a Somali—his wife, his camel, and his weapon."[6]
  Advice: The enumerative structure imposed by this type of headline draws the questioner's and audience's attention by creating curiosity: "What are the three things?" It also sets up the inference that the response, by virtue of its structure, has been well thought out.

- *The use of proof:* "Four fatalities within a year and a half prove we need a light at that intersection."
  Advice: This type of headline communicates directness and responsiveness. However, the evidence you present may not communicate the message you intend. For example, in the headline above, you're seeking to justify the need for the

light. However, a reporter, or anyone else listening to you, could convert your headline to, "City Aware of Intersection Danger for 18 Months." The evidence itself, therefore, can cause you to lose a degree of control. A better headline might be: "Our engineers have studied the traffic patterns at that intersection thoroughly, including the risks, and have recommended that we install a signal."

- *The preamble:* "To answer your question, I need to supply you with a little background information."
  Advice: This option can be effective if the questioner or audience doesn't think you are stalling. Therefore, you may need to offer a reassuring preamble to your preamble: "I want to answer your question directly, but first I need to supply you with a little background information." When dealing with the media, print reporters are more likely to be receptive to the headline than TV or radio reporters, although it can be most effective on TV or radio talk shows. However, regardless of the situation, make sure your preamble isn't too long; otherwise, you might strain both your credibility and your audience's attention span.

- *The argument:* "Because the government is not doing enough to shelter the homeless."
  Advice: The argument communicates directness, and is especially appropriate in response to a "Why?" question. Just make sure that it's your best argument, for sometimes we bury our better arguments deep into the latter portion of our responses.

- *The ricochet* (turning the question on the questioner or questioning the questioner immediately after a brief response): "Why did you ask that?" or "Why do you think I'm spending more time at the plant?"
  Advice: This is probably the most risky type of headline, for it can communicate arrogance, condescension, and disdain. However, I have occasionally seen it used well. Ross Perot, when asked by the media if he felt responsible for Bush's election loss, answered with a quick "No," followed immediately by the ricochet "Do you?" Most people would agree that this worked for Perot, for it was congruent with his image of candor, confidence, and quick-wittedness. Moreover, his ri-

cochet reflected a bias toward the media undoubtedly shared by a good percentage of his audience.

- *The editorial* (regarding the quality or difficulty of the question): "You've asked a very tough question, but. . . ."
  Advice: The editorial is generally a stall for more thinking time (see Chapter 8). When using the editorial, make sure that it sounds neither gratuitous nor patronizing. Consider, for example, "That's a good question." Although the respondent may intend to reinforce the questioner, he may be displaying instead an improperly judgmental demeanor, thereby placing common ground—and credibility—at risk.
- *The show of support, empathy, or compassion:* "I'm sorry you had difficulty with our personnel."
  Advice: The main problem with this type of headline is that it is not used often enough. Although empathy and compassion are discussed at various points throughout this book, suffice it to say that this headline is important when the questioner needs to feel that you are keying in to his emotions before you provide a more substantive response. As you prepare for the Q & A, anticipate the roles you may need to play (Chapter 2). Will you need to be a counselor, problem solver, patient listener, or perform some other role? Once again, anticipating is a prerequisite to finesse.

General Advice Regarding Headlines:

- Whenever possible, use the headline to reinforce your net effects, substance, and image goals.
- Be careful not to state your argument too strongly in the headline if you expect your audience to be at odds with you. Doing so can cause them to become defensive and, as a result, stimulate their desire to refute your position internally or aloud.
- The more pithy the headline, the more likely you'll be quoted. A few humorous examples:

In the 1950s Jackie Gleason, on his TV show, played the memorable character Reginald Van Gleason III, the dissolute playboy. During a courtroom sketch, the judge asked Van Gleason, "Where were you on August 12, 1956?" Replied Gleason, without a moment's hesitation, "Coming home from a New Year's Eve party."[7]

More recently, newly elected Congresswoman Connie Meek, 66, of Miami, when asked to describe her political style, took full advantage of the media flap surrounding presidential candidate Bill Clinton's claim that he didn't inhale marijuana while at Oxford in the late 1960s: "I'm a sweet grandmother capable of impaling."[8]

THE LONG VERSUS THE SHORT ANSWER

In addition to your response options and use of headlines, another crucial dimension of your response is its length. Here, you face a major decision involving a wide range of positive and negative implications for the clarity and interest value of your message, your strategy, and your image. In fact, length itself, regardless of your words, can transmit a broad variety of independent intentional or unintentional messages that can facilitate or impede the verbal message. The following is based on an analysis I conducted of Q & A in 70 different settings, mainly business-related:

Implications of the Long Response

Clarity and interest value

Positive   • The longer the response, the greater the opportunity to clarify and reinforce the point being made.

Negative   • The longer response can be boring, especially if unstructured; too redundant; too technical; or devoid of examples, illustrations, anecdotes, or interesting statistics.

Tactical implications

Positive   • The longer response gives you more thinking time (stalling time) to produce a complete answer.

- It increases the perception that at least a portion of the answer may appear responsive.
- It reduces the number of questions that can be asked (when you don't seek active questioning).
- It can widen the opening for bridging into a proactive theme.
- It reduces the exposure potentially available to the opponent, if any.

Negative
- It can open Pandora's Box, laying the groundwork for damaging follow-up questions.
- It can increase the potential for misstatements and gaffes.
- It provides the audience or opponent with additional time to prepare a rebuttal.
- It can reduce the likelihood of your being quoted (if being quoted is an objective).

Image implications

Positive
- The longer response helps project your knowledgeability or expertise.
- You can enhance your sense of cooperation, including your respect for the question, the questioner, and the audience.
- You can appear more open.

Negative
- It can make you appear unaware of the answer.
- You may appear unwilling to provide an answer.
- You may lose credibility because of your diversionary approach.
- Some long-winded answers can sound too defensive.
- Your long-windedness can demonstrate insensitivity to the audience's level of interest or respect for time.
- Finally, a thin line often exists between long-windedness and preachiness.

Implications of the Short Response

Clarity and interest value

Positive   • The short response isn't burdened by
unnecessary verbiage. It is, therefore, less likely
to strain the audience's attention span.

Negative   • Without sufficient elaboration, the short response
may be too abstract.

Tactical implications

Positive   • The short response is less likely to create the
traps for follow-up questions or rebuttal often
produced by lengthier responses. Therefore, it
also allows the respondent to drop a "hot potato"
issue quickly.

• It allows more time for questions (if active
questioning, including greater interaction with
the audience, is desirable).

• It limits the audience's or the opponent's time to
prepare a rebuttal.

• It increases the likelihood of being quoted (if
being quoted is desirable).

Negative   • It gives the opponent more potential
exposure.

• It allows more time for questions to be asked (if
fewer are desirable).

Image implications

Positive   • Confidence.

• Directness.

• Authority.

• Respect for the audience's time.

Negative   • Too much of a "trust me" tone.

• Caution.

• Arrogance or aloofness.

• Disinterest or indifference.

- Defensiveness.
- Lack of knowledge or depth.
- Lack of cooperation.

Why People Overanswer

Some time ago I met with an executive who was bursting with energy and enthusiasm, fed in part by great confidence in his products. Although he was as delightful a person as you could ever meet, he had one serious problem: when I asked him a question, I could have gone to lunch and returned while he was still answering that same question.

Clearly, one of the major dangers people face in any type of Q & A session is overanswering a question. Therefore, it is appropriate to analyze why people overanswer.

- One reason is that the difficulty of the question requires processing time. You may launch into an explanation to buy time to think about the answer you really want to give. This tactic frequently backfires, as you may never produce the desired answer.

- You may be uncomfortable with silence, and would rather keep on talking than experience the discomfort, however brief, of silence.

- You may become carried away in attempting to impress your audience with your knowledge rather than focusing on your net effects goals (even if appearing knowledgeable is one of your image goals).

- The intellectual depth of the question could stimulate an ego-fed reaction within you that the answer must equal or surpass the question's depth—despite the fact that "Yes" or "No" might in some instances be a perfectly adequate answer.

- You may possess a general lack of confidence reflected in a need to overanswer—a need driven by a conscious or subconscious sense that doing so will produce an enhanced sense of control and possible acceptance.

- You may be concerned that too brief an answer may appear curt or terse; you therefore overcompensate by overanswering.
- You may lack confidence that the answer is sufficiently understood, believed, or well-expressed (although the audience's feedback may have been misread), and thereby engage in unnecessary repetition and detail.
- You may have an inflated sense of how interesting or entertaining you are.
- You may be unjustifiably defensive and defend or justify positions or actions with overelaborate explanations. Defensive overanswering can frequently result in what persuasion theorists call the "boomerang effect": As you are trying to persuade your audience, your overanswering raises additional doubts about your cause instead of convincing your audience of its merits. As Shakespeare wrote, "Methinks the lady doth protest too much." (*Hamlet* III, ii, 242).

Inside advice. Keep your target audience analysis in mind vis-à-vis your net effects, substance, and image goals. Is your answer important to a key decision maker or to your target audience as a whole? If so, you may need to provide a more developed response. If not, it is normally advisable for you to err on the side of brevity. However, you should generally avoid being too brief; otherwise, you might invite any of the negative reactions described above.

STRUCTURING THE RESPONSE

I often refer to a developed response as a "mini-speech," consisting of an introduction (the headline or lead), the body or explanatory material, and a conclusion. A developed answer should reflect overall unity rather than a meandering or disjointed quality. Unity can enhance the audience's understanding and attention, as well as your credibility. Unity can be reinforced by four patterns of organization: (1) *chronological*; (2) *topical*; (3) *problem: solution*; and (4) *geographical*.

Chronological

Question:

What influenced you to open your own bank?

Response:

I've been in banking most of my career. I started out as a teller in the mid-1950s, became a branch manager in the early 1960s, a regional vice president in the late 1960s, headed the consumer division in the 1970s, and was recently second in command in Villanova Trust's commercial division. My banking experience is, therefore, broad. Starting my own bank is the most fulfilling way to capitalize on that experience.

Analysis:

When choosing this approach, you must be careful to avoid providing too many chronological details, or the response can quickly become boring, especially if the headline is not compelling.

Note that the gist of the actual answer to the question comes at the end. Although one could argue justifiably that it belongs in the beginning, putting it at the end provides a good climax to the response.

Topical

Question:

What influenced you to open your own bank?

Response:

Three factors. First, this is something I've always wanted to do since I entered banking 33 years ago. Second, I have broad consumer and commercial experience that I can put to fuller use by starting my own bank. Third, I received tremendous encouragement from my wife, family, and friends.

Analysis:

The topical approach to a response is the most commonly used. Note how the "three factors" headline gives immediate structure to the response. Its terseness grabs audience attention. Note also that this overall response is somewhat tighter than the chronological. This helps make each topical facet or key message of the overall answer ("something I always wanted to do," broad experience, encouragement) easier to retain.

Problem: Solution

Question:

What influenced you to open your own bank?

Response:

Having lived in this area for 20 years and having spent the last 33 years in banking, I detected two clear needs for a new bank in this community: first, a more personalized approach to the customer; second, a greater attention to the needs of small businesses. Our bank will definitely address and meet both needs.

Analysis:

Notice how the respondent initially builds his credentials as a banker and community member. Then note the sense of structure created by the way the need (problem) is presented. Finally, note the strong close that reinforces the banker's theme. This response has unity and closure, and is the strongest business-oriented answer of the banker's three responses.

Geographical

Question:

How is your marketing territory organized?

Response:

By county, into three regions: Delaware, Montgomery, and Chester.

Analysis:

Although this approach is less common than the chronological or topical, it is particularly useful in explaining patterns of organization and processes.

As you think about structuring your response, you may benefit from two principles of persuasion reflected in the examples above. The first is the *"anticlimax versus climax"* approach to a question. "Anticlimax" involves providing the gist of your answer early, often in the headline. This approach helps create a sense of immediate responsiveness and credibility, and generally makes your response more quotable for a taped TV or radio interview. However, as noted in the discussion regarding headlines, a headline that is too blunt or direct can heighten the audience's defensiveness, especially if they disagree with it.

"Climax" involves building toward the gist of your response by creating a climate of curiosity or suspense (first example above). Although this approach can enhance the audience's attention, it should neither be too long nor appear manipulative.

The second principle of persuasion, called *"primacy-recency"* and based on extensive research, implies that we tend to remember best what we hear first and last. Relying on this principle, you should normally begin and end your responses with your stronger arguments. Also, consider beginning and ending any listing of proof as strongly as possible. Finally, if the strength of the argument or proof is marginal, consider leaving it out; otherwise, it could dilute the impact of your stronger arguments or evidence.

PROOF

You may remember when, during the 1988 presidential race, Pat Robertson accused George Bush's campaign of manipulating the timing of the Jimmy Swaggart sex scandal to embarrass Robertson. When Robertson, a Yale Law School graduate, was asked, "Where's the proof?" he produced not a shred, weakening both his campaign and reputation.

As an arbitrator-mediator and a former college debate coach, I have studied the subject of proof or evidence closely. This experience has produced the following practical advice for responding to questions:

1. *Be prepared to prove a controversial point* (especially to your target audience), via testimony, examples, data, or a real exhibit.
2. *Before providing the proof, make sure you sense the audience's desire for it*. Otherwise, your proof, however intrinsically persuasive, could make you appear defensive.
3. *If you have several "pieces" of evidence, choose only the strongest one or two*, making sure they are suited to your target audience—their attitudes, knowledge level, interest, and patience. If they want more, let them request it.
4. *Be prepared to document the source* and, where appropriate,

to explain the methodology behind the proof. But again, do not offer either unless your audience appears interested.

5. *Take appropriate advantage of visual aids.* Have charts on reserve to provide the more technical or detailed inferential proof, and photographs or actual objects to provide more "real" proof.

6. *Avoid proof that may raise a skeptical eyebrow* because it is somewhat irrelevant, dated, lacking in authority, biased, or methodologically flawed.

7. *Most important, be totally honest regarding the basic facts* surrounding both the source of your proof and the proof itself.

Chapter Eight

Challenges to Finesse

S o far, this book has discussed your preparation for and mastery of *Fire Away!* strategies and tactics: the roles of audience analysis, goal setting, memory, and control are now clear. However, the firing line can be confusing; questions may be fired from all directions, jarring your memory and sense of control. At times, you may feel your finesse being challenged. This chapter addresses factors that can undermine your finesse, and offers a broad range of tactics to sustain or reclaim it.

BOUNDARIES AND FENCES

Since the Q & A exchange is frequently a contest between whose agenda will take precedence—yours or the questioner's—it's not unusual for a respondant to need to declare a question out of bounds. The key to preventing yourself from responding to an out-of-bounds question, or to being embarrassed by not answering one, is your skill in erecting verbal boundaries or fences, and your ability to stick to them.

The effectiveness of this skill depends on your ability to read your audience, including their expectations of you and the situation. If the situation is sensitive, boundaries may be ill-advised or need to be erected with consummate finesse. Among the more popular boundaries that can be erected at the beginning of the Q & A exchange or during it:

- "I will not comment on matter X, because it is in litigation."
  Comment: The person is not technically prohibited from commenting; yet whatever is said could be used in the case.

- "I refuse to answer because my response might incriminate me."

  Comment: Invoking the Fifth Amendment may be predicated on genuine concern regarding self-incrimination, the desire not to be cooperative, or both.

- "The question you ask is personal. Regardless of whether the answer is 'yes' or 'no,' this matter is not appropriate for this discussion."

  Comment: This type of response is occasionally used by political candidates to avoid a discussion regarding their sex lives, medical history, and financial holdings. It may not work. For instance, Gary Hart would never have gotten away with it. However, *Playboy* cover girl Shane Barbi did. When asked by a reporter whether she or her identical twin Sia (who also appeared on the cover) was older, she responded: "Ask us about our cup size or our favorite position, but—please—no personal questions."[1] Fences don't come any funnier.

- "For reasons of national security I cannot discuss this matter."

  Comment: This line, and lines like it, have been invoked by several presidents over the years. Sometimes it has been used as a tactic to simply avoid discussing a personally embarrassing point, or to avoid an "I don't know." When this occurs, the president is often accused of "wrapping himself in the flag."

- "I do not want to criticize my opponent. Our policy is not to criticize the competition."
  Comment: This approach, called "taking the high road," is popular in politics and business. It helps convey an impression of statesmanship and confidence in one's own assets. However, it can also degenerate into an "I don't want to criticize my opponent (or my competition), but. . . ."

- "I don't want to add fuel to the fire."
  Comment: Depending on the context, this expression has two possible meanings: (1) that you have fuel to add but won't discuss the matter further (although you may have tipped your hand, intentionally or not); or (2) you're simply staying out of the fray.

- "Today I will answer questions only related to X, because that is my specialty."
  Comment: This approach is common in special briefings and crisis communication conferences. It prevents you from saying, "I don't know," and your organization from being perceived as uninformed, inadequately prepared, or uncooperative. In erecting this or any other boundary, make sure you do not appear too heavy-handed.

- "I have answered all questions regarding this matter before. I see no point in continuing to answer these questions over and over again."
  Comment: This line seldom stifles the media. Frequently the reporter has a different view regarding what questions have and have not been answered—and how satisfactorily. This is why the media hounded Reagan and Bush about the Iran-Contra debacle for years.

One of the more memorable examples of one's failure to take advantage of fences occurred during President Clinton's news conference on March 24, 1993, when he faced questioning regarding restrictions on homosexuals in the military. Although Clinton was awaiting a Pentagon report before announcing his policy regarding gays, instead of simply erecting and adhering to the fence

"I do not want to comment on that matter until I study the report," he got trapped by two follow-up questions. As a result, he implied that he might support segregating the military on the basis of sexual orientation. This point of view drew widespread criticism, especially from the gay community. In addition, his being taken by surprise raised serious questions about the quality of his preparation. The following excerpts from the news conference clarify how he cooked his own goose:

Reporter:

Excuse me, could I follow, sir? The task force was supposed to be created by now. The Pentagon has not created the task force and there's been no report to the Hill, and in fact Senator Nunn has indicated that he thinks some of the compromises that might have been possible, such as not having gays go to sea or be in combat, are not constitutional. Does that give you pause?

Clinton:

Not constitutional?

Reporter:

Would not pass constitutional muster.

Clinton:

Well, I don't want to get into a constitutional debate. But if you can discriminate against people in terms of whether they get into the service or not, based on not what they are but what they say they are, then I would think you could make appropriate distinctions on duty assignments once they're in. I—the courts have historically given quite wide berth to the military to make judgments of that kind in terms of duty assignments.

****

Reporter:

Are you prepared to support restrictions on—to follow up on Andrea's question—prepared to support restrictions on the deployment of homosexual members of the service? And if you are, do you think that fulfills the criteria that you laid out, that discrimination should be on the basis of conduct, not orientation?

Clinton:

That depends on what the report says; that's why I'm waiting for the Secretary of Defense to issue the report. But I wouldn't rule that out, depending on what the grounds and arguments were. Yes?[2]

DISAGREEING WITH THE QUESTIONER

Few people who watched the debate between Ronald Reagan and Jimmy Carter on October 28, 1980, will ever forget Reagan's famous line: "There you go again," directed toward Carter following one of his anti-Reagan attacks. The line was completely devoid of substance; in fact, it was 100 percent pure image delivered in quintessential Reagan style. The net effect: through this amazingly simple tactic Reagan was able to demonstrate a sense of calm command—presidential command—while putting down the president of the United States in a manner considered neither abrasive nor strident.

There will undoubtedly be occasions when you may need to let the questioner (particularly in accusatory situations) know that you are less than pleased with the tone of the question, its logic, or her understanding of the facts. The decision to "take on" the questioner is a judgment call requiring keen sensitivity. In making this decision, you should consider the general tone of the session, and how many times the questioner has elevated your "blood pressure" and undermined your need for control, including possibly your image. If you decide to take on a questioner, remember that you should normally question her logic or facts, not issue a personal challenge. Avoid becoming unduly defensive or combative. Well-prepared lines for any anticipated disagreement can provide you with an added sense of control over the exchange—especially if you have kept your net effects goals (particularly your image goals)—clearly in mind.

These lines may make a bad situation worse, especially if delivered in a challenging, aggressive manner:

"Your premise is faulty."

"What makes you say that?"

"Come on. That's not true and you know it."

"You're not serious, are you?"

"That's a bunch of crap. You actually believe that?"

The *aggressive ricochet*, where you suddenly take the offensive and become a questioner, can be one of the more imaginative but hardly risk-free ways of challenging the questioner (see also the discussion of headlines in Chapter 7). A good example of this tactic occurred several years ago on "This Week" (ABC Sunday) when, at the end of an interview with Senator Ernest Hollings (D-S.C.), Sam Donaldson changed the subject and told Hollings that he had heard that the senator had his suits made in Korea. "Was this true?" Donaldson queried. Hollings, obviously surprised by the question, but with little hesitation, assured Donaldson that his suits were made with American cloth. Hardly the type of personality to be upstaged, Hollings then asked Donaldson, "Since we are getting personal, where is your wig made?" Donaldson remained conspicuously silent.

Another amusing example of the ricochet (laced with a heavy putdown) surfaced during a news conference called by Zsa Zsa Gabor's publisher upon the launching of her autobiography. When asked by a reporter to divulge her age (not disclosed in the book), she said in her own inimitable style, "Dahling, what a stupid question!" Then she demanded of her questioner, "How old are you?" "Thirty-five," she responded. Zsa Zsa, without a hitch in her rhythm, advanced her ricochet and putdown one giant step further: "Well you're stupid to tell it, because you look 28."

These following lines are potentially more acceptable than a risky ricochet or the contentious lines listed above:

"In theory that makes a lot of sense, however. . . ."

"I don't quite see it that way, and let me explain why."

"I have a different way of looking at that" (and go on to explain why without being too aggressive).

"The way we see it. . . ."

"I can't quite agree with that premise."

"You know a lot about the situation, but let me fill in a few blanks that may make it clearer."

"I DON'T KNOW"

There is nothing wrong with saying, "I don't know," as long as it is said with finesse. Specific audience analysis can be an enormously helpful tool in gauging your audience's expectations of what and how much you should know. For example, since one of my more frequent roles is to prepare executives to appear before their boards, not only do I determine in advance the background of each board member, but I also learn as much as possible about both the types of questions each member tends to ask, as well as her questioning style: how likely is she to participate? How frequently? Is she more prone to ask conceptual rather than specific questions? How interested is she in trends? The intricacies of finance? How tight a case does one usually need to make to convince her? To what extent has she been "presold" by other board members or executives? Is her approach to spending conservative or otherwise? How do other members of the board regard her? Her questioning? And the list goes on.

If, for instance, you learn through your audience analysis that a targeted board member is known for asking picayune questions that other board members do not especially value, you may need to spend more time studying the numbers, but with less fear of possible embarrassment if you can't instantly retrieve one in response to the question. Or, if you learn that one board member's pet subject is the effect of the changing value of the dollar on your international sales, a subject that interests other board members, then you should prepare to reduce the likelihood of a potentially embarrassing "I don't know."

Although "I don't know" can indeed be potentially embarrassing, it can also enhance your credibility. A direct, nondefensive "I don't know," especially in response to a question your audience does not *expect* you to know, can be interpreted as "I'd rather she tell us that she doesn't know than line her 'nonanswer' with bullfeathers." In fact, I have often told my clients that, ironically, an "I don't know" can actually be more credible than the actual answer, if known. (However, I certainly don't advise substituting "I don't know" for the known answer.)

Visual aids can be extremely effective in rescuing you from an embarrassing "I don't know" question—especially aids containing complex data or technical information. In fact, I regularly advise my clients to prepare an "on reserve" collection of visuals to support anticipated questions. However, consider these three caveats as you are retrieving the "perfect" visual to reinforce your response: (1) avoid transmitting the self-satisfied signal that you were just waiting for that question; (2) avoid resorting to a visual that could become an unwelcomed target for too much questioning; (3) avoid using visuals that might not reinforce—or might even conflict with—your net effects goals.

Another way to limit the negative potential of an "I don't know" is to create a team presentation or to have your "experts" available "on call." This approach, however, presents three risks: (1) they may not reinforce your key messages; (2) they may contradict your facts, arguments, or themes; or (3) they may be too technical or detailed. However, through careful planning *and practice*, these risks can be abated.

Two typical companions of "I don't know" are the explanation of why you don't know and the "but I'll get the answer for you." Either or both may be helpful, but neither is without risk. In explaining why you don't know, be careful to neither sound defensive nor present a reason your audience won't accept. The "I'll get the answer for you" should only be used if the information is reasonably available and not proprietary. In fact, in some situations you may be well advised to say, "I'm not sure how available that information is, but speak with me after the meeting so I will know how to contact you when I find out." This statement, in effect, lets you off the hook even further, because neither you nor your company may possess nor choose to produce the information requested.

"I don't know" sometimes surfaces when you actually know the answer, or could determine it, but decide not to provide it because it is proprietary, potentially embarrassing, or is in some other manner ill-suited to your agenda. This gambit is patently unethical, and can often be replaced by a boundary or fence, for example, "That is a proprietary matter."

The "I don't know" followed by an opening to pursue your net effects goals is often the preferred route. A fine example of this ploy surfaced during a 1992 news conference announcing that Herschel Walker, the veteran running back and Heisman Trophy winner (1982), was joining the Philadelphia Eagles. Asked his speed in the 40-yard dash, he replied with cool assurance: "I don't know, but I'd bet my salary against yours that there's not a running back [in the entire National Football League] I can't outrun."[3]

STALLING TACTICS

Do you remember the television series "The Honeymooners," starring Jackie Gleason as bus driver Ralph Kramden? If you were a regular viewer, you may recall Gleason's hilarious "humata, humata, humata" stall when caught speechless in some self-imposed predicament. Gleason's shtick mirrors our own sense of embarrassment when the right word or phrase temporarily or permanently eludes us—when we need more thinking time.

With characteristic ingenuity, humans have invented several verbal and nonverbal stalling tactics to provide thinking time to come up with an answer.

One-Liners

• *"Thank you for your question"* may be appropriate if not over-used or gratuitously uttered following a "zinger" for which you do not feel particularly thankful.

• *"That's a(n) good (excellent) question (point)"* may be appropriate reinforcement, especially in a teaching situation. However, it may also sound patronizing and unduly judgmental. It may make other questioners who were not reinforced in this manner feel that their questions were not as good. If the question contains a premise damning you, your cause, or your point of view, the positive reinforcement "That's a good point" could make the audience sense that the questioner's claim may be valid. Moreover, they may sense that you are acquiescing to the questioner's point of view too easily or too gratuitously. As a substitute, "that's interesting" or "that's intriguing" may sound more genuine and be less prone to elicit the negative reactions described above.

• *"I'm glad you asked that question"* may be genuine, and sound it. However, I have frequently seen it expressed when the questioner would have paid money to prevent the question from being asked. This approach can sound more genuine (while you simultaneously extend your stall) by explaining briefly why you're "glad," for example, "because it focuses on a significant issue facing all of us."

• *"Let me take a moment to think about your question"* is one of the more genuine stalls. In fact, it has a confessional tone that can relieve some of the stress related to the question. However, be sure that your stall or pause is not too long—no more than nine months pregnant.

• *"That's a tough (difficult) question"* is another, more genuine stall. Psychologically, it, in a sense, compliments the questioner by acknowledging a challenging question and provides you with cathartic or confessional relief in admitting to its difficulty. The relief may also clear the way for a persuasive response.

• *The temporarily postponed answer (when interrupted during a speech or presentation):* for example, "I'll be covering that issue shortly." In certain situations this tactic may be acceptable, especially if your presentation is interrupted by a question. However, if a high ego, instant gratification-oriented target-audience member is asking the question, your temporarily postponed answer could lead to the defeat of your proposal, or to a permanently postponed raise or promotion. A win-win alternative tactic: give the gist of your response immediately, offering fuller elaboration later in the presentation. The key to making the temporarily postponed answer work for you is your tone; it should not be austere, but cordial.

• *"Let me first ask you a question before I answer yours."* Sometimes this may be a legitimate and positively perceived stalling tactic, especially if your question is necessary to respond properly to the initial question.

Question asked by one of my clients:

Should I take a glass of water to the lectern when I speak?

Question I asked in response:

Do you tend to get dry mouth when you speak?

• *"I'm frequently asked that question."* If you are, why announce it? First, it tells the questioner that her query is not fresh or original. Second, you are diminishing your credibility and the credibility of your response by signaling the audience that you're ready for this one. Third, if the question criticizes you or your position in any way, signaling the audience that it is "frequently asked" may cause them to feel that the criticism has merit—that they may have reason to jump onto the (negative) bandwagon. Finally, if you are "frequently asked" it, you'd better have a good answer.

• *"As I said earlier. . . ."* Although this may occasionally be appropriate, be careful that it isn't "code" for the putdown "if you were listening." Otherwise, this defensive ploy could damage your rapport with your audience.

• *Beginning with an essay* until the answer surfaces is a most common type of stall. Your main concern here should be not to meander; otherwise the audience may realize that you are evading because you don't know the answer or are embarrassed by it.

• *"Well."* A classic Ronald Reagan stall. During preparations for the debate with Jimmy Carter, one of Reagan's long-time advisors asked me if Reagan's frequent use of "well" caused me concern. My answer: "Well, I don't think we should tamper with it. Otherwise, he could become too self-conscious about saying 'well' and become distracted from both the question and the answer."

Repeating the Question

Repeating the question is generally advisable only if a portion of your audience can't hear you. If you repeat the question and everyone heard it the first time, then you will probably be branding yourself as a transparent staller (this is especially true when dealing with a small audience). If, however, it appears that a portion of the audience did not hear the question, you are entitled to a double stall: first by asking if you should repeat the question (two to five seconds), and then by repeating it.

Repeating a question loaded with hostile language (see Chapter 10) directed at you can make you look ridiculous unless you sense that your target audience is on your side, and you repeat it in an appropriately humorous manner, or by ridiculing the questioner (without creating the "boomerang effect"). Usually, however, it is more advisable to rephrase the question.

In friendly situations, repeating a short question may be an acceptable stall. One good example involves an interview between a TV reporter and the first professional female baseball umpire:

Reporter:
Do you regard yourself as a saint? (for breaking the sex barrier to umpiring)

Umpire:
> Do I consider myself a saint? No. Don't you know that all umpires are supposed to be the devil?

Restating the Question

Restating the question may be advisable if you wish to put it in more manageable form. The question may be too long or confusing, or contain a premise, facet, or loaded language you want to avoid. However, when appearing before decision makers, be careful to neither alter the question's intent when restating it nor imply that the original phrasing was less than acceptable.

Requesting Clarification

To request clarification—"Would you please clarify your question?"—may seem only sensible if you sincerely don't understand it. After all, you don't want to risk possible embarrassment related to misunderstanding or not answering the question. Moreover, by asking for the question to be clarified, you also buy yourself more thinking time.

One effective way to ask for clarification is to identify the terms or portion of the question you did not understand. For example, "I'm not sure I understand what you mean by 'the time horizon for cost effectiveness to increase.' " By choosing this active listening approach, you are signaling the questioner and the audience that you intend to be responsive.

Asking for clarification also has its risks—risks that can prompt one to waive the option to ask for clarification and produce instead a less faithful response. For instance, if the questioner is hostile, long-winded, or both, your request for clarification may result in an expanded diatribe and an even more difficult—and unclear—question. In addition, in live radio and TV interviews and political debates, such a request may signal the interviewee's lack of knowledge or, worse yet, weak intelligence, especially if the question seems clear to the audience.

One of the ploys frequently used when fielding an obviously "fuzzy" question is not to ask for clarification, but to begin instead with the disclaimer: "I'm not sure I fully understand your question, but I'll give it a try." This can help let you off the hook, especially if you are later accused of not having understood or answered the question.

"Did I Answer Your Question?"

In a teaching situation, this question may be appropriate, especially when interacting with a student who appears reluctant to provide feedback or ask for clarification. In most other situations, however, it is not advisable. For example, in a public hearing, crisis news conference, or annual meeting where the climate is growing increasingly hostile, asking, "Did I answer your question?" can result in an unsettling chorus of "No's." This question, therefore, not only relinquishes your control, but can also signal a lack of confidence in your response—a cue you normally would not want to transmit to your superiors, decision makers, or the media.

When facing a more friendly situation, what do you do when your answer is central to your persuasive goal and you are not receiving reinforcing feedback from your audience? Instead of asking, "Did I answer your question?" you may be better served by, "Would you like for me to elaborate?" or, "If you wish, I'd be pleased to develop this further." These lines, delivered confidently, demonstrate appropriate respect for the audience.

Nonverbal Stalls

Nonverbal stalls, which can be used in combination with verbal stalls, are often more subtle.

- *The pause*—deliberate, plain, or unadulterated—may be acceptable if the audience feels that the question requires reflection; if not, you could appear stupid, uninformed, or both.
- *Taking a drink of water* as the question is asked, or immediately after, is generally acceptable, unless you're doing it too frequently. If so, you may be leading up to the grand stall—an unplanned trip to the men's or ladies' room.

- *Lighting a pipe, cigar, or cigarette* was formerly more socially acceptable in our culture. However, with more taboos on smoking now, especially on cigarettes and cigars, choosing this stall should be based on a careful analysis of your audience. For example, in the United Kingdom and other nations smoking in meetings is far more acceptable than in the United States.

- *Removing eyeglasses* can connote a more reflective mode. However, I have seen many participants in my Q & A seminars overuse this ploy—so much so that an accelerated videotape replay shows their glasses repeatedly coming on and off with the cadence of a Charlie Chaplin movie.

- *Taking a few steps toward the questioner* as the question is ending or immediately after it is asked can be natural and engaging. However, be careful not to "over-engage" a hostile questioner or to invade your questioner's "space" (see Chapter 12).

- *Returning to a visual aid* is a terrific stall as long as the aid is relevant, well-prepared, and not a target for further unwelcomed questioning.

One final point regarding the stall: don't overreact to the momentary silence between the asking of the question and your response. In fact, the silence created by your pause—if not too protracted—can give you added thinking time, and signal your thoughtfulness (versus glibness) as well as your respect for the questioner.

Chapter Nine

Finesse in Hostile Territory

"...WITH THAT QUESTION, I'VE JUST DECIDED TO ANNOUNCE MY EARLY RETIREMENT...."

Every April and May tens of thousands of America's shareholders make their traditional migration to an annual meeting. For many, the meeting provides an up-close look at management, including the opportunity to better understand the company's progress and plans for the future. For others, it can be good theater—especially if management comes under fire by vocal detractors reinforced by a responsive audience.

As good as the theater may be for the shareholder, these scenarios are no easy act for management. After all, in so many situations, management has worked diligently, resourcefully, and proudly to enhance shareholder value. Only a masochist would enjoy the verbal lashings that surround issues related to financial performance, size of dividends, executive compensation, acquisitions, and corporate responsibility.

The CEO holds no special claim to hostile audiences. Consider the school board chairperson who, in open meetings, regularly confronts outspoken parents with their views regarding such issues as controversial teachers, curriculum, discipline, sex education, and censorship, or the company engineer who has to convince citizens at a public hearing that the pipelines and exhaust stacks of his company's new chemical plant will not endanger the community.

How should you prepare for such encounters beyond anticipating the questions and thinking through the answers? The first piece of advice is to *value composure*. No better example of this comes to mind than the Reagan-Carter debate. As Reagan was preparing for the debate, the Carter camp had convinced a sizable segment of the American electorate that Reagan was too prone to push the nuclear button—that he did not have the temperament to choose "more rational" approaches. To counter this image, Reagan's advisers (myself included) wanted the debate to showcase his reasonableness, advising him that "composure can speak as loudly—or more loudly—than content." Anyone who remembers the debate will recall that Reagan's composed, avuncular manner won the day and strengthened his margin of victory.

The most important advice I can give you in responding to hostility is to *depersonalize the hostility*—to separate your pride or ego from your response and to concentrate as much as possible on your message, the issues, and your responsibility to yourself and your organization. As you do, you need to say to yourself, *"In this situation I am not me; I am the personification of* _____ *First and foremost, I must be their advocate."*

Depersonalizing will help improve your ability to listen, retrieve well from your memory, and provide the detractor with an opportunity for cathartic relief (frequently his principal motive in posing a question or nonquestion). Depersonalizing will also prevent you from engaging in unnecessary debate.

As you face a hostile situation, ask yourself how well you understand the nature of the hostility being expressed. First, is *hostile* a fair term or is *anger, frustration, deep concern,* or some other term more appropriate? Second, if *hostile* is the appropriate term, how widespread is the hostility? Remember, two or three (or more) hostile questioners do not automatically constitute a hostile audience. Remember also that an audience applauding a hostile questioner is not necessarily a hostile audience—they may merely agree with his message at the moment.

As you analyze more precisely the nature of the hostility, ask yourself these additional questions: are you dealing with a person who is, by nature, hostile, or are the circumstances creating or exacerbating the hostility? To what extent might the emotional content of the question or remark be more focused on the issue versus you or your company, or is the hostility mainly personal?

If you find that a sizable segment of your audience is hostile, a key question awaits you: to what extent are they part of your target audience—the people you want most to persuade? If the answer is "not significantly," then you have little to worry about as long as you maintain composure and project respect. If the answer is "significantly," then you are probably facing a tough uphill battle.

HOW TO CULTIVATE HOSTILITY: TEN EASY LESSONS

Wounds from uphill battles are frequently self-inflicted. Therefore, as you analyze the hostility expressed by one or more audience members, you should also analyze whether or not you may be inviting it. This can happen easily if you cause yourself to be perceived as:

1. *Dishonest.* Once your credibility is in jeopardy, restoring it can be an eternal struggle.
2. *Inept.* Perceived competence is a major component of your credibility. Once confidence in your competence is seriously in doubt, it might be time to move on.
3. *Preventing reasonable access.* Not only does lack of access undermine internal morale, it can drive the media bonkers.

4. *Evasive.* Again, a quality that your colleagues, your shareholders, or the media can tolerate on a sustained basis.

5. *Self-centered.* As soon as your boss, the board, the shareholders, or the media perceive your personal agenda to be taking precedence over the company's agenda, your credibility can immediately enter a holding pattern and invite hostility.

6. *Unfair.* Playing favorites, succumbing to selfish motives, or acting in a heavy-handed or too-lenient manner can all generate hostility—very quickly.

7. *Improper.* As an executive you are expected to be a role model. Although occasional improprieties may be tolerated, especially in the presence of prevailing positive qualities, perceived excess can generate a hostile climate.

8. *Patronizing or condescending.* If the audience feels you are talking down to them, or appealing to them gratuitously, watch out!

9. *Defensive.* Assuming responsibility is at the core of our value system. Defensiveness implies a shirking of that responsibility.

10. *Hot-headed.* Losing one's cool is the most dramatic form of both defensiveness and loss of control. If control is lost, we are often prone to wonder about the respondent's psychological state, competence, method of preparation, truthfulness, etc.

HOW TO NONVERBALLY CULTIVATE HOSTILITY: TEN EASY LESSONS

Can your nonverbal communication feed the audience's hostility? Absolutely. Not only via content and tone, but via body language. The following primer will serve you well in getting one or more audience members ticked off:

1. *Tidying up speaking notes with eyes turned downward* as a question is being posed.

2. *Not walking toward the questioner* when a question is asked, especially if you have walked toward previous questioners.

3. *Acknowledging the questioner with a forcefully pointed finger* rather than with a facilitative open hand.
4. *Projecting a stern visage* rather than an engaging smile.
5. *Turning your body away from the questioner* as a question is being posed—or not turning your body toward the questioner in the first place.
6. *Folding your arms defensively across your chest* as the questioning gets tougher.
7. *Elevating your chin and head,* suggesting haughtiness, arrogance, or defensiveness.
8. *Displaying any other negative emotion* (see the discussion of image goals in Chapter 3).
9. *Interrupting the questioner midstream,* especially if the question is neither too long nor repetitious.
10. *Starting to call on a questioner, deciding it is not a good idea, and then switching to another.*

PREEMPTING HOSTILITY: TACTICAL OPTIONS

One way for you to prevent hostile questioning, or at least to soften it, is to preempt the more predictable hostile questions by answering them within the speech, presentation, or opening statement. This approach can prevent you from being accused of deliberately avoiding the issue. In addition, your "preemptive strike" gives you better control in both the phrasing and tone of your remarks. Just as important, the "strike" can produce a framework for responding to hostile questions that may surface despite your preemptive efforts. However, for this approach to work, your preemptive rhetoric must not appear antagonistic, defensive, nor deceptive.

Triangulation

What happens if you show undue disrespect toward a detractor? The accompanying diagram will help answer this question. Arrow A indicates the audience's level of respect for you (10 being

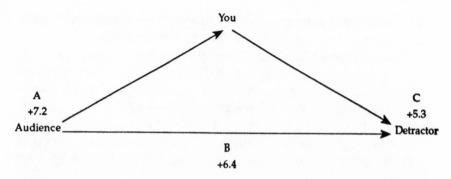

the highest). Arrow B indicates the audience's level of respect for the detractor, and arrow C, yours for the detractor.

At any given point the numbers can change. If, for instance, you say something to the detractor that the audience regards as highly inappropriate, your audience's level of respect for you (arrow A) may drop and their level of respect for the detractor (arrow B) may increase. The key message of this example: although the audience's respect for you may be higher than that for the detractor, when they do respect him, they will react to reinforce that respect.

Persuasive Bonding

In addressing a hostile audience, particularly if they are part of your target audience, *seek out areas of perceived commonality.* Can you build upon the trustworthiness component of your credibility by referring to a shared experience, attitude, value, or goal? Is there a way you can win their trust without appearing phony or manipulative?

Consider this scenario: You are a Ph.D. psychologist representing a leading manufacturer of video games. A study just released by a major university has concluded that video games promote aggressiveness and other forms of antisocial behavior. You are invited to appear on a national talk show with one of the researchers who conducted the study. He's smooth, attractive, and articulate. Moreover, the evidence he presents is so compelling that the studio audience is quickly influenced by him. As you are introduced, and before you utter your very first word, you, by virtue of your position, are perceived as biased. How can you attempt to build your credibility—to at least neutralize this audience that could at any moment become outright hostile?

Do you have children of video game-playing age? Can you refer to a long career of helping people through your private practice? Do you or have you specialized in children of video game-playing age (child and adolescent psychology)? If you answer "no" to any of these questions, the audience's aggressiveness toward you might pale in comparison to that ostensibly spawned by video games. If you answer "yes," you might have a fighting chance.

The Appeal for a Fair Hearing

Many speakers I've worked with enter a room knowing that the audience was "loaded for bear"—so loaded that interruptions and heckling made it virtually impossible to speak. What should you do if this happens to you?

If the chair of the meeting (if there is one) can't secure you a fair hearing, then you may need to make the appeal on your own. As you do, remember that few people are willing to admit that they do not believe in fair play and freedom of speech. Therefore, as you make your appeal, be aware of what you are trying to accomplish psychologically: you are attempting to diminish the conflict between you and your audience by emphasizing the higher-minded bonding (common ground) you share with them over fair play and freedom of speech.

A possible approach: "Please, please. You invited me here (appeal to proper hospitality). I know that we may have differences of opinion, but all I ask for is a fair hearing—just fairness on your part in the true democratic fashion—so that both sides can be heard. In return, I promise to be as to-the-point as possible."

Avoiding a Debate

Few behaviors can affect the hostility meter more dramatically than debating the questioner. The word *debate* in a question-and-answer situation refers to an exchange that extends beyond a simple question and answer. As a debate climate develops, questioner and respondent become contestants, trying to outpoint each other while displaying an "I must win; you must lose" mentality. Such an exchange, while potentially exciting and occasionally effective, more often signals an abject loss of control by the respondent. This is frequently accompanied by the audience's perception of his defensiveness, and feeling that in the heat of the battle he lost sight of his target audience, including his goals.

Achieving finesse in Q & A requires knowing how to extricate oneself from a potential debate. The following advice should prove helpful:

- *Make a commitment not to debate* unless it is absolutely necessary to your net effects goals.
- *Prepare lines in advance* to avoid a debate:

    "We obviously have differing points of view; however, this is not the proper forum in which to debate them."

    "I'm not too sure we can convince each other of our own position, but at least the audience can now reflect on both points of view."

    "We obviously disagree, and that is the value of dialogue such as this."

- *Consider holding a private meeting* to discuss your varying points of view more fully.

The Format and the Hostile Questioner

When you have control over the format, you have added control over the hostile questioner as well as the monopolizer. The annual shareholders' meeting is a good example. The way you conduct the meeting can be a metaphor for your leadership style. If you demonstrate weak control, your targeted shareholders could question your leadership strength. The many control tactics appropriate for the annual meeting—and selectively appropriate for other large forums—include:

- *Inviting questions only from those entitled to speak*, for example, shareholders, registered voters, dues-paying members, etc.
- *Asking that each person identify himself by name.* This tack makes the questioner accountable instead of anonymous.
- *Requesting that only one question be posed at a time.*

- *Requesting questions only—not statements.* If you decide to exercise this option, try not to sound too heavy-handed.
- *Requesting conciseness or placing a time limit* on the question. A one-, two-, or three-minute limit is more likely to be tolerated when more than 150 to 200 people are present and a high level of participation is expected.
- *Placing a time limit on the topic at hand.*
- *Making sure that the discussion is relevant to the topic at hand.*
- *Requesting that each questioner move to a microphone* or wait for an usher to move the microphone to him to ask questions. This helps prevent a hostile questioner or monopolizer from jumping up and down to ask questions and forces him to wait his turn if others want to speak.
- *Having a good repertoire of lines to control the discussion.* For example: "Thank you for your comment," "We'll take that under advisement," "What is your question?" "Please finish," "You have exceeded your allotted time," "Your comment is not pertinent to the issue at hand," "That issue is not appropriate for this meeting and is, therefore, out of order," or "Please sit down and be quiet."
- *Ordering that the person's microphone be turned off* if the situation gets out of control.
- *Ordering security to remove the person.* This is one of your *last* resorts, and must be preceded by one or two warnings. Note: Check with your legal department before deciding on the advisability of this option.
- *Calling a recess or adjourning the meeting.* These are very last resorts; they should be exercised only when the entire meeting appears out of control.

Du Pont's chairman Edgar S. Woolard, Jr., began his company's 1992 annual meeting with the following warning that the meeting might have to be adjourned prematurely:

> Now, a little different note that I feel obligated to make. As you observed coming into the meeting, perhaps, there have been demonstrations going on outside the building. And in the interest of safety, I feel I need to inform you that we had a very regrettable experience in Canada just last Thursday when the Du Pont Canada's stockholders' meeting was totally disrupted by a

Greenpeace demonstration inside the room that forced the meeting to be adjourned prematurely as the Greenpeace participants actually took over the podium.

I feel obligated to inform you of this and can assure you that, in the unlikely event Greenpeace attempts to disrupt this meeting, we believe that we have ample security and are prepared to handle such a situation should it arise. It is unfortunate that these kinds of precautions and warnings are necessary, but Greenpeace appears solely committed to obtaining publicity for themselves and seems to have no interest in constructive dialogue. I am very hopeful we will have an opportunity for constructive dialogue here today and that Greenpeace will be willing to behave like other shareholders. And we welcome that and we will provide you that opportunity.

So I ask everyone to please follow the meeting procedures that you have in hand so everyone can have an opportunity to be heard and we can have a fair and an orderly meeting.[1]

Fortunately for all present, the meeting continued as planned, with active (and civil) participation by representatives from Greenpeace, the Reverend Jesse Jackson, plus frequent badgering by the ubiquitous gadfly, Evelyn Y. Davis.[2]

Eye Contact

As you begin to respond to a hostile questioner, look directly at him. Generally, do not feel obliged to look at him throughout your entire response; doing so could force you into taking one or more follow-up questions, or it could encourage a diatribe. Therefore, try to make a point within your response that allows you to turn your body, head, and eyes toward another audience member, preferably one not seated too closely to the hostile questioner—and preferably a supportive member of your target audience.

Seating Arrangements

Suppose you are expecting at least 100 persons to attend a meeting planned by your organization, one where you expect a fair dose of hostility. Before you commit yourself to a narrow seating arrangement where you can easily spot a hostile questioner, consider one that will easily allow you to shift your focus away from any hostile questioner. Your best option: an arrangement where rows are stretched out from left to right.

The Private Meeting

As annual meetings approach, it is not unusual for the chairperson of a corporation or his designee to meet in advance with a shareholder known to be hostile. The private meeting not only accords the shareholder a measure of respect, it allows him to vent his concerns while the executive attempts to address them. Regardless of whether or not the meeting produces constructive understanding, the executive emerges from it better prepared to anticipate the hostile shareholder's questions.

Offering a private meeting during the Q & A exchange is useful when facing a questioner who rises to express a personal complaint that requires fact-finding. This approach has, for instance, worked well for speakers who, while addressing consumer groups, receive complaints about billing procedures. The key to making this approach work well for you is to have the right line ready, for example, "Since your question is more of a personal nature, let's discuss it one-on-one at the end of the meeting."

Demonstrating Understanding of and Respect for the Opposing Position

Hostility can be diminished by the audience's perception that you understand and respect their point of view. In such instances it may be advisable to verbalize the audience's position clearly and respectfully within your prepared remarks and answers, and then explain, without appearing apologetic, defensive, or gratuitous, why you differ with it.

Hostile questioner:

Who needs this industrial park in the first place?

Chamber of Commerce official:

It seems clear to me that the reasons why you don't want the industrial park in your area are your concerns for how it will affect traffic patterns, contribute to noise and air pollution, and undermine the residential status of your neighborhoods. Allow me to respond to your concerns and to raise some additional points.

Analysis:

A clear and tactful demonstration of understanding. However, be careful not to raise negative points about your proposal that the audience may not be considering. Otherwise, you may be "poisoning your own well."

Empathy or Compassion

The expression of empathy or compassion can signal genuine understanding of the hostile questioner's concern and, in some instances, be all that he expects:

CEO to a senior citizen shareholder:

I'm sorry to hear how our financial performance has affected your income.

Utility executive to a customer:

I understand the frustration you've faced in trying to straighten out your bill and I will. . . .

Congressman during a "town meeting":

(*to a senior citizen whose Social Security check got lost in the mail*) I realize how important that check is to you and I will. . . .

The "Yes-But" Technique

As you listen carefully to a hostile questioner, ask yourself whether or not you can agree with any of his statements or assumptions before taking your own position. This can neutralize the hostility and build common ground and credibility between you, him, and that portion of the audience that identifies with him.

Chamber of Commerce official:

(*at a public meeting*) I completely agree with you that traffic in this area has become too congested. I also agree with you that new development has a lot to do with it. But I ask you to suspend judgment regarding your "no more new development" position until the town leaders decide whether or not a more sophisticated development plan than the one we relied on in the past could work for our community.

Monitoring the Burden of Proof

A hostile questioner stands up in a meeting conducted by you and fires a "shotgun blast"—a fusillade of unsubstantiated accusations against your actions, motives, and character. In addition to following the advice already presented, how do you handle this situation?

- *Avoid going too far on the defensive.* You are under no obligation to defend yourself against unsubstantiated charges. *Remember:* Technically, the burden of proof is on the accuser, although you should not normally invite him to uphold it; otherwise, you might be relinquishing control by allowing him to strengthen his case against you.
- *Keep your target audience in mind* and respond to the claims that may have influenced them the most as you consider ignoring or giving less attention to the other claims.
- *Consider the persuasive value of forceful, flat denial,* recognizing that a more elaborate response can make you appear defensive.

    Hostile shareholder:

    The only reason Ruszenas is on your board is because when he was mayor of East Kaiotz he gave your firm a lot of business.

    You:

    Your statement is completely unfounded and irresponsible. (*Note:* A tone of righteous indignation, as opposed to outright anger, may be appropriate in situations like these.)

- *Decide whether the turning-the-tables tactic will be effective* in these situations. George Bush chose this tactic for Dan Rather during the 1988 presidential race when Rather badgered him regarding his role in Reagan's arms-for-hostages scheme.

    Rather:

    Mr. Vice President, you've made us hypocrites in the face of the world. How could you, how could you sign on to such a policy?

Bush:

(*a few moments later*) It's not fair to judge my whole career by a rehash on Iran. How would you like it if I judged your career by the seven minutes when you walked off the set [in anger] in New York? How would you like that?[3]

Bush's ploy was regarded as a masterstroke that helped him diminish the "wimp" image that had been plaguing him throughout the campaign. In addition, it symbolically put the media in their place.

Humor

The use of put-down humor can be effective in hostile situations, especially if the audience does not identify strongly with the questioner but does identify well with the respondent.

Hostile questioner:

All you care about is profits, profits, and profits. You drive big cars, eat at the fanciest restaurants, take nice vacations, and wear the nicest clothes. When are you going to show more concern for the little person?

Executive:

I'm only 5'4" myself. And by the way, I like your silk tie.

In some situations this respondent would have had his audience in stitches; in others, he would be courting disaster. In essence, good humorists are good risk-assessors.

HANDLING HECKLERS

Heckle: "to harass (a public speaker, performer, etc.) with impertinent questions, gibes, or the like; badger."

—*Random House Dictionary (Unabridged) of the English Language*

Few persons and few situations are "heckle-proof." For centuries, heckling has been the norm in Britain's House of Commons. In fact, a few years ago my wife and I attended the House of Commons' traditional weekly Question Period where Margaret Thatcher, then prime minister, was obliged to defend the controversial behavior of one of her cabinet ministers. Throughout her remarks, the opposition repeatedly shouted "rubbish" and guffawed loudly. During the entire period, Thatcher maintained impressive composure, ignoring most of the heckling as she forcefully—and cleverly—refuted the opposition's position.

Heckling also occurs in situations where reasonable decorum has been considered the norm (e.g., presidential press conferences, financial analysts meetings), and, of course, in less-controlled situations such as public hearings, school board meetings, and protest gatherings.

What do you do if you are confronted by a heckler or a whole gaggle of them? The answer depends primarily on the situation. In some situations you should simply ignore it, both verbally and nonverbally. In others, especially when you feel that your target audience is on your side and the heckling is getting out of hand, you may want to appeal for a fair hearing, or rebuke the heckler in a manner befitting your position and the situation. Or you may choose to give the heckler an opportunity to state his position for a given number of minutes in exchange for an opportunity to carry on without interruption (a very risky option that can work and thereby accentuate your finesse).

Whatever option you select, "Would you please shut up and sit down," George Bush's response to a group of POW-MIA families protesting his campaign speech during the summer of 1992, is generally considered bad form. It displays not only a lack of composure, but a narrow repertoire to draw from to display finesse under fire.

CONTROLLING THE MONOPOLIZER

We've all seen situations in which a questioner either holds the speaker at bay with a long-winded question or continues to ask questions while effectively excluding others. To exercise the proper amount of control in these situations, regardless of whether the questioner is hostile, you have several options. If the questioning is getting too long-winded (as evidenced particularly by the audience's nonverbal cues), you may need to: (1) interrupt with "I understand your question"; (2) restate the question, capturing the gist—or the "spin"—you wish to place on it; or (3) request clarification, as in "Please briefly clarify (or summarize) your question." (*Note:* This third option is risky, since it could relinquish even more floor time to the monopolizer. However, if you've really lost the drift of the monopolizer's question, you may have little choice.)

If the monopolizer is posing questions too frequently, you may need to work harder at attempting to balance the participation. For example, you might explain, without being too harsh, that other people have questions as well. You might also offer to try to get back to him after you have responded to their questions. Or you might suggest a private meeting immediately following the engagement or at a later date. If, however, the monopolizer is a key target-audience member, reasonable accommodation with silent prayer could be your best approach.

YOUR ATTITUDE

Having prepared hundreds of executives and celebrities for the toughest annual meetings, talk shows, news conferences, and media interviews, I can say with confidence that I have seen all of the advice given in this chapter work well. However, at the very core of its capacity to work is your attitude. Hence, my parting advice: hostile questioners, hecklers, and monopolizers often provide hidden opportunities. If you listen carefully, depersonalize the situation, and maintain an "in-control mentality," these people can unwittingly help place your finesse in the spotlight better than anything you could possibly dream up on your own.

Chapter Ten

Your Finesse and Banana Peels™

Scene One:

Democratic presidential candidate and front-runner Gary Hart at a news conference held in May 1987 (following a major news story reporting that, although he was married and in his forties, he had spent the previous weekend with Donna Rice, a voluptuous 28-year-old model).

The question: (one of dozens posed)

Have you ever committed adultery?

Hart's answer:

A self-incriminating refusal to respond.

The result:

Within 72 hours, his soaring candidacy had plummeted and ended with enormous public disgrace, to be followed six months later by another ill-fated campaign.

Scene two:

Al Campanis, executive for 44 years with the Brooklyn and L.A. Dodgers, appearing on ABC's "Nightline" with host Ted Koppel on the 40th anniversary of Dodger Jackie Robinson's entry as the first African-American into the major leagues.

Koppel's question:

Why are there so few blacks in baseball management?

Campanis's answer:

I truly believe that they may not have some of the necessities to be, let's say, a field manager, or perhaps a general manager. . . . Well, I don't say all of them, but they certainly are short [on ability]. How many quarterbacks do you have—how many pitchers do you have that are black?

The follow up:

Koppel tried to bail him out with follow-up questions, but Campanis kept misspeaking, asking, and answering his own question up to the fatal blow: "Why aren't black men, or black people, good swimmers? Because they don't have the buoyancy." (a tired myth)

The result:

Within 24 hours, Campanis apologized, but within 48 hours, the 44-year veteran was fired.

Scene three:

The Senate Caucus Room, Washington, D.C., July 7, 8, 9, 10, 13, and 14, 1987. The witness: Colonel Oliver North, to many the "fall guy" for the Iran-Contra arms-for-hostages fiasco, who breaks his eight-month silence by testifying with limited immunity.

The question:

3,137 questions and answers over the six-day period.

The result:

With enormous composure, a compelling presence, and powerful persuasive resourcefulness, North instantly became a national hero.

Three different situations. Three different results. Yet there were commonalities as well. Hart, Campanis, and North were all highly competent figures in their respective fields. Most important, the fate of each of them was sealed by the manner in which they handled the challenge presented by the Q & A situation they faced. Hart and Campanis failed miserably—Hart because he misbehaved so badly that nothing would have helped him, Campanis because he misspoke ("misthought" and misprepared). North, however, could not have done better; he mesmerized a large portion of the American people and, as a result, won their support for his cause, their contributions to his legal defense fund, and most notably, their hearts.

As we analyze these events, all occurring within three short months, we can also conclude that while North was clearly well-prepared, Hart and Campanis were both victimized by the surprise that comes from not being prepared. Yes, it can take years of hard work to make one's star rise, yet it can fall immediately—and sometimes irreversibly—because of one misdeed or misstatement.

The obvious message here is to prevent surprises through careful planning and practice. The less-obvious message is that specific approaches are available for you to counter the element of surprise created by a hostile, tough, or entrapping question.

BANANA PEELS™

The Banana Peels™ approach for handling tough, trick, and entrapping questions is one method anyone can learn and develop. It was created by me for Ronald Reagan's debates with John Anderson and Jimmy Carter during the 1980 presidential race. Since then, the approach has been refined considerably, and used widely in numerous business-related situations (e.g., highly challenging presentations, media interviews, crisis situations, annual meetings, public hearings, etc.).

The term Banana Peels™ takes its name from an incident (perhaps apocryphal) involving a G.I. who was returning home without a scratch from the front lines following World War II. As his family greeted him on the front steps, he slipped on a Banana Peel and broke his leg.

The Banana Peels™ approach is based on five premises: (1) most—if not all—trick and entrapping questions can be placed in the twelve Banana Peel categories that follow; (2) any trick, tough, or hostile question can actually contain more than one type of Banana Peel; (3) a set of distinct tactical response options applies to each type of Banana Peel; (4) an executive can avoid slipping on Banana Peels™ by learning the categories and response options; and (5) mastering this approach provides the respondent with significantly enhanced control.

Banana Peel 1: The Hostile Question

The hostile question can be one of the toughest. The questioner who poses it intends to create embarrassment. Here the respondent's ego is placed on the alert and can result in defensiveness or loss of composure. However, risky, hostile questions skillfully addressed can be filled with opportunity. How better can a respondent display the ability to think quickly and project command and composure than under the pressure produced by a hostile question?

Hostile Banana Groves

The key to handling hostile questions—and to avoiding stepping on all types of Banana Peels™—is to anticipate them. Therefore, where do hostile Banana Peels™ originally come from? From hostile Banana Groves. Banana Groves help you anticipate the more predictable lines of questioning related to a hostile Q & A exchange. Three major types of Banana Groves—*questions regarding actions, motives, and character*—are illustrated here:

Hostile Banana Grove A: Questions regarding actions

1. Acted in the absence of a clear and present need.
   Example: Why did you build a $40 million office center when there is a glut of high-quality, conveniently located, and reasonably priced space?

2. Acted without sufficient information.
   Example: Why did you take a position on the Supreme
   Court nominee when you admit that you haven't even
   reviewed her major cases?

3. Acted without sufficient planning.
   Example: Why isn't the new telephone system you
   selected adaptable to forecasted technological advances?

4. Acted too slowly (decisional paralysis).
   Example: Isn't the main reason why we lost this account
   because you and your team dragged your feet?

5. Acted too quickly.
   Example: Why didn't you wait the extra week to receive
   the proposal from American Machine? It could have
   saved us nearly $500,000.

6. Acted without sufficient attention to input from
   important constituencies.
   Example: Don't you think that if we had listened more
   carefully to the customer that we wouldn't be in this
   mess?

7. Acted without sufficient attention to quality or safety
   considerations.
   Example: Wouldn't we have been able to prevent the
   return of these thousands of worn discs if we had made
   them slightly thicker?

8. Picked or kept the wrong people.
   Example: No wonder our accounts are down. How can
   you expect a new MBA with no practical marketing
   experience to handle them? Any day I'd trade a
   prestigious degree and a high IQ for a background with
   solid experience and results.

9. Acted contrary to assurances, past practice, established
   standards.
   Example: Why didn't you alert me to the possibility of a
   cost overrun? You repeatedly told me that you would.

10. Acted without sufficient oversight or supervision.
    Example: Don't you feel that if you had paid closer
    attention to the training needs of the nuclear power
    station control room operators that we could have
    avoided this crisis?

11. Acted without heeding the warning signals.
    Example: The maintenance record on the brake system of the school bus that crashed indicates that you took a band-aid approach to the problem instead of replacing the whole system. Why?

12. Acted too harshly (or leniently).
    Example: Why did you fire Joan, a good worker, simply because she was arrested for possessing a very small amount of marijuana?

Hostile Banana Grove B: Questions regarding motives

1. Acted out of financial selfishness.
   Example: As a shareholder, I'd like to know—how can you and your executive team reward yourselves with such a handsome stock option plan when the financial results of this company have been abominable?

2. Acted out of a need for greater control.
   Example: As a board member I feel obligated to tell you that some of us feel that the reason you fired Pollak was because you regarded her as a potential threat to your position. How do you react to this?

3. Acted out of a need for a higher profile/greater visibility.
   Example: As a board member, I'd like to know—how do you react to the allegation that your decision to appear in our company's television commercials is driven more by your own political ambitions than by your commitment to your present position?

Hostile Banana Grove C: Questions regarding character

1. Deceived or lied.
   Example: Your resume indicates that you graduated from Plato University. Yet in checking with their registrar and their alumni association, they have no record of you. Did you change your name, or are you trying to pull the wool over our eyes?

2. Took improper advantage.
   Example: You requested that we underwrite your trip to the national convention, and yet according to informed sources, you didn't attend one session. In fact, you

apparently spent most of the time touring and carousing. How do you explain this?

3. Attempted to "cover up."
   Example: Why were we not informed, as we should have been, that the temperature of the (nuclear) fuel rods had risen well above normal levels and that you had to take emergency action to cool them down?

4. Divulged proprietary information.
   Example: The only way our competition could have learned about our "surprise" advertising blitz had to be through a leak in your operation. Whom do you suspect?

5. Conducted oneself in an improper/immoral manner.
   Example: Did you, without our consent, and contrary to both our policy and established law, bribe the purchasing agent of Ficticco to secure your most recent order?

6. Reneged on a commitment/promise.
   Example: You promised the union an active role in developing with management an employee drug testing program, and yet you acted on your own. Why? How can we assign any credibility to your words or actions when you can't keep a simple promise?

Handling the Toughest Banana Peel: The Hostile Question

The first key to handling a hostile question is emotional control. The more the executive can control her emotions—including her ego and capacity not to take a "hostile" remark too personally—the better. In fact, emotional control or composure can be more important than content.

The second key to handling a hostile question is effective listening. *Nothing can interfere more with effective listening than unchecked emotion.* A controversial facet of a multifaceted hostile question or an emotion-laden accusation can produce an immediate short circuit in the listening process, weakening your ability to access your memory and, thereby, provide a quality response. Therefore, listen carefully, paying close attention to the words, the *apparent* intent, and the stated and unstated assumptions.

The third key to handling a hostile question is quality dissection. Quality dissection involves analyzing the language and assumptions of a question, and then framing your response around the analysis. It can occur only following effective listening. For example:

Question:

"How do you expect more business with your *rotten* customer service record?"

Assumption dissection:

1. You expect more business.
   Analysis: May be true or untrue.

2. Your customer service record is "rotten."
   Analysis: May be fair or unfair.

3. The customer service record is a significant factor in generating more business.
   Analysis: May be true or untrue. Many customers (e.g., mail order) are not aware of a company's customer service record.

Language dissection:

"Rotten"

Analysis: Accusation may stand if not refuted. However, it may be reinforced if refuted too defensively. For example, if you say, "Our record is not rotten" and sound too defensive and do not convincingly prove the contrary, you could end up inadvertently supporting the questioner (the "boomerang effect"). Moreover, you might be repeating the word *rotten* for an audience that didn't hear or remember it when the question was asked. Hence, by giving *rotten* added exposure, you could end up "poisoning your own well."

Not only is it usually inadvisable to repeat the damning premise or term, it is also ill-advised to end your response to a hostile question by referring in any manner to the premise or term. Rather, you should attempt to make the positive force of your response, including the way you conclude it, nullify any lingering negativity created by the question.

Another option in responding to a hostile question is to ignore a term (e.g., *rotten*), a hostile facet (in a multifaceted question), or an assumption. Three reasons stand behind this option: (1) you don't have a good answer; (2) the answer you have, while technically sound, is not potentially persuasive; or (3) you can take the offensive better by not acknowledging the term, facet, or assumption (see the following page).

Remember when handling a hostile question that the name of the game is persuasion. Specifically, your principal purpose is to advance your net effects, substance, and image goals. Therefore, if your "rotten" record is unfairly challenged and truth is on your side, you should bridge as deftly as possible to a genuinely positive (versus a negative or defensive) response:

> We are proud of our customer service record. Despite an occasional concern, which any business experiences, we receive exceptionally strong feedback from our customers—directly and from the surveys we conduct. They perceive us as attentive and efficient, two reasons why our sales have increased by at least 15 percent annually for the past five years.

Banana Peel 2: The Speculative Question

During the Supreme Court confirmation hearings for Clarence Thomas, witness after witness was asked why would law professor Anita Hill, who accused Thomas of committing sexual harassment years earlier, be motivated to step forward and, as tens of millions of Americans watched, have her integrity, psychological state, and sexual sensitivities forcefully questioned by senators who supported Thomas. Clearly, not one witness could plumb her true motives. For this reason several witnesses refused to speculate.

The speculative question is one of the easiest to spot, because it automatically calls for the speaker to engage in conjecture—to resort to a conclusion totally dependent on inference, not fact. Frequently, the speculative question calls for a prediction.

Question to a sales manager:
What do you expect your sales to be next year?
Analysis
- If you overestimate, you may be eventually creating a perceived slump or shortfall.
- If you underestimate, you might be creating a perceived boon (not necessarily positive, for it can confuse planning and expectations).

- If you refuse to answer or ignore the question, you might be sending an inadvertent message declaring low confidence in your sales.
- And, finally, if you find exacting numerical predictions risky (as in the preceding example) a positive, proactive theme line is the bare minimum response you should consider: "We expect sales to continue to increase steadily next year."

Question to a coach:
Will your team make it to the playoffs?
Analysis

- If you say "Yes" too pointedly, you could instill overconfidence in your team.
- If you say "No" or communicate too much doubt, you could jeopardize morale, not to speak of attendance and gate receipts.
- If you indicate "Yes" and those clearly in the know (including the team and the front office) think "No way," then you are at best a dreamer and at worst a liar.
- If you do have a shot at the playoffs and you highlight the resourcefulness of the team and other favorable factors (e.g., other teams in the running not doing well) you will probably score—at least in your answer.

As you tackle a speculative question, don't hesitate to use such expressions as "I'd rather not speculate," "I make it a practice not to speculate," or "Although you are asking me to speculate, let me try to answer your question." By using such expressions you are, in effect, presenting a disclaimer that might help keep you off the hook—and the hot seat.

My favorite disclaimer line surfaced during one of our seminars. An executive was asked to predict stock market performance for the following year. His response: "I no longer make public my crystal-ball gazing; I'm tired of eating crushed glass."

Banana Peel 3: The Hypothetical Question

The hypothetical question is tricky, for it invites the respondent to take a position based on one or more hypothetical assumptions.

Question with one hypothetical assumption:

If sales increase within the next year, would you still propose cutting the advertising budget?

Analysis:

- Do you expect sales to increase next year? If you do, you may wish to affirm that you expect them to. If you do not, you may wish to challenge the assumption or to remind the audience that it is "merely hypothetical."

- On the other hand, you may not necessarily agree with the assumption that a causal connection should exist between sales volume and advertising expenditures. Therefore, you may wish to respond solely to this misassumption.

- If you agree with both assumptions, then your answer is a piece of cake—a "Yes" or "No" plus any embellishment you might choose to add.

Question with three hypothetical assumptions:

Say we acquire Panacea Pharmaceuticals and merge both our and their research and development and domestic sales divisions. Wouldn't the efficiencies that should result from this consolidation significantly strengthen our financial performance?

Analysis:

- *Hypothetical assumption 1:* "Is the acquisition of Panacea Pharmaceuticals a realistic possibility?" If not, challenge this assumption and the response should normally go no further.

- *Hypothetical assumption 2:* "Is the merger of the research and development efforts a realistic possibility?" If not, you may challenge this assumption.

- *Hypothetical assumption 3:* "Is the merger of the domestic sales division a realistic possibility?" If not, here's another opportunity to challenge the assumption.

- *Independent assumptions:* (1) "The combined mergers will contribute to efficiencies." Is this causal claim valid? If not, it may need to be challenged. (2) "The efficiencies will 'significantly strengthen' financial performance." Again, is this causal claim valid? If not, a challenge may again be appropriate.

This Panacea Pharmaceuticals example highlights the trickiness of hypothetical questions. Although it took only 15 seconds to pose this question, it is laced with five interdependent assumptions—a challenge even for those with the most consummate finesse.

As you field such Banana Peels™, you can also rely on such trusty disclaimers as "Although your question is hypothetical, I'll do my best to answer it," or "I'd rather not play Monday-morning quarterback," a handy line when you're asked to second-guess an action already taken.

Question:

If you had read this book before that Q & A exchange, don't you think you would have done better?

Analysis:

While you and I know that the answer is "absolutely," the Monday-morning-quarterback line may be (as I swallow a bit of author's pride) the better face-saver.

Banana Peel 4: The Picayune/Overspecific Question

Unlike speculative or hypothetical questions, picayune questions do not normally challenge our reasoning processes. Rather, they challenge our memory banks (see Chapter 4). Many of us feel embarrassed if we cannot instantly retrieve an elusive number or fact from our cerebral computers.

Command of numbers and details can be enormously impressive. However, I have advised scores of persons who can retain and recite the numbers but have difficulty stating the argument the numbers are supposed to support.

A question I'm frequently asked:

What is the percentage of your corporate versus political business during election years?

Analysis:

- During the last election year (1992) it was approximately 80 percent corporate and 20 percent political (but I don't know the exact number).

- Furthermore, the question asked about "years." The truth is that I hadn't carefully tracked these percentages before the past election. Therefore, I would unhesitatingly give the "80/20" answer. Then, depending on my target audience's interest in the question, I would decide whether or not to explain that I hadn't tracked earlier percentages, or to pursue a key message, or both.

When you're stuck and don't have the requested information at your fingertips, you have five major choices that may be used separately or in combination:

1. *Say nondefensively that you don't have the exact information.*
2. *Offer to make the information available* as soon as reasonably possible (if conveniently accessible and not proprietary or personal).
3. *Present the trend* (e.g., increase, decrease) *without the specific information requested.*
4. *Indicate that the information is either proprietary or difficult to access.*
5. *Pass the ball to a colleague* who "works more closely with this issue."

In the final analysis, quality target audience analysis will help clarify your expectations regarding to what extent you will need to demonstrate command of facts and figures.

Banana Peel 5: The Leading Question

We can all think back to the days of Perry Mason or some other favorite television courtroom lawyer who would confidently object to a question because it was leading the witness. But wouldn't you agree that we probably have less-clear recollections of where we might have been trapped by a leading question? (Were you just trapped?)

The leading question, by its very nature, imposes the questioner's assumptions on you as the respondent, often making it difficult for you to find an out.

Question posed by boss to employee:
Barb (the new president) has done a great job instilling new life into this company, hasn't she?

Analysis:
- You may immediately agree.
- You may not feel that Barb has done a great job, but merely a good or decent job. Therefore, you may:

1. Simply want to say, "yes" to avoid the issue.
2. Question what your boss meant by "great" (choosing to do so may depend on your relationship with her).
3. Substitute your own term, for example, "decent."

- You may disagree.
- You may deflect (ignore) the actual question by simply mentioning one or more of Barb's qualities or actions you do like.
- You may choose to accept the expression *instilling life*, or ask that it be defined.
- You may or may not choose to mention—possibly with a smile— that the question is leading.

Whatever option(s) you choose, remember that effective listening is critical in detecting this type of Banana Peel—an extra slippery species indeed.

Banana Peel 6: The Loaded Question

The loaded question, like most of the Banana Peels™ discussed so far, is normally filled with assumptions. These assumptions are often accusatory, and, if unnoticed, could produce a monumental slip. The complexity of dealing with a loaded question is well-illustrated by the following question and the range of choices one has in responding to it:

Question:
An employee of yours has told us that your company repeatedly and callously ignores safety standards, and that your company's attitude toward safety is a "joke." How do you react to this?

Advice:
- Do you say, "That's one employee's opinion," and stop? Generally you shouldn't, for doing so could sound arrogant. Further, it could offend any target audience members, particularly employees, who identify with the complaining employee. Finally, you don't need for the questioner, especially a reporter, to say, "I can name X number of employees who agree with her."
- Do you say, "That's one employee's opinion," and then give your own position? This approach remains risky for the reasons stated

above. However, the risk potential could be offset by the persuasiveness of your position.

- Should you refer to the question as "loaded?" In some instances, this is most appropriate, but if your target audience might be siding with the questioner, doing so could appear defensive, evasive, or both.

- Do you want to ask who the employee is? In some instances, this may be advisable to determine the employee's vantage point, credibility, and to possibly impugn her credibility. In other situations, doing so could make you appear defensive, and, depending on your tone, even punitive.

- Should you ask the questioner for examples of neglected safety standards, thereby shifting the burden of proof to her? As you contemplate this option, ask yourself whether or not your questioning could result in a persuasive response that might place you in a deeper hole.

- Should you take exception to the damning terms chosen (i.e., *repeatedly, callously, ignore*)? You probably should if truth is on your side, but without repeating them. Otherwise, if you ignore these accusations, especially if they have been stated persuasively, you could allow them to stand.

- Should you "sell" your compliance with safety standards? If truth is on your side, absolutely. In fact, this should constitute the major import of your response.

- What if the questioner is essentially correct? Consider admitting to safety-related problems without being too confessional. Then discuss steps your company is taking to improve the situation.

- What if the questioner is essentially correct and your company has done nothing, and doesn't intend to? You need more than my advice to get you out of this predicament.

Banana Peel 7: The Value Question

One of the first public arguments I can recall took place over 40 years ago in a grocery store in my hometown of Gardiner, Maine. Two of the patrons, both friends, got into a dispute over which ball club was fielding a "better" team, the Boston Red Sox or the New York Yankees. The dispute escalated as each party tried to outperform the other in argument, command of baseball data, and ego. Yet neither had ever taken the time to reach an initial understanding regarding the criteria that would help them define *better*.

Similarly, value questions can provoke controversy or confusion if the crucial terms are unclear.

Question:
Who was the better president, F.D.R. or Lincoln?
Advice:
- If the question per se and the audience are friendly, you might wish to ask them to define their meaning of *better*.
- Alternatively, if you have a definition of *better* in mind, then you may choose to build it implicitly or explicitly into your response.
- In a related vein, you may wish to substitute the word *better* for another term (e.g., "superior") while assuming a degree of added control.

Other Frequently Used Value Terms Often Requiring Definition

Competent/incompetent	Good/bad
Decent	Great
Effective/ineffective	Impressive/unimpressive
Excellent	Poor
Fair/unfair	Strong/weak

Banana Peel 8: The Multifaceted Question

Except for the hostile question, the multifaceted question is usually the most difficult to handle. Why are multifaceted questions used? What factors make them particularly challenging to answer? What tactical options do you have in responding to them? This is a multifaceted question. And now for my answer(s).

We ask multifaceted questions for one or more of three principal reasons, conscious or unconscious: (1) to clear our agenda of questions; (2) to pursue a line of logic reinforced by each facet; or (3) because we are unsure whether or not we will be called upon again.

Multifaceted questions can be particularly difficult to answer if:

(1) there are three or more parts; (2) the phrasing of the collection becomes particularly long (increasing the burden of remembering them); (3) the elements of the question are not well-related to one another; (4) the facets contain more than one type of Banana Peel; (5) the facets vary in type—from Banana Peels™ to a basic question of fact (see example below); or (6) any combination of the above.

To make a multifaceted question more manageable for the respondent, you can announce that you have a two-, three-, or four-part question. This cue helps promote better listening, for without the cue, the facets often pile up by surprise.

The response options are illustrated below:

Question:

How many females do you employ? How has this level changed over the past four years? Why doesn't your firm's employment of females compare with that of competing firms? Why is there only one female on your board?

Advice:

- If each facet can be remembered and answering all won't cause harm (assuming there is ample time), then answer fully.

- On the other hand, if harm can be caused by answering a remembered facet, it may be best to "forget" it. (Although you may risk a possible follow-up question, implying your temporary amnesia.)

- Don't hesitate to ask for a facet to be repeated, especially if you sense you forgot a "safe" one.

- If the questions cannot be realistically answered within the time allotted, politely say so. Then, if possible, respond to each selected facet or to the spirit of the question.

- Sometimes it may be advisable not to respond in the order in which the facets were asked. Journalists often insert a hostile "zinger" into the last facet. For example: "Doesn't all this prove that your management is dominated by male chauvinists?" In such instances, it is normally advisable to render the "zinger" impotent before responding to the facets that preceded it.

- Rather than treating each facet separately, you may be better served by "bundling" them into a single thematic response supportive of your goals.

I have seen many people have fun with the multifaceted question. In one of our seminars, a quick-witted, verbally facile banker began his response with, "First I'll answer your fourth question, then I'll answer your second and third, and then if I have time, I'll answer your first one." An effective ploy if your audience is on your side—or expected to be.

Banana Peel 9: The Vague, Unfocused Question

"What is the meaning of life?" This classic question usually produces a paralyzing sense of puzzlement over how to respond. Another classic that frequently surfaces during a job interview is, "Would you mind telling me a little about yourself?" (Although it is technically a "yes-no" question, if you want the job, you'd better elaborate.)

Vague, unfocused questions can liven up a philosopher's picnic. But they can also drive a detail-oriented person bonkers. Vagueness is rooted in two causes: (1) the abstract nature of the concepts to be discussed, for example, "the meaning of life"; or (2) the fuzziness of the phrasing, including word choice and syntax.

Sometimes vague questions are used to generate follow-up questions. A few years ago I received a call from a political reporter I barely knew who, aware of my active involvement on the national political scene, began our conversation with an unfocused "What's new?" I quickly seized the opportunity created by her question to explain the escalating importance of political debates (since we prepare candidates to appear in them).

The vague, unfocused question, although it can easily throw one off-stride, calls for only two straightforward response options:

Question:
What are your company's plans for the future?
Analysis:
- Treat the question as an opportunity—even as a gift—by answering it the way you wish—consistent with your net effects, substance, and image goals.
- Ask the questioner (if not hostile) to clarify, politely pointing out the words or concepts that need clarification.

Banana Peel 10: The "Yes-No" Question

"Yes-no" questions can initially appear easy to answer. An example: "Have you eaten lunch yet?" Yet they can also be extremely challenging, especially if loaded, leading (as in the classic "Are you still beating your wife?"), speculative, or hypothetical. Three tactical options can reduce the likelihood that a "yes-no" question will make you one of the all-time squirmers.

Question:

Interest rate fluctuations explain why your bank didn't do so well last year: yes or no?

Advice:

- If a simple "yes" or "no" is a safe response, answer accordingly.

- If risky, point out how the forced alternatives of "yes" or "no" can interfere with a presentation of "the full truth." Then answer the question. Lines that can be helpful here are: "This can't be answered in simple 'yes-no' terms," "A 'yes' or 'no' would not do justice to your question," "This issue cannot be treated on a black-or-white basis."

- You could also ignore the "yes-no" framework and answer the question on your own terms, reinforcing your persuasive goals. For example: "Deregulation was an even more significant reason for our difficulty last year, but we've brought a few new products on stream that will make this year far more successful."

The amount of elaboration a response requires following a simple "yes" or "no" depends mainly on the importance of the question to your target audience. If the question is being asked by a superior or target-audience member looking for more than a "yes" or "no" headline, be obliging.

If the headline begins with a "yes" or "no," be careful. For example, if asked whether or not you favored a controversial issue—such as mandatory testing of employees for drugs—and you immediately answered with a definitive "Yes" or "No," your response could have a polarizing effect on your audience, especially if an important segment disagrees with you. In such instances, you may be better served to first highlight the premises you share with your audience regarding the issue, and then state your position—followed, if possible, by an alternate solution:

(If your answer is actually "No.") I fully recognize that the drug problem is very serious—one of the more serious problems our society has faced in our lifetimes. And I understand how it affects the workplace; it affects our sense of security, personal relationships, and morale. However, testing of employees is not the answer because. . . .

A final caveat regarding the "yes" or "no" question: be careful not to walk into a "gotcha" trap by deliberately taking the phrasing of a "yes" or "no" question too literally. The following example illustrates this trap:

Reporter to religious leader accused of an improper fundraising scheme:

Isn't it true that you have established a commission system for your fundraisers?

Religious leader:

No.

Reporter:

But I have evidence here that you have a point system for fundraising whereby certain numbers of points entitle your fundraisers to a wide range of prizes—all the way from electric can openers to trips to the Orient.

Religious leader:

We don't call it a commission; it's an incentive plan.

Analysis:

Because the religious leader deliberately took the word *commission* too literally and was not forthcoming in his initial response regarding the "incentive plan," his evasiveness was not skillful, but transparent.

Knowing how to avoid "gotchas" requires considerable skill, but when the dominant issue is credibility, playing cute can create the perfect set-up for a "gotcha"—or a whole bushel of them.

Banana Peel 11: The "Either-Or" Question

The "either-or" question is a close relative of the "yes-no" question, for it forces only one of two choices.

Question:

Why is the consumer advocate attacking you so forcefully? Is it because of consumer pressure, or because the media have accused her of treating you with kid gloves?

Advice:

- Do you feel that the consumer advocate is attacking you forcefully? If not, you have the option of challenging the assumption.
- You are being asked to speculate on the consumer advocate's motives—to "climb into her brain." Indicate that you can't speculate. "You'll need to ask the consumer advocate" may, depending on your tone, sound appropriate or inappropriately contentious. If a softer approach is preferred, an "I don't know" with a bridge to your positive message may be best.
- With certain "either-or" questions you may want to challenge one or both of the alternate premises (e.g., consumer pressure versus media pressure) and provide a substitute for one or both premises—or provide more than two premises.
- In so doing, you may wish to point out that the question is "either-or," emphasizing that the answer is not that simple.

Banana Peel 12: The Nonquestion

How often have you attended a speech when an audience member stands up during the question-and-answer session and presents a statement or speech instead of a question? These circumstances are prompted by two main causes: (1) the audience member was more interested in expressing an opinion or venting emotion than in soliciting the speaker's opinion; or (2) the questioner may not have noticed that although a question was intended, none was asked.

Nonquestions can be particularly tricky if they are potentially convincing accusatory editorials:

Nonquestion posed at an annual meeting:

You and your board have sold the shareholders down the river by approving a buyout by a bank that is already in serious financial trouble.

Advice:

- Respond briefly and confidently to any claims or assumptions that may have won wide audience support, making sure to reinforce your net effects goals.

- In a friendly situation, or when dealing with a long-winded questioner, politely and gently ask, "And your question is?" Asking admonishingly, "Well, what is your question?" or accusing the person that she didn't ask a question can cause the audience to side with the questioner, unless they've already pegged her as a pain-in-the-anatomy. Moreover, it can give this person more floor time—a potential anathema to your need to exercise control.

- Based on the preceding advice, an insert suited to your net effects goals is often the preferred approach to the nonquestion.

QUALIFIERS

As helpful as the Banana Peels™ approach may be, it can be rendered virtually useless if any of your answers has a ring of certainty that is convincingly challenged by the questioner:

Reporter during crisis interview:
Are you sure that the skin of your aircraft's fuselage was inspected recently?
Airline executive:
Yes!
Reporter:
Then why do the official inspection records indicate that the skin has not been examined for four years?

In this example—and in so many others that come to mind—this executive should have monitored her tone of certainty and been prepared to use a qualifier to avoid the follow-up Banana Peel. Some of the more frequently used qualifiers are: "To the best of my recollection . . . ," "As far as I can determine . . . ," "Based on the information presented to me . . . ," and "According to the most reliable information. . . ."

There is, of course, a flip side to using qualifiers. Too many can damage your credibility by making you appear too cautious or unable to remember information that key decision makers, the media, or the public expect you to remember. Therefore, don't be surprised if a reporter or panelist at a legislative hearing asks pointedly, "What do you mean by 'to the best of my recollection'?" If this occurs, be prepared to explain nondefensively that you are committed to answering the questions as precisely and as responsibly as possible. Be also prepared to explain that facts you may not be aware of could influence the full truth behind your response.

A TIMELY ANECDOTE

The playwright, Charles MacArthur, who had been brought to Hollywood to do a screenplay, was finding it difficult to write visual jokes. So he decided to turn to the comedic genius, Charlie Chaplin, for advice.[1]

Chaplin:
What's the problem?

MacArthur:
How, for example, could I make a fat lady, walking down Fifth Avenue, slip on a banana peel and still get a laugh? It's been done a million times. What's the best way to get the laugh? Do I show first the banana peel, then the fat lady approaching: then she slips? Or do I show the fat lady first, then the banana peel, and then she slips?

Chaplin:
Neither. You show the fat lady approaching; then you show the banana peel; then you show the fat lady and the banana peel together; then she steps over the banana peel and disappears down a manhole.

You are now prepared to deal with Banana Peels™. However, I have no sage advice regarding the "manhole," unless it is a metaphor for what happens if your answers aren't truthful. If that is the case, perhaps the "manhole" metaphor is by itself a more striking message regarding the importance of truth than my pen could possibly capture.

Chapter Eleven

Facing Crises with Finesse

The sinking of the *Titanic*, the *Hindenberg* explosion, the Three Mile Island nuclear reactor scare, the Tylenol tampering incident, the Union Carbide tragedy in Bhopal, India, the ill-fated flight of the *Challenger*, the Amoco *Cadiz* and Exxon *Valdez* oil spills, the syringe-in-the-Pepsi case—each of these crises and perhaps many more are deeply embedded in our long-term memory.

Although these crises are among the more noteworthy over an 80-plus-year time span, crises are occurring every day throughout this world. In fact, today, as I work on this chapter, *The New York Times* is reporting three crises on the first page of its National section: The first, a 24-column inch story (with photograph) regarding the instant death of a 51-year-old Tennessee man from a headache remedy tampered with by someone who replaced the medicine with sodium cyanide.[1] The second, a 23-column inch (with photograph) investigative piece regarding a Massachusetts college post office's role in delivering to a student a suspicious package containing what was to become, two hours later, a gun used to kill two persons and wound four more.[2] The third, a briefer story of a man who killed three coworkers and then himself at the Christmas party of a Miami-based aircraft parts company.[3]

Fires, explosions, spills, dangerous emissions, transportation-related accidents, product defects and tamperings, scandals, terrorist incidents, financial problems, and various forms of protests (including pickets, boycotts, lie-ins, die-ins, etc.) are some of the more prominent types of situations that often evolve into a crisis.

But what is a "crisis"? *Webster's New Unabridged Dictionary* defines a "crisis" as "a serious or decisive state of things, or the turning point when the affair must terminate or suffer material damage."[4] This is a somewhat helpful definition that begs another question: what factors influence the "decisive state" or "turning point?"

Our experience in providing crisis counseling and seminars points to the following factors:

- The element of surprise.
- Real or perceived risk to safety, health, the organization's infrastructure, the environment, financial status, reputation or credibility, or any combination of these factors.
- The fear of erosion of support from such target audiences as clients or customers, consumers, distributors, public officials, the financial community, shareholders, and employees.
- The perception—or reality—of losing some degree of control over the crisis.
- The fear—or reality—of adverse media exposure.
- The fear of personal embarrassment, including potential damage to one's career.

Any combination of the factors listed above necessitates nothing less than superb preparation for the firing line. And the firing lines that grow out of any given crisis can take many forms, among them: responding to questions posed by competing scoop-hungry reporters in one-on-one interviews and news conferences; facing the scrutiny of a legislative committee or subcommittee hellbent on determining fault and the advisability for further government regulation; or giving a deposition or appearing in court to face tough questions based on one or more "deep pockets," crisis-related suits.

Most of what has already been discussed in this book, plus the preparation plans that follow, will help get you ready for the firing line. However, crises, because the stakes can be so exceedingly high, call not only for superb preparation, but also for special preparation. I will assist you in this preparation by presenting the balance of this chapter in the form of a user-friendly advisory memo for dealing with the media.

PLAY THE ADVOCACY ROLE TO THE HILT

In dealing with the media, you are your company's advocate, not simply a resource providing information. Your job, therefore, is to influence the attitudes of your target audiences via carefully defined net effects, substance, and image goals (Chapter 3). Based on this approach, any "information" you share with the media must support your goals. When in doubt, don't share it!

PAY CLOSE ATTENTION TO PREVENTIVE NET EFFECTS GOALS

The extent to which your net effects goals are more positive or preventive depends heavily on whether your organization is perceived more as the victim or the culprit. If perceived more as the culprit, your priority net effects goals are more likely to be preventive, or damage-control oriented. Again, the major preventive goals (discussed in Chapter 3) are:

- Protest.
- Erosion of support (psychological, financial, etc.).
- Deterioration of morale.
- Possible or anticipated misperceptions of fact.
- Release of sensitive or proprietary information.
- Speculation/rumor.
- The perception of negligence.
- Public concern or fear.
- The highlighting of a distracting/potentially embarrassing negative.
- Undue optimism/pessimism.

The priorities you establish based on these goals can help you influence the media and other target audiences while attempting to maximize control over the environment in which you will be presenting your messages (Chapter 6).

A caveat: you can be perceived and treated as the victim one day, and the culprit the next. Hence, be prepared to shift quickly from more positive net effects goals to more preventive ones. A perfect example is the grounding of the tanker *Brear* off the Shetland Islands in January 1993. Initially, the media treated the tanker's owner as the victim, focusing on its loss of power in strong seas. However, within a day, the company was portrayed as possibly more culpable. Several questions were raised, including: had the crew abandoned the ship too early, thereby preventing assistance that tug boats could have otherwise provided? Was the crew too tired to react properly? Were certain potentially relevant repairs to the ship handled in too much of a band-aid-like fashion?

ANTICIPATE MEDIA SLANTS AND BIASES

A critical part of your goal setting (especially your substance goals) and your strategy in implementing your goals is to anticipate the major slants or biases the media may be reflecting, including the Banana Peels™ they might try to place in your path. The following list of slants and biases has been enormously helpful to our clients in taking the offensive to shape credible statements and responses.

"The situation is out of control."

"Company is caught up in a state of denial over the severity of the problem."

"Company is not telling the truth."

"Company is to blame for the problem."

"Company does not possess the expertise to address the problem."

"Company is insensitive to people."

"Company is insensitive to the environment."

"Company is taking too long to respond to the problem."

"Company is unwilling to spend the dollars needed to fix the problem."

"Company is stonewalling/not cooperating with the media."

"Company is not cooperating with the authorities."

"Company is not sufficiently regulated."

As you review this list, ask yourself the following two questions: (1) "Which must be addressed right now?" and (2) "If this crisis escalates or deescalates, which ones will become increasingly important?"

ANTICIPATE POTENTIALLY DAMAGING RUMORS AND LEAKS

Crises are more conducive to spawning rumors and damaging leaks than any other situation. In fact, in several of the crisis situations we have addressed, most of the rumors and leaks were traced back to company employees or former employees most affected by the crisis.

Several interrelated psychological factors contribute to this tendency to feed the rumor mill or leak sensitive information, including particularly:

- Anger, frustration, or vengeance, leading to a tendency to place blame, justified or not, or to disclose confidential or sensitive information, real or fabricated.
- Personal insecurity, leading to the tendency to achieve special in-group status or identity, external recognition as someone who is "in the know," or both.
- Personal hidden agendas, including the desire to see a person, group, or institution fail as a means to achieving one's own goals.

Part of the process of anticipating rumors, and the Banana Peel questions they often stimulate, involves deciding whether your target audiences should be inoculated[5] against them via various preemptive means to reassure them. These include meetings, telephone calls, faxes, courier paks, special 800-number rumor-control hotlines, etc.

Leak prevention is often no less complicated than rumor control. In fact, preventing a deliberate leak can be more challenging; it may depend more on the leaker's fear of being caught than on any measures you might take. Preventing inadvertent leaks, however, can result from keeping your number of spokespersons to a minimum, preparing them well, and reinforcing within your ranks the rule that only the company spokespersons speak with the media. This rule, however, may be difficult to enforce when, for instance, a TV crew greets an unsuspecting employee in his driveway.

Rumors and leaks can also come from parties outside the company; for example, the investigative team. If you sense this possibility, consider speaking with them directly, or enlisting a third party (e.g., a lawyer or trusted public official).

The major rumors we have dealt with are:

Magnification of severity

- Injuries.
- Deaths.
- Damage to infrastructure.
- Environmental impact.
- Economic impact.

Assignment of blame

- The wrong party.
- Scapegoating.
- Too simple.
- Investigative process flawed.

Nature of corporate response

- Too slow.
- Too cost-sensitive.
- Uncooperative (media, government agencies).
- Defensive.
- Untruthful.
- Remedial steps ineffective.

Implications

- Heads will roll.
- Big lawsuits.
- Government will take a greater role.
- Company viability.

UNDERSTAND THE DEBATE-LIKE CONTEXT IN WHICH YOUR REMARKS WILL BE TREATED

Anything you say to the media will likely be treated in the context of a quasi-debate. In addition to soliciting your views (which in many instances may be merely obligatory to appear even-handed) the media usually interview police, fire and ambulance personnel, public officials, and experts. However, the tone of their stories—especially radio and TV coverage—is often set by the raw, unrehearsed emotion of the witnesses, victims, and their loved ones.

Recognizing this provides ample reason for you to jettison any tendency to employ stilted "corporatespeak." You need to replace it by expressing consummate sincerity, empathy, or compassion, complemented by your action-oriented control statement. There is no other road to achieving finesse.

BEWARE THE DANGERS OF ADRENALINE

Few events in business life get the adrenaline pumping more than a crisis. Unfortunately, too many spokespersons and executives, energized by the flow of their adrenaline, are all too prone to meet the media before they are sufficiently prepared. Much too often adrenaline helps bring out the "wing-it"—the overly confident "I can handle them (the media) without preparation"—mentality.

If you are the spokesperson, take notice. If you are preparing the spokesperson, you may need to muster the courage to wrestle him to the ground to impose some added preparation time.

UNDERSTAND THE DIFFERENCE BETWEEN TRUTHFULNESS AND OPENNESS

Whatever you say to the media must be 100 percent truthful—no exceptions. However, you are under no obligation to be totally open. Some information you may choose not to disclose at all. Or perhaps you might later. Remember, the name of the game is control, and your hand—not the media's—is on the faucet of information.

DON'T TALK UNTIL YOU HAVE A "CONTROL STATEMENT"

Regardless of the severity of the crisis, you cannot afford to speak with the media until you are prepared to communicate your company's competence, empathy and/or compassion, cooperation, or any combination of these three factors. In fact, even at the beginning of a crisis situation, however serious, you should be able to marshal the right ideas and words to communicate these three factors—even if you have to qualify your remarks with an "I just learned about this," or "I just arrived here. . . ."

Competence is usually conveyed by the persuasiveness of the action steps you are taking to mitigate the crisis—or at least by referring to a plan and a trained team, even if you are not yet sure of the steps the team is taking or will take. Empathy and compassion are conveyed by the persuasive expression of your company's values in addressing the situation, and by the genuineness and emotional depth of your own and your company's feelings regarding the crisis. Cooperation is demonstrated through your expressed willingness to assist the authorities in charge of abating the crisis, investigating it, and through your reasonable access to and openness with the media.

Finally, don't predict when the situation will be brought under control unless you are 100 percent sure you know, and the answer supports your net effects goals.

AVOID DISCUSSING CAUSE OR BLAME UNTIL ABSOLUTELY NECESSARY

The media thrive on conflict, and blame or finger-pointing serves this purpose exceedingly well. For this reason you need to be especially prepared to deflect the hypothetical and leading Banana Peel (e.g., "if X were inspected more often, this tragedy would not have occurred"), or the pure leading question ("I have it on good authority that the major cause of this problem is Y").

The best way to deflect questions regarding cause or blame and to thereby pursue your "control message" is with a credible "We won't know until the authorities conduct a thorough investigation." Then, if this crisis is continuing, take the offensive by stating in essence that all your energies are currently devoted to addressing the situation. After that, present a strong listing of your action steps, including any progress you can report.

Your effectiveness in deflecting cause questions with the "under investigation" response will often depend on your ability to convince the media and your target audience(s) of three things: (1) the team's expertise; (2) their objectivity; and (3) the rigor of their process. Also, seek an opening to emphasize that "we intend to cooperate with them fully."

PLAN AND PRACTICE HOW TO CONVEY EMPATHY OR COMPASSION CREDIBLY

If one or more persons has been seriously injured or killed, if the health and safety of anyone has been or is being threatened, or if the environment is imperiled, be prepared to express your own and your company's empathy or compassion at the earliest possible opportunity. Doing so credibly is an uncommon skill, especially for most men, since they tend to be culturally conditioned to contain their emotions. To compound matters, dealing with the crisis, no matter how tragic, is often exciting, even heady. Therefore, the ability to switch emotional gears to a more subdued state conducive to communicating empathy or compassion can be a formidable challenge for even the most talented spokesperson.

The following is a sampling of expressions used in a wide variety of crisis situations:

- "Saddened"/"Deeply saddened"
- "Are sorry"/"Are terribly sorry"
- "Feel bad"
- "Regret"/"Very much regret"
- "Our hearts go out to . . ."
- "Our sympathy is extended to . . ."
- "Our prime concern is for . . ."

Two major pieces of advice:

1. *Choose an expression that makes you feel authentic;* anything less is phony. Moreover, saying something that doesn't feel right will likely be picked up as phony by the piercing eye of the television camera.

2. *When time permits, practice the expression(s)* so you can break through any culturally imposed resistance patterns and natural nervousness as you convey your company's feelings with the fullest impact—including full eye contact with the reporter(s).

If your company has developed a set of guiding principles or values, consider referring to those portions most relevant to the crisis. A few examples:

"Nothing is more important to us than the safety of our employees."

"Our company has a long and proud tradition in being a good citizen. Our response to this situation will, I assure you, reflect that tradition."

"Our company is a leader in setting and enforcing standards to protect the environment, and in exceeding those mandated by the government."

"We have been an integral part of this community for X years. Many of us were raised here. Our children attend school here. We worship here."

I am not advising you to select any of the examples presented above. In some situations, they may be eminently credible; in others, they might sound shallow or self-serving. Therefore, I recommend that you prepare in advance empathy, compassion, and value-laden statements with strong credibility potential for the firing line.

A caveat: While expressing your empathy, compassion, and corporate values, beware of the words responsible *and* concern. *Responsible,* to you, connotes your company's commitment to do the right thing. To an external audience, *responsible,* especially if part of a TV or radio soundbite, can make your company appear to be assuming responsibility for the crisis. *Concern,* to you, may be a means of conveying empathy or compassion. However, to many, the expression "we are concerned" can be interpreted as "we are worried," and can thereby undermine the essence of your "control" message.

SELECT TERMS TO DESCRIBE THE CRISIS

If you don't, you may find yourself unwittingly parroting or, by omission, reinforcing the reporter's depiction, which may conflict with your net effects goals. For example, calling an incident a "collision" rather than an "accident" prevents your company from implying that it assumes even a degree of blame.

The following terms have been helpful to our clients in deciding how to characterize the crisis:

Adjectives		Nouns	
Awful	Serious	Accident	Misfortune
Catastrophic	Shocking	Calamity	Mishap
Challenging	Startling	Catastrophe	Mistake
Devastating	Surprising	Challenge	Occurrence
Difficult	Terrible	Collision	Plight

Adjectives		Nouns	
Dire	Tragic	Crisis	Predicament
Distressing	Unexpected	Disaster	Problem
Dreadful	Unfortunate	Emergency	Situation
Fatal	Unpleasant	Event	Tragedy
Grievous	Unsettling	Incident	
Regrettable	Unusual		
Sad			

As you select the appropriate term, consider the following advice:

- You may or may not need to use an adjective.
- Be careful to neither overdramatize nor downplay the situation unduly. The major risk associated with overdramatization is heightening alarm. Downplaying unduly can risk both the empathy or compassion component of your message, and, as a result, your firm's overall credibility.
- Unless appropriate, be careful to neither imply denial nor assume an improper degree of blame.
- As the crisis escalates or deescalates, you may need to select other terms.

WEIGH YOUR WORDS CAREFULLY

So far, I have just scratched the surface of emphasizing the importance of choosing language carefully to convey empathy, compassion, corporate values, and to describe the crisis. The following can be helpful in avoiding the wrong terms and choosing the right ones. However, be careful not to strain your own or your company's credibility by appearing too euphemistic:

These words can overqualify your description of the situation:

Adequate	Feel	Quite	Think
Believe	Pretty sure	Seems to me	

These can overqualify your efforts to resolve the crisis:

Attempt	Maybe	Not yet	Try
Hope	Might	Perhaps	Wish

These tend to accentuate the negative:

Acidic	Caustic	Hazardous	Toxic
Cancerous	Chemical	Problem	Unsafe
Carcinogenic	Dangerous	Risky	Volatile
Careless			

These modifiers connote action when describing your initiatives:

Actively	Immediately	Quickly
Expeditiously	Promptly	Swiftly

These expressions convey a strong sense of commitment:

"Thorough and complete" (investigation/inspection)
"Rigorous" (investigation/inspection)
"We are fully committed to . . ."
"We are doing everything conceivable to . . ."
"Nothing is more important to us than . . ."
"Our highest priority is . . ."

These verbs connote action in addressing the crisis:

Activate	Deploy	Rectify
Address	Eliminate	Resolve
Alert	Mitigate	Respond to
Alleviate	Mobilize	Summon
Clean up	Neutralize	Tackle
Contain		

MONITOR MEDIA COVERAGE THROUGHOUT THE CRISIS

You need to keep continually abreast of how much coverage your situation is receiving, who's saying what, how fairly and accurately, and what visuals are being used (e.g., helicopter flyovers, file footage, live on-scene interviews, a camera crew at the entrance of the hospital emergency room, etc.). Special attention should be paid to whether the major coverage is or can negatively impact your target audience(s). If so, determine whether you can and should adjust your net effects, substance, and image goals. You certainly don't want to be drawn into too much of a reactive mode, but neither can you afford to deny or ignore potentially damaging coverage.

How do you keep abreast of the coverage? If your industry is crisis-prone, select and staff a few rooms with a sufficient number of radios and TVs for monitoring coverage by the leading stations. If your business is not crisis-prone, and radios and TVs are scarce, round some up. As a last resort, ask friends and family to phone in reports on as timely a basis as possible.

CREATE PREFORMATTED MATERIALS TO ADDRESS YOUR MORE PREDICTABLE CRISIS SITUATIONS

Certain businesses can predict the crisis situations for which they may be more vulnerable. For example, the railroad industry, based on historical trends, expects annually a certain amount of derailments and railroad-crossing accidents. Their ability to predict also creates opportunities to classify types of derailments, for example, cargo (safe or dangerous), passenger car, and types of crossing accidents (e.g., cars, buses, trucks, etc.).

This information allows the industry and its specific railroads to: (1) anticipate questions and, as a consequence, prepare credible responses; (2) preformat modules for news releases and opening statements for news conferences; and (3) discuss their investigative procedures thoroughly and credibly. Therefore, through such planning only dates, location, key facts, and a few words or phrases may need to be tailored to address the crisis at hand.

This type of advance preparation not only enhances an industry or firm's potential to influence its target audience(s), it can also reduce significantly the stress level of those dealing with one crisis, and allow their energies to be focused on resolving other, less-predictable aspects of the crisis.

MAKE A COMMITMENT TO REGULARLY SCHEDULED CRISIS DRILLS

Regardless of the sophistication of your crisis response plan or the talent of your crisis team, neither your plan nor your team can remain sharp without practice. The best form of practice is a full, real-time operations and media response drill based on a realistic scenario with surprise updates, including complications.

The second option: a realistic scenario with complications conducted within a more condensed time frame. For example, some of the real-time drills we have worked on have lasted as long as 19 hours, while the condensed versions have been as short as a half-day. Whichever version you choose, the drill should provide the following benefits:

- Smooth out wrinkles in the team's interaction process.
- Highlight needed adjustments in crisis team composition.
- Clarify the relative adequacy of resources required during an actual crisis.
- Promote a "teamthink" mentality (*esprit de corps*).
- Demonstrate the effectiveness of the crisis plan per se.
- Strengthen each team member's leadership and participation skills.
- Strengthen the skills of the spokesperson(s).
- Ultimately reduce management's anxiety level.

Chapter Twelve

Displaying Finesse Globally

MARTEL/DESLAURIERS

Today's business environment is becoming increasingly global. Improved communications technology and jet travel have shrunk the world, particularly the business world. These factors have helped spawn a worldwide economy—one locked in a closed system of economic interdependence. Just as global activity has spread among giant multinational corporations, smaller firms have begun to face the challenge of competition from and cooperation with businesses from abroad.

To this point, *Fire Away!* has discussed fundamentals and effective strategies and tactics to help you take command of even the most difficult Q & A session. However, to return to my initial baseball analogy, the previous chapters all assumed a domestic-based or "home" audience. What happens when you travel internationally for an "away" game? Developing global finesse requires an awareness of the unique challenges that a new cultural setting presents. As *Time* magazine writer Robert Hughes stated:

> The future of [America] in a globalized economy without a cold war will rest on people who can think and act with informed grace across ethnic, cultural, linguistic lines. And the first step in becoming such a person lies in acknowledging that we are not one big world family, or ever likely to be; that the differences among races, nations, cultures and their various histories are at least as profound and as durable as the similarities; that these differences are not divagations from a European norm but structures eminently worth knowing about for their own sake. In the world that is coming, if you can't navigate difference, you've had it.[1]

Knowledge of the pertinent cultural norms is a crucial first step to "navigate difference" in Q & A, no matter where in the world you may be. An otherwise successful meeting can be ruined by a completely avoidable, culturally based misunderstanding.

My firm recently completed a research study, "The Global Q & A Survey," as part of our ongoing mission to develop insights into global business communication. The 22-item questionnaire was sent to scores of executives representing a broad spectrum of businesses with well-established global presence. Each executive had significant experience in the country for which he or she responded to the survey. To complement the survey, I also conducted focused interviews with several other executives. The survey instructions requested that responses be given from the perspective of an American, or a person from an American firm, fielding questions in a business setting featuring questioners from the surveyed country.[2] The results of this research, my personal experiences, plus valuable insights gleaned from publications dealing with issues of international communication, are the foundation for this chapter.

This chapter is not intended to cover every country, situation, industry, or level of business communication you might face. Instead, the sheer multiplicity of variables has forced me to make broad and frequently qualified generalizations. My principal intent, therefore, is to raise your consciousness—to make you aware of the variability of cultural norms, and thereby prompt you to conduct your audience analysis (Chapter 3) from a global perspective.[3]

This chapter is organized into three major sections: (1) universal communication norms and body language; (2) nine common American gestures frequently misinterpreted abroad; and (3) business norms, protocol, and body language in the 10 countries serving as the United States's major trading partners.

AVOIDING MISUNDERSTANDING: UNIVERSAL COMMUNICATION

To understand the influence of cultural norms on behavior, we must first understand what meanings of nonverbal behavior are shared universally. The following list of universal gestures is based on Roger Axtell's excellent book, *Gestures: The Do's and Taboos of Body Language around the World*.[4] Each has particular relevance in a business setting:

- Cupping the ear with one hand is understood almost universally as "I can't hear you."
- Scratching the head to show confusion or skepticism seems instinctive and universally understood.
- Rolling the eyes is a fairly common gesture of incredulity or amazement.
- Holding the nose with thumb and forefinger is universal for "it smells bad."
- Thumbing the nose is a universal insult.
- Yawning is a universal sign of fatigue, boredom, or both. (In many countries yawning in public is considered rude, especially if the mouth is not covered.)
- Hand-clapping or applause is a universal way to express appreciation and praise.
- Shaking the fist signals anger, resentment, and opposition.
- Fist-pounding is generally understood to signal anger and determination.
- Waggling the forefinger back and forth is a fairly common and widespread gesture used to chastise, as if to say "No, don't do that."

- The most universal gesture—one that will rarely be misunderstood and can help in the most awkward situations—is a *smile*.

Following is a collection of the most common gestures you might encounter in Q & A-related business situations, and their varied meanings abroad. These are based mainly on Roger Axtell's work and research conducted by the David M. Kennedy Center for International Studies at Brigham Young University.

Shaking Hands

Home: A greeting. Firm, solid grip.

Away: While generally adopted as a greeting worldwide, the Japanese bow and Southeast Asians press their palms together in a praying motion. Middle Easterners and many Orientals prefer a gentler grip—a firm grip in their cultures can imply aggressiveness.

Eye Contact

Home: Look directly into another's eyes when talking. To do otherwise might suggest lack of confidence, insincerity, self-centeredness, and other negative connotations.

Away: Japanese and Korean cultures teach the opposite—to avert the eyes and avoid direct eye contact. Direct eye contact may be considered intimidating or even suggest sexual overtones.

Waving

Home: To signal hello or goodbye, or to gain a distant person's attention.

Away: Throughout much of Europe this action signals "No!" Europeans customarily raise the arm and bob the hand up and down at the wrist. Italians curl their fingers inward, back and forth with their palm up.

"V" for Victory

Home: The index and middle finger displayed in a "V" is understood virtually around the world to mean "victory."

Away: Be careful in the United Kingdom, the exporter of Winston Churchill's famous "V" for victory. This gesture, when done with the palm facing inward toward the face, means "Up yours!"

The "O.K." Gesture

Home: Used frequently and enthusiastically to signal "okay." It is formed by making a circle with the thumb and forefinger while the other three fingers point upward.

Away: In France, this gesture means "zero" or "worthless." In Japan it can mean "money." In places like Brazil, the former Soviet Union, and Germany it is the symbol of a private bodily orifice, and is therefore crude.

Thumbs Up

Home: To signal various forms of approval, including "Good job," "O.K.," or "Great!"

Away: In Australia, if the thumb is pumped up and down, it is equivalent to saying "Up yours!" Also, in North America, the upright thumb may be used to hitchhike, while in countries like Nigeria it is considered rude. In Europe and Japan, it is used when counting, indicating "five" in Japanese and "one" in Europe.

Spatial Relationships

Home: Normally we stand at arm's length (about 24–30 inches apart).

Away: Eastern cultures stand even farther apart, while Latin Americans and Middle Easterners tend to stand closer to one another—sometimes even toe-to-toe or side-by-side, brushing elbows. To move away, as is the instinct of a North American, can signal unfriendliness, and, in Q & A, defensiveness (both home and away).

Touching

Home: Americans are generally not touch-oriented. Good friends may occasionally touch a forearm or elbow, and very good friends place an arm around a shoulder. However, casual acquaintances seldom hug.

Away: Orientals usually shun body contact. Latins enjoy body contact—the Latin *abrazo* or embrace is a common greeting between new acquaintances. In Russia, the "bear hug" is a common greeting among good friends (and is being seen more frequently in American business and nonbusiness settings). In Arab nations and in Southeast Asia, male friends, while walking down the street, might hold hands as a sign of friendship.

Nodding and Shaking the Head

Home: Throughout most of the world, nodding the head (up and down) means "yes" and shaking the head (side to side) means "no."

Away: In Bulgaria, the custom is just the opposite. Nodding the head means "no" while shaking the head means "yes!"

Our firm's research survey provided other generalizations regarding body language and other norms related to a business presentation:

- *Keeping your hands out of your pockets* when presenting or fielding questions. Although generally acceptable in the United States and Canada in less-formal situations, it is considered impolite in social and business situations in such diverse locales as Germany, Belgium, Indonesia, France, Finland, Japan, and Sweden.
- *Not interrupting a presentation to ask questions.* In Latin America, Europe, or Asia it is rarely done, even when invited at the outset to do so.
- *Waiting to be invited to use first names.* The quick jump to use of first names mainly occurs in the United States, Canada, Iceland, and Australia. In most other cultures the foundation of a deeper relationship needs to be established.
- *Direct or to-the-point questions are preferred* in most countries.

- *Avoiding lengthy presentations.* American, Canadians, northern Europeans, and the Japanese greatly appreciate punctuality and regard for time, and become intolerant of unduly long presentations. However, the length of time devoted to a presentation versus time for subsequent Q & A depends heavily on the situation.
- *Americans have a tendency to highlight superlatives in their presentations and in Q & A*—"first," "bigger," "largest," "grandest," "best." Many cultures, notably the British, tend to dislike this. The Japanese are also more modest, more humble, and, therefore, less tolerant of what could be perceived as American boastfulness.

The remainder of this chapter is devoted to country-by-country profiles of the cultural and business norms, and presentation and Q & A expectations of the United States's 10 major trading partners.[5] The profiles are arranged in the order of the country's ranking as a trading partner. Treat the remainder of this chapter as an atlas by skipping to those countries most pertinent to you.

CANADA

Canada, geographically the second-largest country in the world (after Russia), has experienced a major transformation in its economy since World War I. The economy evolved from one based primarily on agricultural production and the export of agricultural products and raw materials to one based primarily on its manufacturing and service sectors, as well as a mining sector of continuing importance. Canada's economy now reflects an affluent, high-tech, industrial society and resembles the United States in its per-capita output, pattern of production, and market-oriented economic system.

The economy strengthened under the leadership of former Prime Minister Brian Mulroney. A strong proponent of foreign investment and privatization, his most significant achievement was the negotiation and passage (1988–1989) of a free-trade agreement with the United States. The agreement, to be implemented in stages throughout this decade, will create a North American free-trade zone expected to strengthen Canada's economy further. However, some Canadians fear that the measure could undermine Canada's sovereignty and national identity.

Canada is rich in natural resources. A world leader in value of mineral exports and production, it exports many of the minerals needed for modern industrial economies. Its soils, especially rich in the three prairie provinces of Alberta, Saskatchewan, and Manitoba, make Canada one of the world's largest exporters of agricultural products. Forests cover much of the land, and Canada is the world's largest exporter of newsprint and a leading supplier of lumber, pulp, paper, and wood products.

Canada has a total population of more than 27 million, or approximately one tenth that of the United States. About 80 percent of this number live within 100 miles of the U.S. border on the south; approximately 89 percent of the country is virtually unsettled. Because of these vast tracts of virtually uninhabited northern forests and tundra, Canada has one of the lowest population densities in the world. The great majority of Canadians were born in Canada, and most are of European descent. The ethnic composition of the population today is the result of successive waves of immigration by various European national groups.

Canada has two official languages, English and French. These have equal status in affairs of the federal and provincial government and federal courts. More than 60 percent of Canadians speak only English, and significant minorities speak only French or are bilingual. A few speak neither language. The majority of new immigrants prefer to learn English rather than French, and to enroll their children in schools where instruction is in English.

Most Canadians are friendly and open to visitors. They are proud of their cultural heritage, which includes French, British, and other European influences. Although there are many similarities between Canada and the United States, Canadians may be prone to point out that they are different from United States citizens.

Atlantic Canadians are regarded as conservative and traditional. They are very patriotic, since their area was one of the first to become part of Canada. French-speaking people are often more outgoing and open than those of British descent.

Quebec, due largely to its historic cultural and linguistic ties to

France, Switzerland, and Normandy, reflects the greatest European influence within Canada. Women who are close friends may embrace, and both men and women often exchange kisses on both cheeks as a greeting. Since not all of Quebec is French, greetings in predominantly English areas are similar to those in other parts of Canada. Throughout Quebec, first names and informal language forms are not used by adults, except with close friends or relatives. Conversation is direct and polite.

The majority of the people in Ontario, the prairie provinces (Manitoba, Saskatchewan, and Alberta), British Columbia, and the Yukon and Northwest Territories speak English. However, British Columbia, especially metropolitan Vancouver, has been experiencing a sizable influx of immigrants from Hong Kong (110,000 between 1984 and 1991), infusing $2 to 3 billion a year into Canada's economy.

Business Norms & Protocol

Business norms are highly similar to the United States. The business day is 8:00 A.M. to 5:00 P.M. or 9:00 A.M. to 5:00 P.M., Monday through Friday.

Presentation and Q & A Expectations

Our research concluded that there are no significant differences between the presentation and Q & A norms that prevail in the United States and Canada.

JAPAN

Despite enormous differences in language and culture, both Americans and Japanese clearly recognize that their economies are, to a significant degree, mutually dependent. For this reason, Japan will continue to be both one of our major trading partners and more formidable competitors.

The Kata Factor

Shikata (she-kah-tah), the Japanese term for the Kata Factor, is the "way of doing things" in Japanese, with special emphasis on the form and order of the process. It incorporates both the physical and spiritual laws of the cosmos, referring to the way things are supposed to be done to maintain harmony in society and in the universe. Another important influence of the Kata Factor, dating from the 7th century codification of Japanese idealized virtues by Prince Shotoku, is the Japanese "village mentality." It prevails in the form of groups and factions in business, politics, education, and elsewhere, and serves as a major means to maintain harmony.

There is, in essence, only one "right" way of thinking—the "Japanese" way. Every action is either right or wrong, natural or unnatural. Kata means nothing is left to chance or personal inclinations; kata applies to everything—down to the arrangement of food on a tray.

One key to successful business relations in Japan is understanding the Japanese mind. And that means understanding the concept of the kata, or "form." In his book *Japan's Secret Weapon: The Kata Factor*, Boye Lafayette De Mente states:

> Kata are the cultural molds that create and control the behavior of the Japanese, and are the source of both their strengths and weaknesses. All relations with Japanese are influenced by kata, yet few foreigners are aware that they exist! Knowledge of the kata strips away the cultural cloak hiding the Japanese from the outside world, and provides a clear view of the heart and soul of the famed Japanese Way. Dealing effectively with the Japanese—in personal or business matters—often requires knowing how and when to induce or compel them to break the kata and behave in a nonJapanese way.[6]

The Kata Factor has strongly influenced Max Downham, NutraSweet's vice president for mission and strategy. Having conducted business in Japan for nearly a decade, he points to four major norms influencing business relations with the Japanese:

• The Japanese are very formal, and evince a cultural inclination to be very polite.

- A significant difference between their culture and ours is their consensus style of management. This aspect basically means that they will not react quickly, while making certain that the reaction conforms to the thinking of the entity they represent.
- Rapport and trust must be earned over a long period of time. Therefore, if rapport and trust exist between the presenter and questioner, the communication exchange is likely to be more complete and effective.
- To support their consensus style of management, the Japanese are outstanding in collecting, processing, and distributing information on a global basis, particularly within their respective organizations.

General Norms

- A bow is the traditional greeting between Japanese. Persons wishing to show respect or humility bow lower than the other person. The Japanese shake hands with Westerners. While some appreciate it when Westerners bow, others do not, especially when the two people are not acquainted.
- Since the Japanese are formal, titles are important in introductions. The family name is used with the suffix *san* in the same way that "Mr." is used in North America. A Mr. Ogushi in the United States would be called *Ogushi-san* in Japan. The use of first names without a title is reserved for family and friends.
- Greetings usually depend on the relationship. For example, a clerk would greet his superior or a stranger by saying "*Konnichi wa*," but might greet a fellow worker or friend with a popular English phrase, "Hi."
- The act of gift giving is also a traditional part of the Japanese culture. Gift giving is important because a gift says a great deal about the giver's relationship to, and respect for, the recipient. It is, therefore, especially crucial in business relationships.
- Food and drink are the most common gifts, because gifts for the house would quickly clutter small homes.
- When exchanging gifts, let the Japanese host initiate the act. The gift you give may be refused several times, then

accepted. Present it wrapped and with both hands. Wrap it with the appropriate colors. White, gold, and red are happy colors for births and graduations; black and white or black and purple are for funerals; and gold and silver are for weddings. Avoid gifts in numbers of four or nine, as they symbolize suffering or death. Never give a gift on the fourth day. Keep records to avoid repeating a gift.

- Gift giving reaches its peak at the end of each year, when giving the right-priced gift (the price is more important than the item) to all the right people (family, friends, officials, and business contacts) sets the tone for the coming year. If entertained in a home, bring flowers in an uneven number, edible items, wines, or something appropriate from your country. Gifts are given and accepted with both hands and a slight bow. Some people, especially the elderly, may consider it impolite to open the gift right away.

- Laughter does not necessarily signify joy or amusement; it can also be a sign of embarrassment.

- Businessmen wear suits and ties in public. Conformity, even in appearance, is a characteristic of Japanese people.

- Although Japanese is the official language, English is taught in all secondary schools and is often used in business.

- The Japanese place a great value on nonverbal language or communication (e.g., the bow). In fact, one is often expected to sense another person's feelings on a subject without verbal communication. Westerners often misinterpret this as a Japanese desire to be vague or incomplete. The Japanese may consider a person's inability to interpret feelings as insensitivity.

Business Norms & Protocol

- The Japanese prefer oral to written communication.
- Expect to exchange business cards, preferably printed in English and Japanese.
- Discuss a subject from every possible angle.
- Meetings in Japan are longer and more frequent than in other countries because of the process of consensual decision making.

- Japanese businesspeople prefer compromise and conciliation to confrontation.
- Business hours are typically 8:00 A.M. to 5:00 P.M. or 9:00 A.M. to 6:00 P.M. Overtime is common. The average Japanese worker spends 10 percent more hours on the job than does an American.

Presentation/Q & A Expectations

- The Japanese tend to be thorough in studying the presenter's background before the presentation. In fact, they may invest more time studying the background of the presenter or her firm than the details of the deal.
- Seniority plays a very large role in Japanese society and in business. This influences who asks the questions. Specifically, the most senior member will ask the question. Exceptions sometime depend on the Japanese person's understanding of English.
- A very clear priority is usually given to the presentation, with the Q & A session being allocated from as little as 10 percent to usually no more than 25 percent of the total time. This, of course, varies based on the situation and topic.
- The Japanese are not as likely to be aggressive in their questioning. This does not mean that tough questions will not be couched in polite terms. However, a clear status relationship between buyers and sellers can lead to more aggressive questioning by the buyer in the early stages of negotiations.
- The exchange between the presenter and questioner(s) is likely to be reported thoroughly (to conform with their consensus management style).
- If the presentation or discussion has been very long, the questioner, who could be experiencing some fatigue, may understand less and yet not ask a follow-up question. Therefore, key points should be built into responses early and simply.
- Because of the comparative difficulty of the Japanese language, a presenter may think that she articulated an answer or response well, only to determine or discover later that little or no understanding exists.

- In general, the Japanese prefer shorter answers. Answers given by the Japanese may often seem vague when the respondent is attempting to avoid a firm commitment (due to her consensus-oriented style).
- The Japanese (not unlike the Mexicans) do not like to say "no"; therefore, determining their true position on an issue may be confounding.
- In general, questions are likely to be well thought out and will reflect the longer-term objectives of the questioner.
- It is generally not appropriate to interrupt a presentation unless invited to do so at the outset. However, the formality of the occasion, the nature of the presentation and the familiarity of the parties will determine whether interruptions are permissible.
- Always use the last name with the appropriate title.
- If the presentation is conducted in a smaller meeting room, cultural preferences seem to indicate that being seated during Q & A is appropriate. However, in a larger environment, standing is often preferred. This, however, may be more situational than culturally based.
- Since the Japanese are very space conscious and tend to stand even further apart than Americans, their norms do not support the advisability of the respondent moving closer toward the questioner during Q & A.
- Humor is rarely used in presentations.

Body Language

- It is impolite to yawn in public.
- One should sit erect, with both feet on the floor. Legs may be crossed at the knee or ankles, but it is inappropriate to place an ankle over a knee.
- Beckoning is done by waving all fingers with the palm down.
- Shaking one hand from side to side with the palm forward means "no."
- The mouth should be covered when using a toothpick.
- Chewing gum in public is considered impolite.

- Gestures with broad arm movements are considered impolite.

MEXICO

A Spanish-speaking friend of mine, an executive formerly based in Mexico for 10 years, describes the Mexican mind as "virtually impenetrable." He is referring to the extent to which Mexican behavior is, in essence, an amalgam of deeply ingrained influences rooted especially in its long and varied Indian heritage (Aztec and Mayan) and Spanish past. Therefore, as we cross the border into Mexico, we are stepping into a culture, including a business culture, dramatically different from ours.

Probably the first thing to keep in mind when crossing the border is that Mexicans are a very proud people with a strong sense of nationalism. They are highly sensitive to criticism, even from non-Mexicans who have lived there for years. Moreover, anti-American sentiment flows broadly, although it is less apparent in more sophisticated, trade-based businesses.

Although the general atmosphere in Mexico is friendly, gracious, and easygoing, the pace of business is spirited and the attitude cosmopolitan. Personal relationships are the keystone of Mexican commerce, and local representation (a lawyer, banker, agent, etc.) is often recommended. Negotiations can take place via telephone and letters; however, most business is conducted through the unofficial channels of one's connections.

Successful business relationships depend on a high level of mutual trust and compatibility. While senior management might be impressed by your presentation, they could decline your offer simply because they do not find you congenial.

Seniority is a major factor in Mexico. In large and small companies, the boss is often called *Patron*. This term implies a paternalistic relationship between management and its employees. This relationship assumes that if the employees give their all to the *Patron's* organization, they will be cared for indefinitely in what my friend calls a "mantle of structured protection."

Business Norms & Protocol

- Be prompt for your appointment, even if you expect to wait before the meeting actually begins. If the meeting is held in Mexico City, be sure to take into account the great potential for long, congestion-related traffic delays.

- Mexico City's traffic problems have become a boon to the cellular telephone business. Having one helps an executive communicate the reason for a delay and when to expect her arrival.

- To establish rapport, employ a warm and personable approach. Take time to get to know your business associate. Demonstrate interest in her family, whether you are telephoning, writing, or meeting in person.

- Demonstrate your knowledge of Mexican culture and consider making favorable comments on the country's achievements. However, do not make comparisons between the United States and Mexico.

- Mexicans, even if fluent in English, prefer that business be conducted in Spanish. However, if your command of the language is not impressive, Mexicans, unlike the French, will appreciate your use of a few familiar words or phrases. Since Spanish is a far less precise language than English, this poses an additional challenge for an American fluent in Spanish.

- Do not refer to yourself as an American.

- Mexicans, like Germans, are very formal in addressing people with specialized or advanced degrees. For example, if the person is an engineer, she will be addressed as "*Ingeniero* (Engineer) last name," Doctor last name, and *Licensiado* last name (tantamount to being authorized by college degree to practice in a certain area, e.g., law).

- The person's middle name is her surname.

- Mexicans reflect a deeply embedded Mexican tradition of punishing the messenger. For this reason, they have difficulty communicating and receiving bad news. Even in long-term, trusting business relationships, it is not uncommon for a Mexican to say "yes," but really mean "no."

- Working luncheons, lasting one to three hours, are popular for building relationships and for maintaining those already built. If a Mexican orders an alcoholic beverage and invites you to do the same, try to comply, for doing so is a trust-enhancing gesture. However, if in Mexico City, monitor your consumption carefully. At 7,000 feet above sea level, the alcohol can go to your head very quickly.

- For established relationships, the "power breakfast" is becoming increasingly popular in Mexico City, especially since traffic is more tolerable earlier in the day.

- Once an agreement has been reached, respectfully request that it be confirmed in writing. Verbal agreements are often born of politeness, only to be reversed later by letter.

- A sense of rivalry exists between Mexico City and Monterrey, Mexico's more capitalistic industrial base, situated approximately 650 miles to the north, only 125 miles from the U.S. border. There the business-related cultural norms are also different. In Monterrey one can expect more openness and directness than in most of Mexico. This includes the likelihood that a "yes" means "yes," and a "no" means "no."

- Humor is often welcomed in business settings, but, unlike in the United States, it must not be critical of Mexico's government.

Presentation/Q & A Expectations

- In business settings, it is normally inappropriate to begin a meeting until the senior person arrives, even if the meeting must be delayed as long as one to two hours.

- The meeting, especially if it occurs early in a relationship, should begin with an extended socially oriented discussion, focusing on such topics as family and your travels in Mexico. Avoid topics such as illegal aliens, drug trafficking, and the Mexican-American War.

- The senior person should be the central focus of your attention throughout both the presentation and Q & A. Defer to that person to ask the first question.

- Interruptions during the presentation are highly unlikely, unless specifically invited. If questioning occurs, it will be initiated by the senior person.

- Questioning is likely to be less aggressive, a pattern rooted in the culture's overall tendency to avoid confrontation.
- Make sure that your responses do not cause the senior person to lose face, the most costly *faux pas* you could commit. If you need to take exception, do so in the privacy of the senior person's office.
- Mexicans, like most Latins, enjoy listening to themselves. Therefore, in a Q & A setting, don't be surprised if the questioner is very lengthy with a philosophical preamble, a multifaceted question, or a nonquestion—or reflects some combination of these approaches.
- Graphs, charts, computer printouts, samples, and models in your presentations can help surmount initial suspicion.

Body Language

- Mexicans tend to stand close to each other while talking. Do not move away.
- Once you get to know a person well, an embrace (*abrazo*) might be appropriate, or a kiss on the cheek for a woman.

UNITED KINGDOM

Due largely to the convenience of jet travel, a common language, and advances in communications, the business relationships between American and British firms over the past decade have grown at an accelerated pace. In fact, Burger King, Howard Johnsons, Pearle Vision, and Pillsbury—all former American firms—are headquartered in the United Kingdom.

In the last two years, I have made eight trips to Great Britain, including three lasting a week or more. Each trip has accentuated my awareness that while the British and Americans share a common language and, to a significant extent, a common value system, the differences between our cultures are nonetheless dramatic. These differences, as the following synopsis will reveal, are especially pertinent to how we make presentations, field questions, and generally interact in the business world.

Business Norms & Protocol

- Unlike Americans, who are generally egalitarian, the British are very status-oriented. One's pedigree (i.e., family, history, social status, and education) can greatly influence who interacts with whom and how, as well as opportunities for career advancement.
- Consider rank important. This influences who enters a room first, where people sit, and to whom one speaks.
- Consider appearance important—including form and manners.
- Wearing a striped tie in Britain (which usually represents regiments or schools) when you are not entitled to it is considered improper.
- The British consider shirt pockets full of pencils, pens, plastic rulers, and cigarettes unsightly.
- Address individuals by their titles (Dr., Mr., Mrs., etc.); use first names only after a friendship has been developed. However, due largely to American influence, this norm appears to be changing to favor more immediate use of first names.
- Address business after a little small talk.
- The British are more prone than Americans to smoke in business settings—and without the typically American "May I smoke?"
- Use space as a matter of privacy and distance. Closeness is usually not a typical practice, even in a familiar situation. The British normally keep their office doors closed, a polite insurance of privacy.
- The British prefer the business dinner over the business lunch.
- The British appreciate visitors who have some knowledge of their history and political system.

Presentation/Q & A Expectations

- Standing is common during a presentation; however, sitting is appropriate in small groups.
- The British dislike the "hard sell."

- Presentations tend to be less tightly structured than typical American business presentations.
- A presentation generally should be less than an hour (40 minutes maximum), with 25 percent of the time devoted to Q & A.
- The British use many terms differently than their American business associates (e.g., a "cost estimate" is a "bill of quantity" and a "pension plan" is "superannuation scheme").
- Senior managers will often "break the ice" with initial questions.
- It is considered generally impolite to interrupt a presentation with questions.
- The British may consider it improper to acknowledge a questioner by name, unless the presenter knows the names of all the questioners.
- Questioning may be aggressive in terms of content, though polite in approach.
- In both presentations and Q & A, the British often place a greater premium on eloquence and smoothness of delivery than on hard logic.
- The British generally prefer shorter responses.
- Humor is appreciated; is often dry and witty (and clean).
- In Scotland, get to the point quickly. Scots tend to be direct, frank, and straightforward people who work with facts. Unimpeachably honest, they will quickly and abruptly cease dealing with anyone who appears not to be.

Body Language

- Gestures are similar to those found in the United States.
- Avoid excessive hand gestures when speaking.
- Keep a good distance between participants when meeting or conversing.
- Avoid extreme or emotional displays of enthusiasm. The British value moderate behavior and emotional reserve.
- Shake hands firmly.

- The British are not comfortable with physical touching to emphasize a point or to underline a feeling.
- Eye contact should be maintained during a conversation.
- Pointing at people is to be avoided.
- Whispering is considered impolite.

GERMANY

In 1990 Germany was the largest trading nation, surpassing even the United States and Japan. Its economy, Europe's strongest, accounts for about 35 percent of the economic output of the 12-nation European Community (EC).

Germany is relatively poor in natural resources. Its economic success is based mainly on the production of sophisticated manufactured goods, notably motor vehicles (cars, trucks, and buses), chemicals, and complex machine tools. Almost a third of its national income is derived from exports, mainly to its EC partners.

With its unification and the collapse of the Communist regimes in Eastern Europe, Germany is expected to play an important economic role in that region. However, since unification, the economy of the former East Germany has declined rapidly. Most of its manufactured products are not competitive in the open international market. Its previous trading partners—the nations of the former USSR and the countries of Eastern Europe—lack the hard currency to purchase its exports. Its industrial plants and equipment need modernization. Its infrastructure (roads, highways, telephone system, railroads, utilities, sewage and waste disposal) is also in poor condition.

The modernization of these facilities requires a large infusion of investment capital, which will come mostly from West Germany. These economic problems are compounded by a badly damaged environment and a lack of administrative structures such as local and state governments and courts. The service sector of the economy—hotels, restaurants, leisure facilities, independent artisans, and shopkeepers—is also poorly developed.

Due to the lack of self-sufficiency in food and raw materials,

Germany's economic well-being, like that of Great Britain and Japan, depends heavily on successful competition. It must import food and raw materials, and pay for them by exporting manufactured goods. The nation's largest manufacturing firms include the Daimler-Benz corporation and the Volkswagen company—both major producers of cars. Electronic manufacturing is dominated by the giant Siemens and Bosch corporations. The chemical industry is dominated by three large corporations: Bayer, Hoechst, and BASF. The German chemical industry exports more than half of all its manufactured products.

Although German is the official language, English is required in school and is widely understood. Russian is learned in many of the eastern states. Visitors who attempt to learn German are appreciated, especially those who learn it well.

Business Norms & Protocol

- Expect appointments to be made well in advance of meeting dates.
- Stand when a host enters the room and remain standing until you are offered a seat.
- Stand when a woman enters a room.
- Begin meetings punctually.
- Germans are formal in both social and business relations, and use titles and surnames.
- If your host does not state the purpose of the meeting, the presenter should do so shortly after being introduced.
- Germans will tolerate no disorder in status, time, place, appearance, or behavior.
- Germans consider demeanor during discussion very important, and may be embarrassed by compliments.
- They prize privacy highly.
- Germans will hold you to a contract if you lead them to believe that one exists.
- They expect visitors to take the initiative in exchanging business cards—at any time during meetings.
- Germans prefer visitors who appear calm under pressure.

- They expect all agreements to be put in writing.
- They admire longevity in companies.
- Humor is best avoided.

Presentation/Q & A Expectations

- Germans expect presentations to be precise in every detail.
- They expect collateral materials to be well-organized, factual, and devoid of typographical errors.
- Germans are extremely intolerant of hands in pockets when one is presenting.
- They favor "soft sell" over "hard sell."
- Generally, presentations will not be interrupted for questions.
- Usually 25 percent of the time allocated should be allocated for a Q & A session.
- Generally, speakers stand and move very little during a presentation.
- You should make your responses direct and faithful to the question. Germans like detailed responses, with data and other types of proof.
- There is a strong trend to use visual aids.

Body Language

- Shake hands vigorously.
- Wait for a woman to extend her hand before you extend yours.
- Men will often kiss a woman's hand when meeting.
- Stand up when an older person, or one of higher rank, enters a room. Men stand when a woman enters and sit after she is seated. Before leaving, one should shake hands with all members present. The highest-ranking individual should be offered the first goodbye.
- Signify good luck by making two fists—thumbs tucked inside the fist—and gesturing as if lightly pounding on a table.

FRANCE

Like its neighbors Germany and the United Kingdom, France became an industrial power in the 19th century. Then the iron and steel industry and heavy engineering developed near the great coal mining areas (north, Lorraine, centre), and the textile industries matured (wool in the north, cotton in Alsace and Normandy). The 20th century saw the birth of new industries that were going to play an ever-more important role in the economy, especially the automotive and electrical engineering industries.

Today, all types of industrial activities are found in France. Many traditional industries (e.g., footwear, textile, shipbuilding, consumer electronics, and electrical goods) are experiencing difficulties due to competition from recently industrialized countries. Meanwhile, new high-tech industries (e.g., aerospace, computers, telecommunications, chemicals, and pharmaceuticals) are growing in prominence.

The size of companies varies considerably: there are French multinationals with worldwide interests (e.g., Elf-Aquitaine, Alsthom-Alcatel, Michelin, Air Liquide, Saint Gobain, Rhône-Poulenc, L'Oreal, and Renault), and thousands of small- and medium-sized industrial concerns.

France's industrial map is undergoing major changes. Formerly, industry was mainly concentrated in the northern half of the country, but a shift is occurring toward areas that used to be essentially rural. This is happening largely due to the development of the agri-foodstuffs industry (in the west and southwest) and the high-tech sector (Mediterranean region and southwest).

The French believe that their success is judged by their educational level, family reputation, and financial status. Extremely proud of their culture, heritage, and nation, they are among the more nationalistic countries in the world.

Business Norms & Protocol

- Engage an interpreter if you do not speak French fluently, or speak it only minimally.
- Punctuality is a sign of courtesy. The French prefer to get down to business quickly, but may be slow in making decisions (see below).

- Business cards are to be handed to the receptionist. They can be printed in English or French, with academic degree(s) and/or title(s).
- Shake hands (but not strongly; use a light grip and a single quick shake) when meeting and departing. A firm handshake is considered impolite.
- Address individuals with titles/and or degrees formally.
- Rank is important when entering a room and being seated.
- Stand when being introduced.
- Small business gifts can be exchanged as long as they are not construed as bribes.
- The private life of a French person is guarded, and any discussion of family, marital status, or place of residence may be received unkindly.
- A visitor should accept any courteous gesture. If the host motions the visitor through the door first, she should proceed. "After you" gestures are self-defeating.
- The French normally disdain the business lunch.
- They generally like low light in their offices, while Americans prefer bright offices.
- In France it is common to smoke in offices, but uncommon to snack or eat at one's desk.
- Decision making in France is frequently centralized, reserved for upper to top management. The gap between top and bottom management levels is often large. The owner or top manager of a smaller concern also embraces the concept of centralization of power. Decision-making power rests in one individual who literally directs all change. A visitor must, consequently, expect a considerable amount of his or her waiting to be for lower-level bureaucrats to gauge the position of upper-level decision makers.

Presentation/Q & A Expectations

- Standing is the norm for business presentations.
- Expect presentations to be factual, rational, formal, professional, and complete.
- Always wear a jacket and tie when presenting, even if the room is not air conditioned.

- As with people from other EC countries, the French become intolerant if a presentation goes beyond 30 or 40 minutes, with 20 to 30 minutes left for Q & A.
- In a business setting or presentation with a large potential client, defer to the senior manager to set the tone. In a mixed industrial-type audience (e.g., an association meeting) the questions can originate anywhere.
- Humor is best avoided in more formal business presentations.
- Questions normally follow a presenter's remarks.
- The French, like the British, enjoy repartee and challenging the speaker, often with aggressive questioning. This aspect of the French culture is often misinterpreted by U.S. managers as anti-American.
- Because of the norm discussed above, a visiting presenter must be persistent in holding her ground, relying on logic and strong selling points. In so doing, the presenter should be meticulously coherent, informative, and well-organized.
- Soft sells often succeed where extravaganzas and emotional spectaculars hold less promise.
- Shorter, logical arguments are common as responses. French answers, however, may be lengthy and unstructured.
- Unlike Americans, who like compliments and usually offer positive comments first, the French tend to distrust compliments and rarely say anything more enthusiastic than *"pas mal"* ("not bad"). American effusion sounds hypocritical to the French, while the French lack of feedback can leave Americans worried that they're not performing well.
- It is polite for eye contact to drift from the questioner to the larger audience.

Body Language

- The French use body language sparingly. Typically, the French use facial expressions to lend additional meaning to what is being said or heard. Arm waving or lively hand talk is not part of normal business communication. The hand gesture that means "okay" to Americans means "zero" to the French. The "okay" sign for the French is thumbs up.

- They maintain a reserved distance from others. In general, the French stand close together while talking to each other; however, the case in business is different—a reserved distance is maintained between negotiators. Old friends or small merchants may narrow the gap, but a visitor should respect the privacy of space. Physical touching—"moving in" on the French—is generally not acceptable.
- Speaking with food in one's mouth is considered impolite.
- Helping oneself to cheese twice is considered improper.
- Feet are not to be placed on table or chairs.
- Toothpicks, nail clippers, and combs should never be used in public.
- Be discreet when you sneeze or blow your nose, and always use a handkerchief or tissue.
- Avoid yawning and scratching in public.

SOUTH KOREA

Since the Korean War, the South Korean economy has been revitalized and greatly expanded with the aid of capital investment from the United States and, since the mid-1960s, from Japan. During the 1960s and 1970s the economy grew at a rate between 7 percent and 10 percent a year. Economic growth continued during the 1980s (except for negative growth in the year 1980). Overseas construction contracts, particularly in the Middle East, provide a significant source of income.

Manufacturing provides most of South Korea's exports. Early postwar industrial development focused on Korea's low labor costs and included such labor-intensive industries as electronics, footwear, and textile manufacturing. Today, Korean-made television, videocassette recorders, and textiles successfully compete with those made in Japan. Emphasis is also being placed on industries producing high value-added items, such as petrochemicals, steel, ships, cement, and automobiles and trucks.

Koreans are an ethnically homogeneous Mongoloid people

who have shared a common history, language, and culture since at least the 7th century A.D., when the peninsula was first unified. The official language of both North and South is Korean, although many words have been borrowed from the Chinese and Japanese languages. English is taught in the schools, and many people, especially in the business community, have a good understanding of it. Education is the most valued aspect of Korean culture; it is considered the key to success, respect, and power.

Business Norms & Protocol

- The Korean business organization is hierarchical, as opposed to the consensus-oriented Japanese system. For this reason, a premium is placed on seniority, and decisions can be made more rapidly than in Japan.
- The emphasis placed on building trust before consummating a business relationship is similar to that practiced by the Japanese.
- Rank plays a significant role in the success of Korean relationships. Rank is based primarily on seniority within an organization, age, and alumni relationships, especially those formed at the more prestigious universities (e.g., Seoul National University, Korea University, and Yonsei University).
- Many of Korea's more prominent business and government figures were educated in the United States and speak fluent English.
- Respect for the elderly is extremely important.
- Koreans work best with visitors through local representatives. It is important to remember special occasions within the agent's family (e.g., graduations, birthdays, marriages) with gifts (usually money).
- Gift giving as a means of obtaining favors is very important, especially in the workplace.
- Accepting a gift carries the responsibility of reciprocity. Do not open the gift in front of the giver.
- Koreans often make a car and driver available to visiting executives.

- They expect punctuality.
- Use only surnames when greeting and throughout the business relationship unless invited to do otherwise. In Korean the family name comes first, so Kim Hung Bae is addressed as Mr. Kim.
- Koreans ask personal questions to determine others' status, but generally do not conduct as much background research regarding the businessperson or her company as the Japanese.
- In social situations, an initial "no" does not necessarily mean "no" (e.g., when inviting a Korean to dinner). However, a "no" stated within a business meeting generally means "no." Silence in the absence of an immediately positive decision can also mean "no."
- A bow is the traditional greeting, but it is usually accompanied with a handshake between men. The left hand may support or rest under the right forearm during the handshake to show respect, especially for a senior or older person. The handshake is made with a medium-firm grip. The senior person offers to shake first, but a junior person bows first.
- Women tend to have a minor role in big business, although their role in cottage industries may be more pronounced. However, the wife is in charge of the family's finances. In fact, it is not uncommon for married Korean females to be savvy, aggressive investors.
- Business cards are exchanged between professionals when meeting for the first time. The cards should be presented and accepted with both hands after a handshake. The American's card should be printed in English and Korean.
- Criticism and public disagreement are considered very serious, for it is most improper to damage another person's reputation. In fact, Koreans may withhold bad news or adverse opinions out of respect for the feelings of others.
- It is impolite to refuse refreshments when they are offered. Coffee tends to be very strong; decaffeinated coffee is rare.
- Koreans are extremely modest when speaking about themselves. For this reason, compliments are modestly and graciously denied, although they are generally appreciated.

- Success depends greatly on social contacts.
- Korean businesspeople frequently hold meetings in coffee shops.
- Business hours are typically 8:00 A.M. to 5:00 P.M. or 9:00 A.M. to 6:00 P.M. Overtime is common. Like the Japanese, the average Korean worker spends 10 percent more hours on the job than an American.

Presentation/Q & A Expectations

- The senior Korean person should be the principal point of focus throughout the presentation and Q & A. Moreover, that person generally dominates the questioning.
- If the presentation is significant, a senior American businessperson should be present. Otherwise, the presentation could be perceived more as "testing the waters" than as serious intent.
- A clear priority is usually given to the presentation, with the Q & A session being allocated as little as 10 percent, though usually no more than 25 percent, of the total time. This, of course, varies based on the situation and topic.
- Like the Japanese, Koreans are not as likely to be aggressive in their questioning. This does not mean that tough questions will not be couched in polite terms. However, a clear status relationship between buyers and sellers can lead to more aggressive questioning by the buyer in the early stages of negotiations.
- If the presentation or discussion has been very long, the questioner, who could be experiencing some fatigue, may understand less and yet not ask a follow-up question. Therefore, key points should be built into responses early and simply.
- Koreans, like the Japanese (and the Mexicans), do not like to say "no"; therefore, determining their true position on an issue may be confounding.
- In general, questions are likely to be well thought out and will reflect the longer-term objectives of the questioner.
- It is generally not appropriate to interrupt a presentation unless invited to do so at the outset. However, the formality

of the occasion, the nature of the presentation, and the familiarity of the parties will determine whether interruptions are permissible.

- In general, Koreans prefer shorter answers.
- Humor is rarely used in presentations.

Body Language

- It is impolite to yawn in public.
- Neither women nor men hug in public.
- One should sit erect, with both feet on the floor. Legs may be crossed at the knee or ankles, but it is inappropriate to place an ankle over a knee.
- Shaking one hand from side to side with the palm forward means "no."
- The mouth should be covered when using a toothpick.
- Chewing gum in public is considered impolite.
- At home, Koreans do not smoke in front of elders.
- Gestures with broad arm movements are considered impolite.
- Laughter can be very deceiving, indicating not only a reaction to humor, but also embarrassment, anger, or sadness.

THE NETHERLANDS

The Netherlands has a strong, highly industrialized, and efficient economy based on private enterprise. The traditional base of the economy—commerce, the maritime industry, dairy farming, and flower growing—has been significantly expanded and modernized. In addition, its multinational base has grown—some of the larger multinationals are Dutch (e.g., Shell, Unilever, and Philips).

Rotterdam is the biggest port in the world, on which German industry is highly dependent. Throughout the country you can find the newer industries, including chemicals and oil refining. Electronics and steel also play an important role. The country, with only 15 million inhabitants, has benefited from the skilled and productive labor force to convert raw materials into finished, high-value exports.

The Dutch government, benefiting from great political stability since World War II, has actively promoted foreign investment through a hospitable business environment, including free trade zones (unique to Europe), and few barriers.

The Dutch are proud of their cultural heritage, including their rich history in art, music, and politics. The Netherlands is regarded as a very clean country by foreigners, although the Dutch themselves complain increasingly about uncleanliness. Although the country is fairly small, significant cultural differences are found within it's boundaries: Amsterdam is old and culturally rich, while Rotterdam is new—the city where, according to a Dutch friend of mine, Cees van der Wel of AVRO Television, "No-nonsense workmanship was invented." "We earn the money and in Amsterdam they spend it," inhabitants of Rotterdam say, claiming as a joke that shirts in their city are sold only with rolled-up sleeves.

Business Norms & Protocol

- Never refer to the Netherlands as Holland once you get into the eastern part of the country. Holland is only the western part of the country.
- Although Dutch (of Germanic origin) is the official language, English is mandatory in the schools. The older generation also speaks German, but since old (WW II) sentiments are still slumbering, it's not much of an advantage to open a conversation in German. Never make the mistake of saying "Deutsch" to the Dutch.
- Punctuality is demanded.
- Business cards are exchanged.
- Seniority is important.
- People are generally friendly. They introduce themselves and shake hands when greeting and departing. They are generally helpful—very willing to aid any foreigner.
- The Dutch value politeness.

- Doing business will probably be formal from the beginning—almost British. In the Dutch language, there is—as in French and German—a distinction between the formal "u" and the informal "jy" (the German *Sie* and *du*).
- In a related vein, the Dutch often use formal titles in conversations and presentations. The German formalities are regarded as overdone, so avoid calling somebody "Sir (or "Madame") Doctor." "Sir" or "Madame" alone plus his or her last name will do. A formal atmosphere might even be evident in offices. Management people within the same firm refer to each other without using their first name: "As Mister Van Gogh was just saying. . . ."
- Such formalities can disappear quickly once the business transaction is over. As my Dutch friend says, "Then foreign businesspersons will discover that even the Dutch have first names."
- Doing business in the Netherlands takes time; therefore, one should get to know the client. The Dutch are known for being tough negotiators. This may be rooted in their long history of trading worldwide as a sailing nation, and their experience negotiating with former colonies. They call themselves the "Chinese of the West."
- Negotiations proceed in an orderly fashion (with little or no haggling) and may be completed quickly.
- When men stand as women enter a room and wait until they are seated, it is a sign of being well-educated. This is not done so much in meetings, but more in restaurants.
- Women precede men through doors and offer their hands first.
- There is always coffee—any place, all day long. Decaf is rarely available.
- If invited out, reciprocate. If invited to a home, bring flowers.
- The business lunch is fairly common. To impress a foreign visitor, Dutch businesspeople might take you to a Michelin-rated restaurant. Rolls with a glass of milk are common (more in Rotterdam than in Amsterdam). My Dutch friend puts this custom in perspective:

    A few years ago the prime ministers of all the countries belonging to the EC were gathering in a Dutch city. The negotiations took longer than expected. The best lunch the Dutch can offer was waiting, cooked by the best chefs, but the Dutch no-nonsense prime minister—originating from Rotterdam—skipped the lunch and ordered rolls, milk, and buttermilk instead. First the work had to be done; this is the Dutch way of life. Relaxation comes afterwards. The French president Mitterand wasn't too pleased.

- The Dutch like to entertain and be entertained.
- Cracking jokes—after business is completed—is highly appreciated.
- Dinner at night could be helpful. Accept invitations and return them later, but be careful not to overdo it. The Dutch see themselves as rather Calvinistic—a sober lifestyle is a virtue in this country. Your host may invite you to a festive dinner, but doing the same in return may be interpreted by your hosts as going a little too far. Once a deal is made, it is less likely to be a problem.

Presentation/Q & A Expectations

- The senior Dutch person in charge opens the meeting officially by welcoming the guests. This is often rather formal and can get quite time-consuming. But once the formalities have been addressed, the meeting soon becomes more informal.
- Less-structured meetings are often kicked off by small talk, with topics such as hotel comfort, the smoothness of the trip, and a favorite Dutch topic, the weather. Even talking about a recent soccer game might be appropriate.
- Straight politeness might be the best description for doing business in the Netherlands.
- Presentations are to be well-structured: charts, numbers, graphs, and models can help convince your Dutch business partner to go along with your proposal.
- Being precise is a big advantage.
- Try to establish eye contact with each and every person taking part in the meeting. A businessperson who avoids eye contact is regarded as not being fair, open, or honest.

- Following your presentation, the Dutch may seem hesitant to pose questions. Help them out with the first one and the rest will follow automatically.
- The Dutch have a tendency to be very direct. Questioning, therefore, might get tough.
- Although rudeness should be avoided, it is expected that you will give open answers. Being straightforward is regarded as a virtue, without, of course, verbally slapping people in the face.
- The Dutch value careful, even intensive, listening, without impolite interruptions.
- Always ask permission before lighting up a first cigarette, or refrain from smoking altogether.
- Don't talk with your hands in your pockets.
- Talking with accentuated gestures is often regarded as oversell.

Body Language

- Shake hands with everyone, including children.
- Avoid touching the other party during a conversation.
- Cover your mouth when yawning.
- Raising one's voice is considered improper.
- Chewing gum is very impolite. Never offer chewing gum to anybody.

TAIWAN

Formerly known as Formosa, Taiwan, located 100 miles off the southeast coast of mainland China, is the main island of the Republic of China (Nationalist China). Taiwan became known to the West in the 16th century when the Portuguese named it Formosa ("beautiful").

Taiwan's economy remains strong with the largest foreign reserves in the world. Since 1987, political economic reforms have increased exports and permitted foreign investment. As the island develops, most industries are becoming labor- and capital-intensive. Their major products are textiles, clothing, electronics, footwear, toys, ships, and such traditional handicrafts as ceramics, silks, plus bamboo and paper items. Domestic hydroelectric power resources are inadequate, and increasing amounts of electricity are generated from imported petroleum and nuclear power plants.

In small businesses, the most important relationship in Taiwan is the family. Usually, a husband and wife operate the business together under an outwardly patriarchal appearance. However, the wife has significant, but understated, authority (understated in deference to her husband).

The official language in Taiwan and mainland China is Mandarin Chinese. English is widely understood in business settings and is a popular second language for students. It is generally spoken in the capital city of Taipei. Moreover, Western influences in the culture are becoming increasingly evident. It is expected that soon every Taiwanese will understand and speak at least some English.

Business Norms & Protocol

- A nod of the head and a smile are considered appropriate when meeting someone for the first time. Close friends and acquaintances generally shake hands. A slight bow shows respect, but should not be exaggerated.
- Use titles (e.g., Dr. Yu or Mr. Lee) or full names when addressing an individual, especially the elderly. As in the United States, first names may be used once the individual gives permission.
- Gifts are given during New Year's celebrations. Use both hands when exchanging gifts and other items. Gifts are not opened in the presence of the giver.
- Stand when a guest, a superior, or an elderly person enters a room.
- Businessmen wear western suits and ties; businesswomen commonly wear dresses.
- Cleanliness and neatness are most important.
- Westerners are treated with special courtesy and respect; those who reciprocate are appreciated.
- Men and women avoid affection in public.

Presentation/Q & A Expectations

Henry Pollak, president of American Machine and Tool Company, has conducted business in Taiwan for 12 years. His insights can be most helpful in preparing for a presentation and Q & A:

> *May won tee* means "no problem." When one hears this, one knows that there very well could be a problem. "Can't do" isn't part of the Taiwanese language. The Taiwanese will try to accomplish and accommodate virtually anything requested within reason (and sometimes beyond reason). They tend to say "yes" first and a diffident "no" later if, in fact, there is no way they can accommodate.
>
> For cultural reasons, it is sometimes embarrassing for the Taiwanese to indicate that they don't understand. In fact, the term *may won tee* is often used when the respondent does not understand. For this reason, it is important to (1) question, (2) make sure the respondent understands the question, and (3) make sure the questioner understands all of the problems that are going to be encountered so that all parties are aware of the possible levels of accommodation.

Other Q & A norms, based on our research:

- Direct eye contact is expected.
- When pointing to a questioner, use an open hand; pointing with an index finger is considered rude.
- Questioning tends not to be aggressive.
- Interruptions are not common.
- Responses should generally be complete but to the point. This helps reduce language barrier-related problems.
- Moving closer to the questioner is uncommon.
- Nonverbal feedback immediately following a response is common.
- Humor is appropriate if clearly understandable and appreciated by *all* present.

BELGIUM

A very densely populated country, Belgium is situated at the center of a major urban and economic axis that encompasses much of western Europe. Modern agricultural practices, a vibrant economy, and an advanced social welfare system provide a high standard of living for its people.

Belgium is located at the crossroads of Latin and Germanic Europe. The northern part of the country, loosely referred to as Flanders (Vlaanderen), has a predominantly Dutch (Flemish)-speaking population. In the southern region, known as Wallonia (Wallonie), the main language is French. From these two peoples Belgium has derived a rich cultural heritage, as well as a tradition of sectional antagonism that is still a dominant feature of its national life.

Because of its geographic position and history, Belgium is a microcosm of European history, giving it a strong inclination toward European cooperation and integration. In fact, Belgium is a founding member of NATO (1949), and the European Community (1957). NATO's headquarters are in Brussels, as are most of the EC's governing institutions.

Belgium has a highly developed economy based on trade, industry, and services. The country's location near one of Europe's major trading arteries, the Rhine-Meuse-Scheldt delta, its dense network of railroads, highways, and navigable waterways, plus the presence of EC and NATO headquarters have helped the Belgians develop a strong, diversified, economic base. With the decline of mining and other traditional industries, the service sector now dominates the Belgian economy, employing nearly 60 percent of the work force.

There are no free trade zones. Major trading partners are the European Community (EC) countries and the United States. The government is stable and ample opportunities for funding and starting new businesses are available. The work force is highly skilled, possesses a strong work ethic, is educated, and tends to be multilingual.

Business Norms & Protocol

- Most Belgians speak English.
- Business takes time, and you must take time to get to know the client.
- Schedule appointments in advance and be punctual.

- Use titles when being introduced (Mr., Mrs., Miss); never use first names. Only relatives and friends are greeted by first names.
- Business should be conducted in the office; meals are a time for socializing.
- Business gifts can be exchanged at the end of negotiations; these can be desk sets, leather, or high-tech items. Gifts are opened in front of the giver. Be sure to write a thank-you note after receiving a gift.
- Speaking or laughing loudly is considered inappropriate.
- Belgians are suspicious of new people, but proven friends become almost part of the family.
- Personal discussions or discussions regarding the linguistic division of Belgium should be avoided.
- Many businesses close down in July or August.

Presentation/Q & A Expectations

- Speakers will generally stand.
- Come straight to the point and respond faithfully to the question. If you fail to, you could be severely criticized, or ignored.
- Be prepared with facts, figures, and other types of proof.
- Responses may be longer than in the United States, but with greater detail and precision.
- Belgians consider casual American behavior (e.g., talking with your hands in your pockets) rude and a sign of poor breeding.
- Presentations generally last no longer than an hour, with up to 25 percent allocated for Q & A.
- It is uncommon to interrupt a presentation with questions.
- Belgians tend to be restrained in providing verbal and nonverbal feedback.
- They consider pointing with an index finger rude (e.g., as when acknowledging a questioner).
- Belgians dislike the American "hard sell."
- Humor in presentations should normally be avoided.

Body Language

- In both meeting and departing, Belgians give quick and lightly pressured handshakes. Be sure to shake hands with everyone in the group, including secretaries.
- Cover your mouth when yawning.
- Do not chew gum in public.
- Do not smoke if an ashtray hasn't been provided.
- When entertained or invited out, reciprocate.
- Men should walk nearest the street when accompanied by a woman.
- Never talk with something in your mouth (food, gum, or a toothpick).

Chapter Thirteen

Combating Silence

O ne day a communications officer from a large corporation called me to discuss a problem that surfaced during their past management meeting: once the senior officers had delivered their speeches, few of the several hundred officers and managers seated in the audience rose to ask a question. Their silence was deafening, for a major goal of the meeting was to facilitate two-way communication. Why do situations like this occur—and, I might add, why do they occur so frequently?

THE FORMAT

Turn first to the meeting format. Is it so laden with speeches, despite allocated time for Q & A, that the audience's spirit to participate is dampened? I am quite accustomed to seeing a program filled with 40- to 50-minute presentations followed by a 10- to 20-minute Q & A session. However, in many instances, the time allocations for remarks and Q & A should be reversed. Give a speaker 45 minutes and chances are he'll use it up, regardless of whether or not he needs it. In fact, most 45- to 50-minute presentations given to me in preparation for a major meeting should be trimmed by 30 to 50 percent. This is especially true if the major goal of the presentation is to persuade rather than educate.

If you insist that you need 40 or more minutes, consider dividing your presentation into segments. For example, you may choose to stop your presentation for Q & A after 10 to 25 minutes and at the end. This approach has several advantages: (1) it allows the audience to feel more involved; (2) it provides you with feedback regarding your presentation; and (3) it gives you a better sense of your audience as you continue the presentation. The only disadvantage: it requires you to be a skillful moderator during each Q & A segment, especially to know when and how to return to your presentation.

Another format option (selected by the above-mentioned firm that contacted me) is to shrink the size of the original audience by scheduling a series of smaller breakout sessions following the remarks. These sessions should be more facilitative for two reasons: (1) they are devoted exclusively to Q & A; and (2) they provide a more intimate and informal environment where the questioner feels less exposed to so many people.

Still another alternative: select a professional facilitator. This person would interview the executives in a talk show format interspersed with occasional unannounced visits by the host facilitator in the audience (à la Phil Donahue) for comments and questions. This approach can be especially effective in promoting "buy-in" of an idea, or bridging credibility gaps between any two or more segments of an organization. In the final analysis, it can produce a more spontaneous and authentic feeling than carefully tailored and rehearsed presentations.

MANAGEMENT'S TONE

Another major reason why the audience may be reluctant to participate is the tone of management's remarks. Although an executive may want his presentation to stimulate discussion or even controversy, the tone of the content and delivery is either one-way or *fait accompli*. Despite the executive's request for questions or feedback at the end, the inadvertent nonverbal message he transmits is, "We really don't need your input; this is a take-it-or-leave-it proposition."

Such a situation involves what communication researchers call "conflicting communication." Specifically, a "conflict" exists between the *verbal message* ("We want your feedback") and the *nonverbal tone* ("We don't . . ."). According to the research, under such circumstances we tend to place much more credence on the nonverbal message than on the verbal one.

What specifically can management do to make sure that the Q & A session doesn't turn to dead silence? If management is sincere in its desire to facilitate Q & A, then it should consider laying out the Q & A agenda within the presentation itself. For example:

Executive:

I'll discuss with you now some new ideas we're thinking about to improve the efficiency of our distribution system. We're *not sure* how well they *might work* or *whether they will work at all*. So I will look forward to your feedback on these ideas during the Q & A.

Analysis:

Note the tentative tone highlighted by the italics. The ideas do not have the ring of *fait accompli*, and the speaker's request for feedback sounds genuine.

Once the presentation has been made, you have additional options to make the Q & A more conducive to two-way communication.

• *Project a more approachable image.* You can come out in front of the lectern, lean on it, sit on the edge of a table or stool, or walk into the audience. To complement this image, a man may remove his jacket, loosen his tie, and roll up his sleeves. A woman's options regarding attire are more limited. But, whatever options you choose, be careful not to come across as too manipulative.

• *Verbally, you may need to break the ice with a line that genuinely invites participation:* "The purpose of this conference is to promote two-way communication and we really need your feedback," or "Every question is a good question."

• In the same vein, whenever possible, *learn and use the questioner's name* (without sounding forced or patronizing). This can make the communication more personal and less intimidating.

• *Avoid transmitting unduly negative feedback to comments and ques-*

tions. Recognize that this feedback can be communicated both verbally and nonverbally (e.g., a dismissive tone). Instead, find ways to convey positive feedback without sounding patronizing. For example:

> *Unduly negative feedback:* "I can't agree with that at all," "What makes you think that?" (*in a challenging tone*), and "That's ridiculous."

> *Positive feedback:* "That's a very helpful suggestion," "Perhaps we *should* give more thought to your idea," or "I'm not sure that we looked at it that way."

• It is best that you *decide beforehand how much you wish to engage the audience verbally*—how much give and take you want—beyond simply answering their questions. As effective as the give and take may be, a commitment to it requires that you monitor your tone very carefully. The risk of being too argumentative, autocratic, or both often increases in proportion to the length of the exchange.

• *Consider the value of questioning over asserting,* particularly if you genuinely want to know what is on your target audience's mind. By questioning, you are demonstrating interest in their point of view. By asserting, you are seeking to inform or persuade, not to learn.

• *Put your quality listening traits on full display.* For example, cutting one of your managers off midstream can be the kiss of death. Not only will it offend him, but the other managers could be offended as well.

• *Put your active listening traits on full display.* For example, following a participant's comment, especially if it seems significant and not necessarily easy to grasp, say, "Let me make sure I can capture the essence of what you're saying," and then summarize your understanding, allowing the participant to affirm or clarify.

• *Don't take yourself too seriously.* Be prepared to indicate lack of knowledge ("I didn't know that"), admit fault ("I really screwed that one up"), and display tentativeness ("I'm not quite sure how we should proceed"). Self-deprecating humor—as well as humor in general—can also be effective:

> *Heavy person late for a Q & A session:* "I'm sorry I'm late, but when the waitress placed the dessert tray next to my table I didn't know until I paid the check that it wasn't all mine."

• *Be willing to display a certain amount of openness by referring to feelings or personal experiences*, including shared experiences. This helps your audience sense your trust in them and helps build their trust in you. Put another way, the more closed you are, the less approachable and facilitative you will be.

• *Be prepared to demonstrate concern, compassion, or empathy in a genuine manner.*

AUDIENCE RELUCTANCE

No matter how approachable and facilitative management's tone may be, two other audience factors can impede a lively Q & A session: speech anxiety and the fear of embarrassment.

Speech anxiety certainly doesn't end at the edge of the stage. *Questioners can experience it as well,* particularly in large group settings that can stimulate a paralyzing sense of self-consciousness. This feeling can be exacerbated if the person has to stand, identify himself (shedding the security of anonymity), and walk to a microphone placed in the aisle.

The fear of embarrassment can be just as strong an impediment—or even stronger. For example, since employees attending company forums are understandably conscious of their job security and opportunity for advancement, they do not want to pose a question that sounds "stupid," angers the superior, or comes off as showing off or "kissing up." Hence they choose silence.

BACK-UP TACTICS TO COMBAT SILENCE

Although you plan to do everything to make your address and Q & A session as participative as possible, you must be prepared to deal with "the terrible silence" if it occurs. These tactics could prove helpful:

• *Talking to yourself.* You complete your remarks, receive polite applause, invite questions in a friendly, positive manner, and then enter the zone of deadly silence. This can be handled with normal discomfort, but without fluster, by saying to your audience, "While you are thinking about what questions to ask, let me raise and answer a few that are frequently asked by our managers," or "Let me break the ice by asking the first question, as you prepare to ask the second."

• *The survey says.* To break the ice, consider asking your audience questions. Begin with easy, closed-ended, survey-type questions such as, "How many of you have seen the videotape on our new distribution network?" Then slowly begin to solicit attitudes: "How many of you think the network will help?" "Why?"

• *The invisible plant,* that is, planting questions or comments in advance. This approach can be especially effective if the person is someone the group respects and whose participation doesn't appear preplanned. There are four ways to keep the plant "invisible": (1) make the question or comment unabashedly candid; (2) make it challenging; (3) employ some combination of (1) and (2), remembering that challenging questions generally bring out the best in us; and (4) don't read the question.

• *The Harding hopper.* President Warren G. Harding conducted his press conferences by requiring reporters to submit questions in advance. He then assembled the press corps, selected the questions he wanted to answer, and while they watched, tossed the others into a wastebasket. Imagine the media and public outcry if this approach were attempted by a president today. However, this approach has survived in business and professional meetings where the speaker or program chairperson removes from a container questions prepared in advance. Often the questions are prescreened to prevent duplication and ensure clarity. Although the hopper may encourage persons reluctant to ask questions to do so, it is hardly conducive to an open, natural, spontaneous, two-way flow of communication—especially if the questioner's name is not disclosed.

• *Mingling.* You've tried everything and the Q & A session is nevertheless bombing. Your one remaining option is to invite the audience to ask their questions as you mingle with them following your remarks.

Chapter Fourteen

Practice Fuels Finesse

W hether you are preparing for a high-stakes presentation, annual meeting, media interview, crisis news conference, legal or legislative hearing, or job interview, I can't emphasize enough the importance of practice.

OVERCOMING RESISTANCE

People who resist practice sessions usually voice one of these four objections (followed by my abbreviated response):

Objection 1:
How will I find the time?

Response:
This is a priority; you have no choice!

Objection 2:
I'm good with Q & A.

Response:
Perhaps you are, but in this situation you need to be "extra good"—you need to be sharp!

Objection 3:
I'm more comfortable in the Q & A session than in the presentation.

Response:
Comfort is not the issue; the issue is maximum credibility and persuasive impact!

Objection 4:
A practice session will make me uptight—too self-conscious.

Response:
Not if it is planned and executed well—with your input.

PLANNING AND EXECUTING THE PRACTICE SESSION

A productive practice session requires careful planning based on the following three criteria that will serve as the basis for this discussion: (1) the format should be tailored to your comfort level and learning style; (2) for high stakes engagements, the environment should simulate as much as reasonably possible the circumstances of the actual event; and (3) key resource persons should be available to provide feedback.

The Format

When John Kennedy prepared for his first debate against Richard Nixon in 1960, he was lying in bed, reading the questions prepared on index cards, responding, and then tossing them aside. When Jimmy Carter and Ronald Reagan prepared for their debate with one another 20 years later, each practiced in a fully outfitted, mock television studio with a stand-in playing his opponent. The difference between Kennedy's method and Carter's and Reagan's is not related to advances in video technology; rather, it is more attributable to each man's temperament and how it influenced his approach to preparation.

In choosing a format, you need to understand what aspects of it work or don't work well for you. The following questions and advice place this issue in perspective:

Question:

When do you want the session to take place?

Advice:

Whenever possible, the first practice session should take place sooner rather than later. This provides several advantages, including more time to reflect on your strategic approach, address additional research or message development needs, and practice using key points in other settings leading up to the engagement. Further, it prevents any last-minute panic that can undermine your performance.

Whether or not you practice the day of your performance is up to you. Sometimes, especially in crisis situations, you have no choice. When you do have a choice, a few warm-up questions on the day of your engagement can be helpful.

Question:

How long should the session last?

Advice:

They often take longer than one expects—usually 2 to 6 hours.

Question:

Should you discuss target audience(s), goals, key messages, and strategy before you field questions?

Advice:

Absolutely!

Question:

Do you want to receive feedback following each response, or do you prefer to cover a round of questions first?

Advice:

Feedback following each response is usually a more thorough approach, but is less time-efficient than conducting it following each round. A combination approach, based on the importance of a certain response or group of them, may be advisable.

Question:

Do you want to videotape your responses and then analyze them via replay on an individual response or round basis?

Advice:

Although a full replay on either basis is often desirable, when pressed for time, replay the more important responses, especially the ones that gave you the most difficulty. Therefore, keep a thorough log based on your VCR's clock or counter.

Question:

As you analyze your responses for content, do you want immediate feedback regarding strategy and style, or do you prefer that later?

Advice:

Normally it is best to provide it following each response, but only after issues regarding the appropriateness, accuracy, and completeness of the content have been resolved. Ronald Reagan, in preparing for his debate with Jimmy Carter, preferred feedback following each round, starting with substance, then moving to strategy and style (my role). Although the sessions were videotaped, because of time pressures we did not engage in videotape replay analysis.

Question:

Do you want to engage in self-analysis before inviting feedback from others?

Advice:

By doing so, you will set the tone for your receptiveness to criticism, and can preempt the feedback you'd rather not hear first from others.

Question:

Should you identify the criteria to be used during the feedback session, for example, listening skills, use of headlines, congruence with net effects goals, clarity, responsiveness, "Banana Peel" skills, credibility, persuasiveness, appropriate length, etc.?

Advice:

Absolutely! However, make sure you do this in a manner that doesn't increase the executive's anxiety level. For example, you may choose to highlight the two or three criteria you regard as most important. However, net effects goals should always be included.

Question:

Should you take notes during the feedback session, or should someone else do this for you?

Advice:

Entirely a personal decision. However, for a high-stakes situation, someone should keep a record of additional work required to shape the responses as well as major advice you need to be reminded of shortly before the engagement.

Question:

Should a transcript of the practice session be made for more in-depth analysis?

Advice:

Although time-consuming and potentially costly, doing so can be very helpful, not only to identify weaknesses, but also to capture in writing responses and phrases that were especially effective.

The Environment

Question:

How should the practice setting be arranged?

Advice:

Initially, the practice session(s) should normally be conducted in a more informal setting with emphasis given to how well-prepared you are on substance, strategy, and style. Then, as the engagement approaches, a fuller simulation of the actual engagement may be appropriate.

Most of the annual meetings, major news conferences, talk shows, and debates for which our firm has prepared executives and candidates involve full simulations with television cameras and lights, the exact lectern to be used during the engagement, the same type of chair, the identical room layout, etc. Yes, these simulations can be expensive; however, in high-stakes situations, they are usually worth it for two major reasons: First, they can help you alleviate the fear of the unknown; that is, a quality simulation is tantamount to a full dress rehearsal in which details are addressed and the element of surprise is significantly preempted. Second, the simulation often imposes a sense of focus and discipline over the practice session—qualities that may not be as obvious during the more informal sessions.

Whenever possible, a full simulation should be preceded or followed by a visit to the actual site of the engagement. In fact, simulations we work on frequently take place at the actual site of an internal board or committee meeting, an annual meeting, a sales conference, or a news conference.

The Resource Team

Question:

Who should attend the practice session?

Advice:

Too many people in the practice session quickly calls up the "too many chefs can spoil the broth" analogy. A chorus of discordant views complemented by well-meaning but unduly harsh critics can result in a reliable recipe for disaster.

To prevent disaster and make the team work for you, consider this advice: invite only those persons who are likely to contribute constructively. When in doubt, "don't mail the invitation." Consider giving each team member "homework" in advance, for example, preparing questions, issue positions, or both. This prevents them from taking a "wing-it" approach to the session, and increases your chances that the more significant questions will be asked. Encourage them to meet separately, in advance, to review questions and proposed answers. This can help prevent unnecessary overlap as well as time-consuming—and potentially confusing—conflict. Make sure your team knows the ground rules before the practice session begins, including who is in charge.

Do Questioners Rehearse?

Absolutely. Consider this *Time* magazine account of Dan Rather's preparation for his *cause célèbre* interview with George Bush before the 1988 Iowa caucuses:

> The day of the interview Rather had three one-hour rehearsals with six people involved in the broadcast. He was coached as if he was a candidate preparing for a debate or a pugilist preparing for a fight, rather than a journalist going into an interview. Howard Rosenberg, a producer from CBS's Washington bureau, played Bush. "We knew it was going to be a brawl," said [Richard] Cohen [senior political producer of the "CBS Evening News").[1]

Although Rather was wise to rehearse, the one thing missing from his rehearsal was the counterattack question posed by Bush (Chapter 8). In sum, Rather didn't rehearse enough.

POST-PERFORMANCE FEEDBACK

Notice that I didn't title this discussion "post mortem." As you know, this term means "after death," hardly an appropriate way to describe your performance if you faithfully followed my advice. Whatever term you prefer, any important performance should be followed by a feedback session. This session can be especially valuable if a videotape, audiotape, or transcript was made of your performance.

Don't conduct the feedback session until your defenses are down and your disposition toward self-improvement is high. And when you do, remember that your constructive critics may need feedback from you to indicate your receptiveness to their feedback.

Chapter Fifteen

Preparation Plans

F inesse on the firing line requires a comprehensive, systematic, control-oriented approach to prepare for both questioning and responding—an approach that contrasts sharply with the "wing-it" mentality that is all too often doomed to mediocrity or failure. This section, designed to be very user-friendly, provides preparation plans and special advice for the following types of Q & A:

- The Q & A session following a speech or presentation
- The one-on-one print, TV, or radio interview
- The news conference
- The TV or radio talk show
- Testifying at a legislative or government agency hearing
- Being deposed

THE Q & A SESSION FOLLOWING A SPEECH OR PRESENTATION

The Q & A session following your speech or presentation is a prime opportunity to advance your persuasive goals, whether you are promoting an idea, product, or service. Therefore, instead of letting your guard down following your remarks, be ready to persuade further, especially since the Q & A session allows you to address issues that interest your target audience the most. To be ready, prepare for the session carefully, relying on the preceding chapters and the following preparation plan.

Goals and Opportunities

1. Rank which of the following statements represent your two or three major goals for the Q & A session:

A. To provide informed/credible answers supportive of your overall position/presentation.
B. To represent the corporation's or organization's views as its key decision makers would want them expressed.
C. To encourage the purchase of your product or service.
D. To discern the audience's views regarding the issues at hand.
E. To provide the audience with the sense that you support two-way communication with them.
F. To diffuse the audience's concerns.
G. To facilitate and maintain control of the discussion.
H. To avoid gaffes, misstatements, or volunteering too much. (circle your particular concern).
I. Other.

2. Do you regard the Q & A session mainly as an opportunity or an obligation? Why?

Advice:

Don't participate in the session until you have a positive attitude regarding how it can help you accomplish your net effects, substance, and image goals.

Target Audience

1. Using the scale below, how would you rate your target audience's regard for each of the following channels of persuasion?

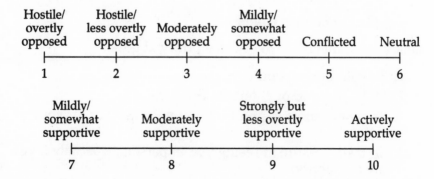

    A. You
    B. Your corporation
    C. The company or division of the corporation you represent
    D. Your industry, business, profession
    E. Your principal message

2. Why do you think they react to each channel in the manner you have indicated?

3. How would you describe your target audience?
    A. How relevant are the following factors?
        1. Age
        2. Sex
        3. Socioeconomic status
        4. Education
        5. Religion
        6. Race
        7. Whether or not they are parents
        8. Whether or not they live in a certain area
        9. Other
    B. How do you intend to incorporate the more relevant factors into your message?
        Advice:
        If the stakes are high and your audience is small (e.g., under 25), you should attempt to focus your analysis on each audience member.

4. What is their level of familiarity with the issues you plan to address?
    A. Should you adjust your message to their familiarity level?
    B. If so, how?

The Audience's Goals

Rank your audience's two or three principal goals.

1. To gain information
2. To be inspired or entertained
3. To demonstrate support for you personally or for your point of view
4. To take pleasure in seeing you in person (especially if you are a celebrity)

5. To secure an opportunity to meet you and develop a personal relationship with you
6. To experience cathartic relief through questioning
7. To exploit your appearance as a forum for expressing a contrary point of view
8. To embarrass you
9. To destroy the meeting
10. Other

Key Messages

1. What key messages do you intend to reinforce during your Q & A session?

   Advice:

   Normally, you should not have more than three or four key messages. Place them on a piece of paper you can refer to during the Q & A.

   A. What is their relative order of importance?
   B. What proof or support can you provide for each key message?
   C. What visual aids do you need to support your key messages?
      1. Photographs or real exhibits
      2. 35mm projector
      3. Overhead projector
      4. Flip chart
      5. Other

   Advice:

   - Make sure you can access the visual quickly.
   - Don't forget the spare bulb, pointer, and marking pens.
   - Consider placing transparencies (also called *foils* or *overheads*) in cardboard frames for easier handling.

Image Goals

What major image goals do you wish to achieve as a result of the Q & A session?

1. What image traits should you consciously avoid? (e.g., defensiveness, aloofness, anger, condescension, etc.)

2. How specifically do you intend to achieve your image goals through:
   A. The responses per se?
   B. Your demeanor?

Format and Norms

1. Will other speakers be on the program?
   A. Who?
   B. What will be their order of appearance?
   C. What will they speak about?
   D. What is the audience's regard for them according to the above scale?
2. Who will moderate the Q & A session and how?
   A. How will the questions be delegated to a speaker for a response (for a panel or symposium)?
   B. How long is the session expected to last?
   C. How will it be introduced and ended? By the moderator or host or by you?
   D. Should you be prepared to identify any topics as off-limits?
   E. What signal system should you have with your host for extending or ending the session?
   F. Is some type of reception planned following the Q & A? How long will it last?
3. Will you be sitting or standing for the Q & A?
   Advice:
   Most persons I advise prefer standing when this option seems appropriate, stating that it gives them a greater sense of command or control.
4. If standing is your preference, where should you stand?
   A. Does a lectern reinforce or undermine your image goals?
   B. If you leave the lectern, will you need a special microphone?
   C. Will you be well-illuminated?
   Advice:
   If you wish to appear engaging or approachable, leaving the lectern is probably advisable, unless doing so will place you

in the dark or cause you to upstage another speaker when you prefer not to.

5. What are the dimensions and layout of the room, including the seating arrangement?
   A. Can you be assured that there will be no noise penetration from the adjoining room?
   B. Will audience members address you from their seats or come to an aisle microphone?
   C. Will they have name tags or tent cards you can read from your position, or should you ask them to identify themselves and their affiliation?

   Advice:

   Referring to them by name (without sounding patronizing) can make the interaction more personable and the questioner more accountable. That is, the anonymous questioner is generally less accountable.

6. Will the media be present?
   A. Who?
   B. Will they participate in the questioning?
   C. Will they want to interview you separately?
   D. What questions do you expect from them?

   Advice:

   The media will sometimes want to interview you before you have an opportunity to mingle with your audience. If mingling is more important, you may wish to ask the media to wait, or arrange for the interview later.

7. Will or should any parties be deliberately excluded from the session? Why?

8. What approaches are you prepared to take in case you run into a hostile audience or audience member?

9. What approaches are you prepared to take if your audience is silent?

10. If you plan a team presentation, have you decided who will respond to which lines of questioning? Are you prepared to explain why you are handing the "ball" off to a colleague?

11. Do you intend to practice your individual or team presentation? If so, when and how?

THE ONE-ON-ONE PRINT, TV, OR RADIO INTERVIEW

Media interviews, even for the media-savvy, are frequently a source of concern. When interviewed, we often wonder or worry whether the interview will turn out fair, positive, accurate, and focused on our key messages. The reporter also has concerns—she wants the interview to be truthful, candid, and interesting, and can feel frustrated when one of these qualities is missing. This preparation guide should help reduce your concerns and meet your goals.

Goals and Opportunities

1. Rank which of the following statements represent your two or three major goals for the interview.
   A. To generate a favorable story.
   B. To control the interview.
   C. To represent your corporation's or organization's views as the company's key decision makers would want them expressed.
   D. To advance a particular point of view regarding an issue or story.
   E. To elevate your personal exposure.
   F. To elevate the corporation's or organization's exposure.
   G. To avoid gaffes or other types of blunders.
   H. To avoid unnecessary disclosures.
   I. To avoid/generate controversy/confrontation (*circle choice*).
   J. To develop a productive relationship with the reporter.
   K. Other.
2. As the interviewee, do you regard the interview mainly as an opportunity or an obligation? Why?
   Advice:
   Do not grant the interview until you clearly define its potential benefits.

Target Audience

1. How would you describe your target audience? What demographic and knowledge-level factors of your target

and general audiences are most relevant to each key message?
1. Age
2. Sex
3. Socioeconomic status
4. Education
5. Religion
6. Race
7. Political preferences
8. Whether or not they are customers
9. Whether or not they are parents
10. Whether or not they live in a certain area
11. Other

2. How do you intend to incorporate the more relevant factors into your message?

3. Using the scale below, how would you rate your target audience's regard for each of the following channels of persuasion?

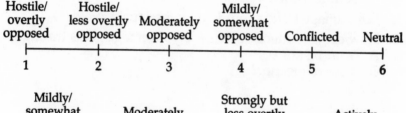

A. You
B. Your corporation
C. The company or division of the corporation you represent
D. Your industry, business, or profession
E. Your principal message

4. Why do you think they react to each channel in the manner you have indicated?

5. What is their level of familiarity with the issues you plan to address?

6. Should you adjust your message to their familiarity level? If so, how?

Key Messages

What key messages do you intend to convey and reinforce?

A. What is the relative order of importance of your key messages?
B. What proof or support can you provide for each key message?

Advice:

For seated print and radio interviews, your key messages can appear on a sheet in front of you. Just be sure that the purpose of the sheet is not too obvious to the reporter.

Image Goals

1. What major image goals do you want to achieve as a result of the interview?
2. What image traits should you consciously avoid?
3. How do you intend to achieve your image goals through:
   A. Your responses?
   B. Your demeanor?

Norms

1. How much time should you make available for the interview? How will you enforce this?
2. What is the basic slant of the interview? Soft or hard feature, straight news report, or investigative report?
3. What ground rules, if any, should you establish regarding off-limits topics?
4. Should you invite someone else to be present as a resource or witness?
5. Should you tape record the interview?
6. Where should the interview take place?
7. To what extent do you want to control the setting (e.g., remove confidential items, place items you wish to discuss

within easy view, make the environment neater than usual, etc.)?

8. To what extent will you agree to speaking "off-the-record," "not for attribution," or on "background?" (See the Inside Advice section below.)

Special Preparation

1. How much do you know about the reporter?
   A. Have you been interviewed by her before? What was your experience?
      Advice:
      Don't assume that your experience will be similar from one interview to the next.
   B. What is her general reputation for competence and fairness?
   C. What is her interest, knowledge level, and attitude(s) regarding your company and industry?
   D. What is her interview style (e.g., friendly, aggressive, etc.)?

2. If you need to learn more about the reporter, what sources are available to you?
   A. Clippings or videotapes
   B. Colleagues who know the reporter or her reputation
   C. Published ratings

3. How much do you know about the channel, station, or publication? How credible is it?
   A. Is it identified with a particular slant?
   B. How have you or your firm dealt with it before?

4. When is the reporter's deadline?

5. Should you make background materials/exhibits available?

6. If the reporter is interviewing you as part of an ongoing story, what has been its drift? Who has spoken? What have they said?

7. What lines of questioning and specific questions (including Banana Groves and Banana Peels™) should you expect?
   A. Are you fully prepared?
   B. If not, what steps should you take to make sure that you are?

8. Following the interview, what type of access should you provide to the reporter?

Inside Advice

1. Since a live interview cannot be edited, you have more potential control over content than with a taped interview.

2. When consenting to an interview, request a list of the topics to be covered. In fact, if the interview is expected to be friendly, your communications specialist may even want to ask for questions in advance. But be ready to be turned down. However, in certain countries (e.g., Japan) it is common for a business reporter to present her questions in advance.

3. There is no such thing as a dead microphone or tape recorder. Moreover, assume the camera is *always* on.

4. Beware of the "pregnant pause," in which the radio or TV reporter holds the microphone in front of you after you've finished your response, hoping you will extend your answer and possibly place you closer to a Banana Peel. If this occurs, look the reporter in the eye with a confident, friendly smile (not grin) and wait for the next question.

5. The interview is not over until you and the reporter have gone your separate ways.

6. If you don't want to be quoted in a print interview directly, yet want to cooperate, you may comment if the reporter agrees that your remarks be treated according to one of the following three provisions:
   A. *On background.* Here you will not be referred to by name. Instead, you might be referred to as "a company source," or as "a reliable source close to the situation."
   B. *On deep background.* This proviso implies an understanding between you and the reporter that every effort will be taken not to imply or to allow the inference that you are the source. This can be particularly restrictive to the reporter—so much so

that information given "on deep background" may not be usable.

C. *Off the record*. This means that the information presented is not to be linked to you in any way. I do not believe in "off the record" remarks, although this proviso remains a matter of continuing controversy among communications professionals.

In choosing any of these three options, make sure that you and the reporter share the same understanding of each option, including clarity regarding when each begins and ends.

7. To increase the chances of being quoted, begin your responses with a strong headline. Such sentences generally are brief, contain one or more words with a strong connotation, carry a particularly graphic metaphor, or reflect some combination of these factors. You might want to prepare and practice your headlines in advance. As you prepare "soundbites" for taped radio or TV interviews, do not refer explicitly to the question, for questions per se do not usually appear in taped news reports. Therefore, your response should be presented as a self-standing statement.

8. Avoid saying, "No comment," especially on TV or radio; otherwise, this expression can taint you with the perception of guilt. If you choose not to comment, be prepared to explain why in a nondefensive manner.

9. Shorter answers are normally more advisable than longer ones. Whenever possible, analyze the actual news program to determine how long the responses tend to be rather than rely on a general principle that your answers should be no longer than "x" seconds. Remember, if the reporter wants more information, she will ask for it.

10. Know how to end the interview. When the interview is arranged, ask your assistant or public information officer to determine—or negotiate—how long it should take. Reinforce the agreed-upon time (and any other ground rules) right before the interview begins. Arrange for your assistant or communications staff member to signal you shortly before the interview is scheduled to end.

THE NEWS CONFERENCE

The news conference—especially a crisis conference—may place you in a lion's den where reporters will seem to compete aggressively to exact from you every available pound of flesh. Your ability to survive the conference—*and to succeed in it*—requires control, credibility, and composure. Moreover, the leadership you display during the conference can be a metaphor for the leadership you and your colleagues are displaying in addressing the crisis.

Goals and Opportunities

1. Rank which of the following statements represent your two or three major reasons for calling the news conference.
   A. To make a positive announcement.
   B. To respond to a negative story or crisis situation.
   C. To offer a single consistent message.
   D. To secure maximum media exposure.
   E. To limit the number of one-on-one media interviews.
   F. Other.
2. How confident are you that the conference is advisable?

Target Audience

1. How would you describe your target audience—those people beyond the confines of the briefing room whom you need to influence?
   A. How relevant are the following factors?
      1. Age
      2. Sex
      3. Socioeconomic status
      4. Education
      5. Religion
      6. Race
      7. Political preferences
      8. Whether or not they are customers
      9. Whether or not they are parents
      10. Whether or not they live in a certain area

11. Other
B. How do you intend to incorporate the more relevant factors into your message?

2. What is their level of familiarity with each of the issues you plan to address?
A. Should you adjust your message to their familiarity level?
B. If so, how?

3. Using the scale below, how would you rate your audience's regard for each of the following channels of persuasion?

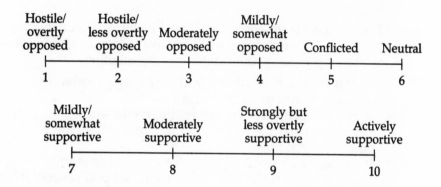

A. You
B. Your corporation
C. The company or division of the corporation you represent
D. Your industry, business, or profession
E. Your principal message

4. Why do you think they react to each channel in the manner you have indicated?

The Spokesperson

1. Why has this spokesperson been chosen? Is she the best person to face the media?
2. Has your company or organization taken sufficient steps to control who is permitted to speak to the media?

3. Rank which of the following statements represent the spokesperson's major goals:
   A. To generate a positive story
   B. To demonstrate corporate credibility
   C. To represent the corporation's or organization's views as its key decision makers would want them expressed
   D. To control the interview
   E. To avoid gaffes and other types of blunders
   F. To avoid unnecessary disclosures
   G. Other

4. If you are the spokesperson, do you regard the interview mainly as an opportunity or as an obligation?

   Advice:

   Even in a crisis situation, you should be focused primarily on using the conference to convey positive substance and image messages regarding your company or organization.

5. If this is a crisis situation, are you currently perceived more as the victim or as the culprit?
   A. If you are perceived as the victim, could this perception change to your being perceived as the culprit? If so, how?
   B. If you are perceived as the culprit, how fair is this perception? If unfair, to what extent can you reverse it?

6. Are other people available to provide technical support for your remarks?

7. How prepared are they to face the media and support your key messages?

8. Do you intend to begin the conference with an opening statement? If so:
   A. What key messages should it contain?
   B. How long should it be?
   C. Who should provide input into it?
   D. Who has final approval?

   Advice:

   Generally, an opening statement (usually no longer than five minutes) is advisable to lay out your key messages and provide a framework for responding to the more-predictable crucial questions. To reflect the desired tone or image it should be practiced separately from the Q & A dry run. In addition, it should be distributed to the media, often with a news release.

Key Messages

What key messages do you intend to convey and reinforce during the news conference?

1. What is the relative order of importance of your key messages?
2. What proof or support can you provide for each key message?

Advice:

Keep a key message sheet in front of you, making sure that the purpose of the sheet is not too obvious to the reporters.

Image Goals

1. What major image goals do you plan to achieve as a result of the conference?
2. What image traits should you consciously avoid?
3. How do you intend to achieve your image goals?
   A. Through the opening statement and your responses
   B. Through your demeanor

Advice:

In a crisis conference, you must be particularly wary of projecting defensiveness, anger, loss of control, and loss of composure. If the conference is called to report on a matter involving injury, loss of life, or a health hazard, or to make a negative employment-related announcement (e.g., to announce a major layoff or plant closing), then it is generally advisable to express empathy or compassion early in the opening statement and to reinforce it during the Q & A.

Format and Norms

1. Where should the conference be held? Why?
   Advice:

   Make sure you have a lectern, enough seating, and adequate lighting. Also, the room should be available for camera crews to set up 30 to 40 minutes before the conference begins. Light refreshments may be advisable.
2. When should it take place?

Advice:

Normally, news conferences occur at approximately 10 A.M. to take advantage of the daily news cycle. However, in a crisis situation, a news conference can be called at any time—even several times—throughout the day.

3. How should you announce the conference?
   A. By telephone
   B. By news release
   C. By fax
   D. Some combination of the above

   Advice:

   Choose whichever method seems most efficient. In fact, all three methods occasionally work well together. You should normally announce the topic in advance. This allows news editors to decide which reporters to send and whether or not camera crews should accompany them.

4. Who should introduce you and end the conference?
   A. What kind of signal system should the introducer have with you to indicate that the conference should end?

   Advice:

   Usually news conferences should end when the questions are beginning to die out or sound too repetitious—or if the climate is deteriorating into seemingly irreversible hostility.

   B. Should the introducer signal you if you are overanswering the question?

   Advice:

   Using a "third base coach" to signal you is probably advisable if you tend to overanswer.

5. What topics should be prohibited (e.g., for legal reasons, or when facts are not yet available), and why?

6. Who should be permitted (and not be permitted) to attend? How will attendance be reinforced?

7. Should you ask reporters to identify themselves by name and affiliation?

   Advice:

   If you don't know most of the reporters, this may be advisable to allow you to identify which ones can most likely reach your target audience.

8. Should you record the conference on audio- or videotape?

Advice:

Whenever possible, you should. Doing so gives you a verification record of what you said and a fine opportunity to analyze your performance.

9. Should you allow a tour of the facility or scene of the crisis?

Advice:

This decision often needs to be weighed very carefully. Whatever the case, your answer should be "no" if the scene continues to pose a hazard. As soon as photographers and camera crews take pictures of a crisis that developed on your premises, they increase the likelihood that the story will reflect negatively on your company or organization. Therefore, your verbal refusal may be less negative than the graphic potency of the pictures taken or videotaping made during the tour.

Some companies we represent have proprietary processing systems. If this applies to your company, a "no" with the explanation that the processes are proprietary can prevent a photograph or videotape from getting into your competitors' hands.

Special Preparation

1. How much do you know about the reporters expected to attend?
   A. Have you been interviewed by any of them before? What is your experience with them?
   B. What is each major reporter's general reputation for competence and fairness?
   C. What are the major reporters' interests, knowledge level, and attitudes regarding your company, the industry, and the issue at hand?
   D. What do you know about the interviewing style of each?

2. If you need to learn more about a reporter, what sources are available to you?
   A. Clippings or videotapes
   B. Colleagues who know the reporter or her reputation
   C. Published ratings

3. How much do you know about the channel, station, or publication?
   A. How credible is it?
   B. Is it identified with a particular slant?
   C. Have you or your firm dealt with it before?
4. If you are being interviewed as part of an ongoing story, what has been its drift? Who has spoken? What has been said?
5. What questions (including Banana Groves and Banana Peels™) should you expect?
   A. Are you fully prepared?
   B. If not, what steps should you take to make sure that you are?

THE TV OR RADIO TALK SHOW

Don't let the comfortable living-room atmosphere of a talk show set deceive you into thinking that a talk show is any less formidable than most interview settings. Depending on the host, the other guest(s), the format, and, of course, you and your subject, even the most ostensibly benign talk show can quickly become brutal. The key to finesse on talk shows is to understand them well, especially since, as this guide illustrates, preparation often involves great attention to detail.

Goals and Opportunities

1. Rank which of the following represent your two or three major goals for the show.
   A. To advance a particular point of view regarding an issue or story
   B. To represent the corporation's or organization's views as its key decision makers would want them expressed
   C. To encourage the purchase of your product or service
   D. To elevate your own personal exposure
   E. To elevate the corporation's or organization's exposure
   F. To avoid gaffes, misstatements, or volunteering too much (*circle your particular concern*)

G. To avoid/generate controversy/confrontation (circle choice)

H. Other

2. Do you regard the interview mainly as an opportunity or as an obligation? Why?

Advice:

Don't appear on the show until you have a positive attitude regarding what you can potentially accomplish.

Target Audience

1. How would you describe your target audience?
   A. How relevant are the following factors?
      1. Age
      2. Sex
      3. Socioeconomic status
      4. Education
      5. Religion
      6. Race
      7. Political preference
      8. Whether or not they are customers
      9. Whether or not they are parents
      10. Whether or not they live in a certain area
      11. Other
   B. What factors are most relevant to each key message?
   C. How do you intend to incorporate the more relevant factors into your message?
2. What is the audience's familiarity level with each of the issues you plan to address?
   A. Should you adjust your message to their familiarity level? If so, how?
3. Using the scale below, how would you rate your target audience's regard for each of the following channels of persuasion?

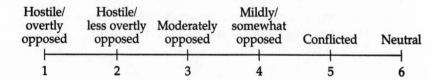

Hostile/ overtly opposed	Hostile/ less overtly opposed	Moderately opposed	Mildly/ somewhat opposed	Conflicted	Neutral
1	2	3	4	5	6

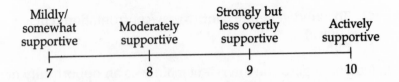

A. You
B. Your corporation
C. The company or division of the corporation that you represent
D. Your industry, business, or profession
E. Your principal message

4. Why do you think they react to each channel in the manner you have indicated?

Key Messages

What key messages do you intend to convey and reinforce during the show?

Advice:
For a radio talk show, you may choose to place your key messages on a sheet of paper in front of you. Be sure that the purpose of the sheet is not too obvious to the host, especially if the circumstances are not friendly.

1. What is the relative order of importance of your key messages?
2. What proof or support can you provide for each key message?

Image Goals

1. What major image goals do you wish to achieve as a result of the interview?
2. What image traits should you consciously avoid?
3. How do you intend to achieve your image goals through:
   A. The content of your comments and answers
   B. Your demeanor

Format

1. What is the length of the show? The length of the segment on which you will appear?
2. Will it be live or taped? If taped, when will it be shown?
3. How large a portion of your target audience is expected to watch it?

   Advice:

   > In certain circumstances, you may wish to encourage viewership via internal announcements, Mailgrams, etc.

4. Are other guests expected to appear?
   A. Who will they be?
      1. Will their message be related to yours?
      2. If so, will this require special preparation?
   B. How will they appear?
      1. Live with you?
      2. On a split screen from a "remote" location?
      3. By voice only, via telephone?
   C. When will they appear—before or after you? How will this influence your presentation?

   Advice:

   > If, for instance, your adversaries will be appearing after you, it may be wise for you to preempt them by refuting their point of view.

5. Will the show include:
   A. A live audience questioning segment?
   B. A call-in segment?
6. If the answer to A or B above is yes:
   A. When will the segment occur?
   B. How long will it last?
   C. What lines of audience questioning can be expected?

   Advice:

   > Often live audiences for talk shows are selected based on interest in a specific topic. In fact, sometimes interest groups successfully "stack" talk-show audiences and call-in segments with informed, articulate advocates. Don't hesitate to ask the producer for background information regarding how the live audience is selected.

7. How do you expect to be introduced?

A. By the host saying to the camera, "Our guest today is . . . ?"
B. By an off-camera announcer introducing you?
C. During an interaction with the host that includes a "welcome to the show"?
D. By the host firing a "zinger" at you to throw you immediately on the defensive?

Advice:

If the introduction is friendly, be prepared to nod and smile as soon as you are introduced. Otherwise, the audience may sense that you are detached. Also, be prepared to respond with a "nice to be here, _____ (host's first name)." If you're hit by a zinger, be prepared to respond forcefully to the claim *without attacking the host*. If the reason for your appearance is to defend a negative story, avoid "nice to be here."

8. What is the seating arrangement in relation to the overall set design, including the location of cameras?

   Advice:

   Secure a diagram in advance. Sometimes you can choose where to sit when more than one guest is appearing at the same time. If you regard your appearance as more of an opportunity than a risk, you may wish to sit closest to the host. This is usually the "power seat" for two reasons: (1) the camera can capture you most easily; and (2) by sitting there you can engage the host more easily than can, for instance, the guest seated three chairs away.

The Host

1. What is the host's general reputation and the reputation of the show?
2. What is the host's questioning style?
   A. Mild-mannered?
   B. Aggressive?
   C. Hostile?
   D. A combination of the above?
   E. Other?
3. To what extent does the host take/suggest a stand?
4. How much control does the host exercise over the interaction?

    A. Significant?
    B. Moderate?
    C. Varied?
    D. Little?

5. To what extent does the host:
   A. Allow guests to complete responses?
   B. Provide fair rebuttal opportunities?
   C. Control interruptions?
   D. Control monopolizers?

6. What specific questions or lines of questioning can you expect?

7. What types of Banana Groves and Banana Peels™ will the host likely rely on?

8. What other tactics does the host use?
   A. Shaking head in disbelief?
   B. Asking the audience "do you believe that?"
   C. Hurling accusations at guests?
   D. Using the cliff-hanger zinger right before a commercial break?

Advice:

> The preceding eight questions can be best addressed by watching and analyzing one or more shows before you appear. Avoiding surprises is an important prerequisite to achieving talk-show finesse.

Special Advice

1. Be prepared to avoid distractions on the set (technicians moving around, cameras, etc.) by focusing squarely on the host or on the person talking. Do not look into the camera unless you are addressing a call-in viewer.

2. Generally, you should not debate the host. Remember, even if members of your target audience may be listening, their loyalty to the host may be stronger than their loyalty to you.

3. Don't refuse make-up if it's offered and one of your key advisers considers it necessary.

4. When sitting, assume a comfortable position, but be prepared to demonstrate energy, involvement, and

conviction by leaning forward and gesturing, and through facial expression and vocal emphasis.

5. Be prepared to compete to be heard. The show may require you to display an atypical amount of aggressiveness (not aggression).

TESTIFYING AT A LEGISLATIVE OR GOVERNMENT AGENCY HEARING[1]

Testifying before a legislative committee or regulatory agency may be an important opportunity to exercise control over the destiny of your business, product, service, or cause. In fact, testifying—especially on a voluntary basis—may be a sign of status and influence. In addition, as the types of government regulation increase, you may need to speak before a government agency to obtain or retain a permit, license, or other benefit. Before you do, you will need to understand the purpose of the hearing, its norms, and its players.

Determine the Type of Hearing

In preparing to testify at a legislative or government agency hearing, the first step is to focus on the type of hearing. These can be broken down into three categories:

1. *Legislative type:* Hearings before a legislative committee or regulatory body to consider adopting, amending, or repealing legislation, regulations, or a policy statement, or issuing a report. Testifying before Congress concerning pending legislation is an example of this type of hearing.

2. *Adjudictory type:* Hearings before government agencies that could affect personal or property rights, liabilities, or obligations. This includes a wide variety of proceedings including rate setting, environmental or land use permitting, and licensure revocation or suspension hearings. Normally this does not take place before legislative bodies.

3. *Investigative type:* Hearings before a legislative committee or regulatory body inquiring into certain conduct or events. The Watergate, Iran-Contra, and Clarence Thomas hearings fall into this category.

The Hearing Landscape

1. What is the stated purpose of the hearing?
2. Are there reasons, other than the stated purpose, that the hearing is being held? Knowing the political or bureaucratic landscape can be critical to your success.
3. What are the goals of those conducting the hearing? Remember, particularly with legislative bodies, that there may be multiple and divergent goals of the various individuals conducting the hearing.
4. What will be the length of the hearing? Will there be other hearings on the same subject?
5. Will the hearings be open or closed? If open, will the media attend?
6. How many other witnesses are expected to appear? Will they be supportive or adversarial to your position?
   A. When and in what order will they appear?
   B. Will their appearance, including the order, influence your message? If so, how?
7. Will the individuals planning and conducting the hearing regard you as a friendly, hostile, neutral, or expert witness?
8. Do you need to be accompanied by an attorney? (*Note:* Where someone's livelihood or reputation is at stake, competent counsel can be invaluable. This is particularly important in quasi-criminal investigations or where questions of immunity or "taking the Fifth" might be relevant.)
9. What is the expected attendance pattern of the panelists?
10. How strongly does the chair exercise her leadership authority? Under what particular circumstances?
11. Do you expect a supportive panelist to speak out on behalf of your position or to attempt to "rescue you" if another panelist treats you unfairly?

12. What specific ground rules apply regarding:
    A. Whether opening statements have to be read or can be delivered extemporaneously?
    B. Whether time limits will be placed on opening statements and questioning?
    C. Who is permitted to ask questions (e.g., just committee members, the committee's counsel, others)?
    D. Whether there will be an opportunity to be called back to testify, if desirable?
13. Is the issue of immunity relevant to the proceedings, and will it be offered?

Goals and Opportunities

1. Rank which of the following represent your two or three major goals for the hearing.
    A. To advance a position or a cause (*offensive strategy*)
    B. To get through the hearing with minimal damage (*defensive strategy*)
    C. To support/oppose legislation or regulatory approval (*circle the appropriate choices*)
    D. To defend or promote your reputation
    E. To advance your career, for example, to secure speaking engagements, job offers, book/ movie contracts, legal defense fund donations, etc.
    F. To generate strong media coverage
    G. To elevate the exposure of a company or organization
    H. To protect confidentiality/secrecy
    I. To avoid gaffes and other types of blunders
    J. Other

2. Do you regard the hearing as more of an opportunity or an obligation? Why?

3. How important is the hearing to the ultimate legislative or regulatory decision or recommendation to be made by the panel?
    A. Extremely important
    B. Very important
    C. Somewhat important
    D. Not important

Target Audience

1. Is your target audience:
   A. The panel?
   B. Certain panelists?
   C. The entire legislative or regulatory body?
   D. The media?
   E. Another specific group or constituency?

2. How would you describe your target audience(s)?
   A. What demographic and knowledge-level factors of your target and general audiences are most relevant to each key message?
      1. Age
      2. Sex
      3. Socioeconomic status
      4. Education
      5. Religion
      6. Race
      7. Whether or not they are parents
      8. Whether they live in a certain area
      9. Other
   B. How do you intend to incorporate the more relevant factors into your message?

3. What is your target audience's familiarity level with each of the issues you plan to address?
   A. Should you adjust your message to their familiarity level?
   B. If so, how?

4. Using the scale below, how would you rate your target audience's regard for each of the following channels of persuasion?

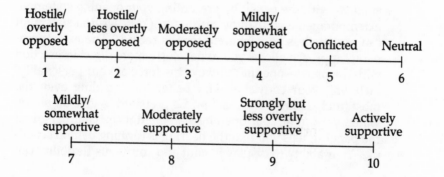

A. You
B. Your corporation
C. The company or division of the corporation you represent
D. Your industry, business, or profession
E. Your principal message

5. Why do you think they react to each channel in the manner you have indicated?
6. Where specifically does each panelist stand regarding your proposal? Why?

Key Messages

What key messages do you intend to convey and reinforce during the hearing?

1. What is the relative order of importance of your key messages?
2. What proof or support can you provide for each key message?

Image Goals

1. What major image goals do you wish to achieve?
2. What image traits should you consciously avoid?
3. How do you intend to achieve your image goals through:
   1. Your opening statement and responses?
   2. Your demeanor?

Advice:

Generally, in legislative hearings, it is far more advisable to *communicate* with the panel, by presenting your opening statement extemporaneously, than by reading it. (Your written statement can nonetheless be submitted for the record.) The extemporaneous approach allows you to develop a more direct interaction with the panel—one that conveys the force of your personality, including your conviction—far better than reading even the most finely tailored manuscript. Be prepared to give an abbreviated version of your opening statement if the chairperson of the panel signals you that the hearing is running behind schedule. Your ability to display instant and courteous flexibility can be most impressive. Note, however, that extemporaneous statements may be dangerous in adjudicatory or investigative-type hearings when a premium is placed on verbal precision.

Special Preparation

1. How much lobbying will be necessary before testifying?
   A. What information gleaned from the lobbying effort should be reflected in your opening statement and responses?
   B. What questions (including Banana Groves and Banana Peels™) can you expect—and from whom?
2. To what extent should the testimony of the other supportive witnesses be coordinated?
3. What can you learn in advance about the hearing demeanor of each panelist, including the chair?
   A. Aggressiveness in questioning style
   B. Skill as a questioner
   C. Tendency to use the hearing as a soapbox
   D. Compliance with the ground rules
   E. Relationship with the other panelists
   F. Other
4. Are large exhibits (e.g., charts, enlarged photographs) allowed and advisable?
5. Should you be accompanied by your spouse or another prominent supporter? (Remember the stoic, supportive presence of John Dean's wife, Maureen, during the Watergate hearings, and Clarence Thomas's wife, Virginia, during the hearings leading up to his confirmation.)
6. What is the overall layout of the room, including specific seating arrangements? If possible, visit the room and become well-acquainted with it before you testify.

Inside Advice on Cross-Examination

Since legislative and regulatory hearings are often dominated by lawyers, it is not unusual for them to put their cross-examination skills on full display—especially if the media are present. The following advice, although directed to the questioner, can give the respondent added insight into the questioner's tactics:

- Keep your questions clear, concise, and closed-ended to control the communication—and the questions' pressure on the witness.
- Take full advantage of silence—especially following a dramatic admission.
- Focus mainly on the crucial issues.
- Don't ask a crucial question until the foundation for it has been firmly laid.
- Avoid conveying the impression that your emotions rule your reason.
- When your point is made, stop!

Format and Norms: A Checklist

1. Will the hearing be open or closed?
2. What will be the length of the hearing?
3. What other supportive and adversarial witnesses are expected to appear?
   A. When, and in what order?
   B. Will their appearance, including the order, influence your message? If so, how?
4. What is the expected attendance pattern of the panelists?
5. How strongly does the chair exercise her leadership authority? Under what particular circumstances?
6. Do you expect a supportive panelist to speak out on behalf of your position or to attempt to "rescue you" if another panelist treats you unfairly?
7. Will an attorney be present? If so, what will be her role?
8. What specific ground rules apply regarding who is permitted to ask questions, prior submissions, the opening statement, the process of questioning, and the opportunity to be called back to testify?
9. Do immunity provisions for witnesses apply?
10. Will time limits be placed on opening statements and questioning?

11. Do opening statements have to be read or can they be delivered extemporaneously?

BEING DEPOSED[2]

A deposition presents a pretrial opportunity for a party in a lawsuit to question, under oath, adverse parties or witnesses for the purpose of discovering facts. Most commonly, adversaries depose each other in litigation. In many instances the person being deposed is provided with little direction regarding what to expect or how to prepare. This plan should prove helpful in both regards.

Goals and Opportunities

1. If you are being deposed, rank what you consider to be the goals of your adversary's attorney:
   A. Assess your demeanor.
   B. Assess your credibility.
   C. Undermine your credibility.
   D. Get a definitive statement of your understanding of the facts.
   E. Contrast your recollection of the facts with other facts that your adversary may have learned in discovery.

2. Rank which of the following represent your two or three major goals for the deposition.
   A. To advance a position or cause (offensive strategy)
   B. To get through the deposition with minimal damage (defensive strategy)
   C. To divert blame
   D. To defend or promote one's reputation
   E. To protect confidentiality/secrecy
   F. To avoid gaffes and other types of blunders
   G. Other

3. How important is your deposition to the ultimate legal issue to be decided by the court?
   A. Extremely important
   B. Very important

C. Somewhat important
D. Not important

Preparing for Your Deposition

1. What can you learn about your examiner—reputation, questioning style, etc.?
2. Where will the deposition take place? Who will attend?
   Advice:
   Review, with your counsel, documents and other materials about which you expect to be examined, particularly those that you may have written, plus any affidavits that you signed during the litigation.
3. On what basic facts of the case will you be questioned?
   Advice:
   Avoid educating yourself—solely for the deposition—about matters in which you were not involved.
4. What is the legal context in which the case has arisen?

Target Audience

1. Is your target audience:
   A. The court?
   B. The jury?
   C. Your adversary's attorney?
   D. Your adversary?
   E. Your own organization?
   F. Other?
2. How would you describe your target audience(s)?
   A. What demographic and knowledge-level factors of your target and general audiences are most relevant to each key message?
      1. Age
      2. Sex
      3. Socioeconomic
      4. Education
      5. Religion
      6. Race
      7. Whether or not they are parents

8. Whether they live in a certain area
9. Other
B. How do you intend to incorporate the more relevant factors into your message?
3. What is your target audience's familiarity with each of the issues you plan to address?
A. Should you adjust the style of your message (not the facts) to their familiarity level?
B. If so, how?
4. Using the scale below, how would you rate your target audience's regard for each of the following channels of persuasion?

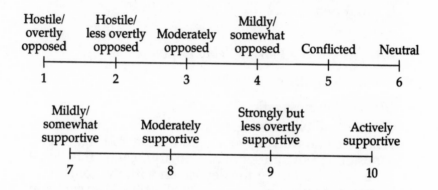

A. You
B. Your corporation
C. The company or division of the corporation you represent
D. Your industry, business, or profession
E. Your principal message
5. Why do you think they react to each channel in the manner you have indicated?
6. Where specifically does each target audience member stand regarding your deposition? Why?

Key Messages

What key messages do you intend to convey and reinforce during the deposition?

1. What is the relative order of importance of your key messages?
2. What proof or support can you provide for each key message?

Image Goals

1. What major image goals do you wish to achieve as a result of the deposition?
2. What image traits should you consciously avoid?
3. How do you intend to achieve your image goals through:
   A. Your responses?
   B. Your demeanor?

Advice for the Person Being Deposed

Nonsubstantive matters

1. Dress in business attire.
2. Counsel will typically agree to the "usual stipulations." These include waiving your right to read and sign the deposition in the presence of a notary, sealing the deposition, and filing the deposition with the court. Normally, you should agree with all of these, except you should consider reserving your right to read and sign the deposition, particularly if you expect questions relating to technical matters, complicated facts, or if you simply want to make sure the transcript is accurate.
3. Under the "usual stipulations," counsel objects to improperly framed questions. Therefore, your attorney may object to the examiner's inquiries. Nonetheless, unless your counsel instructs you not to answer, you must answer all questions, even those to which your counsel has objected.
4. Listen to your counsel's objections, because some lawyers use objections to prompt their client, although this is considered improper.
5. Counsel may agree to go "off the record" during the deposition. This means that the court reporter will not

record what is being said at the time. Usually, counsel goes "off the record" to avoid burdening the record with inconsequential information, such as scheduling matters and minor disputes.

6. If the questioner is referring to documents that she suggests you wrote or reviewed, you should ask to see them.

7. If documents are shown to you, read them. Do not assume that you recall what they say, even if you reviewed them before your deposition.

8. You may refer to exhibits during your deposition.

9. You are absolutely entitled to consult privately with your attorney at any time during the deposition.

Substantive responses

1. Listen to the entire question before formulating your answer.

2. Pause before answering each question to consider exactly what is sought.

3. Answer questions in complete sentences.

4. Answer the question asked of you. Do not answer more than what is asked. Do not volunteer information. If you believe the questioner is seeking particular information, although the question posed is not properly phrased to elicit the information that you believe is sought, *answer only the question posed*—not the one you believe the questioner is trying to ask.

5. Be as specific as your memory allows. If you are not sure, do not guess, speculate, or present as fact something you think is "probably true."

6. If you do not know an answer, say "I do not know."

7. If you knew an answer to a question at one time, but you no longer recall, say "I do not recall."

8. If the examiner's questions contain statements of fact with which you disagree or that mischaracterize your prior testimony, state that you disagree with the premise of the question, then state why.

9. Do not let the examiner put words in your mouth.

10. Do not argue with the examiner.

11. Avoid categorical expressions such as *always* or *never*.

12. Avoid expressions such as *in all honesty, in candor,* and *truthfully*.

13. If you are interrupted, wait for the interruption to end before you complete your answer. Then say, "Before I was interrupted, I was about to state. . . ."

14. Avoid levity.

15. Avoid expressing anger.

16. If asked "Do you have something to add?" and you do not have additional information, state this and do not volunteer additional information.

17. After a witness answers a question, some attorneys pause, hoping the witness will feel uncomfortable with a period of silence, and thereby expand upon a prior answer. Avoid doing so. Do not try to "fill" a pause with volunteered testimony.

18. If you make a mistake, correct it immediately. It is better to correct a mistake promptly, rather than later.

19. If you are caught in an inconsistency, real or perceived, state your present recollection, if asked. State the reason for the inconsistency only if you are asked.

20. Do not consent to supplying additional information requested by the examiner. State that you will "consider" any request made of you, but do not commit beyond that.

Epilogue

The Ethics of Q & A

The English poet and critic, Alexander Pope, once said, "He who tells a lie is not sensible how great a task he undertakes, for he must be forced to invent 20 more to maintain that one." Wise and timeless advice for sure. Yet pressures facing today's executives can often blur the distinction between truth and falsehood. When push comes to shove, can a white lie told by an executive to an audience, reporter, or government panel help preserve the corporation's image and his or her own career path? Possibly, but the risks are, as Pope implied, entirely too great.

In reviewing our ethical standards as communicators, we must draw a clear line between truthfulness and openness. Truthfulness means that whatever we say is, to the best of our knowledge, factual and free from distortion. Openness implies the extent to which the faucet of factual and interpretive information should be opened. Therefore, as communicators, we should be absolutely truthful, while our openness should be relative or situational.

In establishing a personal set of standards for ethical communication, we should adhere to the following advice:

- *Be secure enough to say "I don't know"* rather than feign knowledge—and possibly expose your charade unwittingly—thereby compromising your credibility.
- *Combat any tendency to distort reality* through the selective use of language, examples, numbers, or statistics.
- *Scrutinize your logic* for any tendency to engage in fallacious reasoning.
- *Double- or triple-check your sources* for accuracy, proper context, reputation, and recency.

- *Check the methodology behind any studies* on which your case depends.
- *Avoid any temptation to fabricate examples or other data.*
- *Be prepared to acknowledge persons who deserve credit* for the good ideas or expressions you are using.

When setting our standards for ethical communication, we can derive added insight and guidance from the well-chosen words of William Penn: "Truth often suffers more by the heat of its defenders than from the arguments of its opposers."

Endnotes

INTRODUCTION

1. Michael Novak, "Let the Questions In," *Hemispheres*, November 1992, p. 43.

CHAPTER 2

1. *Philadelphia Inquirer*, November 28, 1991, p. 24-A.
2. "CNN Daybreak," December 24, 1992.
3. *Philadelphia Inquirer*, June 23, 1992, p. B3.
4. Professor Joseph J. Tecce of Boston College has published several articles regarding blinking in academic journals and is frequently quoted in the popular press.
5. Adapted from Myles Martel, *The Persuasive Edge* (New York: Fawcett Columbine, 1989), pp. 175–76.
6. *The Wall Street Journal*, April 14, 1992, p. 3.

CHAPTER 3

1. *Washington Post*, March 27, 1988, p. A8.

CHAPTER 4

1. Kenneth L. Higbee, *Your Memory: How It Works and How to Improve It*, 2nd ed. (New York: Prentice Hall, 1988), pp. 21–22.
2. Ibid, p. 24.

CHAPTER 5

1. *Newsweek*, November 30, 1992, pp. 62–63.
2. *Philadelphia Inquirer*, December 31, 1992, p. D1.
3. Albert Mehrabian, *Silent Messages* (Belmont, Calif.: Wadsworth Publishing Co., 1971).
4. This book will not provide advice regarding attire, especially since styles change so often and are dependent on regional tastes.
5. Eliot Aronson, *The Social Animal* (San Francisco: W. H. Freeman, 1980), pp. 237–70.
6. Verbatim transcription from CNN telecast, March 1991.
7. Theodore C. Sorensen, *"Let the Word Go Forth"—The Speeches, Statements, and Writings of John F. Kennedy 1947 to 1963* (New York: Delacorte Press, 1988), p. 75. The exchange took place during the president's news conference of May 8, 1963.
8. I spotted this exchange on a framed poster in Lindy's Restaurant, New York City.
9. *Newsweek*, December 14, 1992, p. 23.

CHAPTER 6

1. *The Daily Telegraph* (London), June 11, 1992, p. 23.
2. Transcription based on videotape of "Donahue," June 1, 1980.

CHAPTER 7

1. CNN's "Inside Business," January 24, 1993.
2. Transcription provided by White House Office of Communications.
3. Tape, n.d., supplied by the Dow Chemical Company.
4. "Larry King Live," December 24, 1992.
5. *The New York Times*, November 5, 1991, p. A12.
6. *Newsweek*, December 28, 1992, p. 14.
7. Williams A. Henry III, *The Great One: The Life and Legend of Jackie Gleason* (New York: Doubleday, 1992), p. 99.
8. *Newsweek*, December 14, 1992, p. 23.

CHAPTER 8

1. *Newsweek*, January 4, 1993, p. 13.
2. *The New York Times*, March 24, 1993, p. A9.
3. *Philadelphia Inquirer*, June 24, 1992, p. D1.

CHAPTER 9

1. Transcript of Annual Meeting of Stockholders, E. I. DuPont de Nemours & Company, April 29, 1992, pp. 2–3.
2. Ms. Davis is well-known on the annual meeting circuit for trying to— and often succeeding in—taking control of the meetings. Speaking in a thick but wholly understandable German accent, she normally relies on hostile questions, lengthy diatribes, and extreme displays of self-promotion. No question about it, she makes good theater. But more important, knowing how to handle her and personalities like her, without provoking them further or generating audience sympathy for them, can be the ultimate test of not only your control, but your finesse.
3. *Time*, February 8, 1988, pp. 16–20.

CHAPTER 10

1. *The Little, Brown Book of Anecdotes* (Boston: Little, Brown, 1985), p. 111.

CHAPTER 11

1. *The New York Times*, December 15, 1992, p. A21.
2. Ibid.
3. Ibid.
4. *Webster's New Unabridged Dictionary*, 2nd ed. (Cleveland: Dorset & Barker, 1979).
5. *Inoculate* is a medical metaphor used by communication experts to connote a deliberate attempt to build up audience resistance to counterarguments.

CHAPTER 12

1. *Time*, February 3, 1992, p. 47.
2. Our research reveals that there are no significant differences in presentational and Q & A norms between businesses based in the United States and Canada. Hence, throughout this chapter *American* refers to firms based on the North American continent.
3. As globalization of the business world advances, I am sensing a gradual assimilation of norms. Therefore, well-tuned cultural awareness requires ongoing vigilance to changes, however pronounced or subtle.
4. Roger Axtell, *Gestures: The Do's and Taboos of Body Language around the World* (New York: John Wiley & Sons, 1991). The advice offered by *Diplomat* magazine's "Do's & Don't's" column was also helpful.
5. The rankings are based on the U.S. Department of Commerce, Survey of Current Business (March 1992). Luxembourg is listed with Belgium as the 10th major partner. However, because its trading role is only a small percentage of Belgium's net balance of trade, it is not profiled separately.
6. Boye Lafayette De Mente, *Japan's Secret Weapon: The Kata Factor* (Phoenix, Ariz.: Phoenix Books, 1990).

CHAPTER 14

1. *Time*, February 8, 1988, pp. 16–20.

CHAPTER 15

1. I am most indebted to Larry Beaser, Esq., of the Philadelphia law firm Blank, Rome, Cominsky & McCauley, for his assistance in developing this plan.
2. I deeply appreciate the significant assistance of George Kruger, Esq., of the Philadelphia law firm Blank, Rome, Cominsky & McCauley, in developing this plan.

Contributors and Supporters

To the following persons who, over the years, have provided scores of opportunities for me to develop and apply the concepts presented in this book:

Aram Aghazarian
Griffin Allen
Jack Armstrong
Sharyn Arnold
Mike Bailey
Andy Balbirer
John Ballantyne
Buddy Barfield
Neil Bauer
Joe Belfatto
Steve Benoit
Kayla Bergeron
Sue Bernheim
Mark Blair
Joaquin Bowman
Bruce Boyle
Tim Carron Brown
Joyce Buford
Al Butkus
George Butler
Les Butler
Joe Cannon
Delphine Carroll
Kathy Cashin
Jim Cavanaugh
Rob Cawthorn

Michael Chastenet
Tom Churchwell
Kim Clay
Dick Collins
Marguerite Copel
Vic Coppola
Gene Cordes
Marian Crawford
Jerry Cropp
Paul Curcio
Elliott Curson
Matt Davis
Zack Dawes
Tom DeBow
Paul Diamond
Fred DiBona
Tobey Dichter
Robert Dole
Kit Donahue
Brian Dovey
Peter Dowd
Max Downham
Craig Engesser
Dick Evans
Blaine Fabian
Cheryl Fair

Don Fair
Mike Feigeles
Dan Fellner
Mark Fenner
John Field
John Fisk
Steve Gadomski
Lou Gambaccini
Kevin Gardner
Trixie Gardner
Nancy Gargano
Margaret Gaspard
Carl Gerstacker
Nic Gibbon
Dane Gilbert
Amanda Gimble
Linda Gohlke
Mike Grobstein
George Grode
Harry Groome
Fred Hafer
Gretchen Harrison
Betsy Hill
Liz Hilton
Robbie Hoffman
Jack Horner

Marc Howard
Susan Howard
Jeff Hoyak
Jeff Hughes
Richard Hughes
Susan Hullin
Tod Hullin
Alan Hyman
Allan Kalish
Karl Kamena
Marci Kaminsky
Loren Kaye
Carolyn Keefe
Mike Kennedy
Graham King
Jeane Kirkpatrick
Dick Klein
Ralph Knotts
David Komansky
Sari Koshetz
Miles Kotay
Frank Kotsonis
Midge Kovacs
Kathy Lamensdorf
Michael
   Lamensdorf
Ron Lehrer
Steve Lesnik
Patti Lewis
Rick Lieb
Dan Lovely
Jack Lyness
Derek Lyth
James MacAleer

Philip Magaldi
Amy Margolis
Jim Marsh
Ben Martel
Jessie Martel
Ron McCall
Dan McCarthy
Jim McCarthy
Dennis McKeever
Bob McNeil
Emmy Miller
Dan Molesky
Rich Monaghan
David Morley
Ann Marie Morris
Bob Moser
Ira Nathanson
Rich Nelson
Debbie Nute
Maggie O'Neill
Neil Oxman
Jim Panyard
Chris Perry
Henry Pollak
Dennis Randall
Ronald Reagan
Russell
   Redenbaugh
Eliot Richardson
Jeff Richardson
Ellen Roberts
David Robinson
Charlie Rockey
Art Rosenberg

Sam Ross
Don Rumsfeld
Frank Ryan
Marty Satinsky
Ron Schmid
John Schroeder
Bill Schuette
Sharon Shaffer
Stuart Shapiro
Lee Smedley
Thym Smith
Jay Snider
Shanin Specter
Joe Stevens
Bill Stewart
Judith Swedek
Toni Sweeney
Patrick Sylvester
John Thomas
Jan Tratnik
John Vlandis
Catherine Votaw
Jenny Wade
Chris Wagner
Karol Wasylyshyn
Almeta West
George Westerman
Joe Westner
Gaylon White
Pete Wilson
Bernie Windon
Dick Wirthlin
Rick Wooten

In memory of:

Otto Bos
Frank Clarke

Rege Filtz
Bob Pollak

About the Author

Myles Martel, Ph.D., president of Martel & Associates, is one of the world's premier executive communication advisors. Scores of business leaders rely on his counsel for communication planning and strategy, and for such high-stakes challenges as major presentations, speeches, testimony, media appearances, and crises. Among his major clients are 3M, Dow Chemical, Merrill Lynch, Texaco, and Eastman Kodak.

Dr. Martel came to national prominence in 1980 as Ronald Reagan's personal debate advisor. The author of four previous books, his work has been quoted extensively in numerous leading publications, including *The Wall Street Journal, USA Today*, and *The New York Times*. He has also appeared on numerous television and radio talk shows, including "ABC Nightly News," "Nightline with Ted Koppel," and the "CBS This Morning."

For further information on services provided by Martel & Associates, write or call:

Martel & Associates
One Aldwyn Center
Villanova, PA 19085
215/525-5959

Index